GOING FOR IT!

Going for It!

How to Succeed as an Entrepreneur

VICTOR KIAM

Collins
8 Grafton Street, London W1
1986

William Collins Sons & Co. Ltd
London · Glasgow · Sydney · Auckland
Toronto · Johannesburg

BRITISH LIBRARY CATALOGUING IN PUBLICATION DATA

Kiam, Victor
Going for it: how to succeed as an entrepreneur.
1. Success in business
I. Title
650.1 HF5386

ISBN 0 00 217603 3

First published in Great Britain 1986

Photoset in Linotron Times by
Rowland Phototypesetting Ltd
Bury St Edmunds, Suffolk
Made and printed in Great Britain by
William Collins Sons & Co. Ltd, Glasgow

Contents

Acknowledgements

I would like to thank Dick Lally, whose ability to organize my thoughts and assistance in getting them down on paper were an invaluable aid in the writing of this book.

I would also like to express thanks and appreciation to all those who, over the years, have given me the inspiration to try to succeed. In particular, I would especially like to thank Arthur Emil, Wally Heinze, Sandy Kaplan, Al Peterson, and Bob Simons.

To Ellen, who having lived with
an entrepreneur, became one, and
who has compromised, sacrificed,
and brought me so much joy.

And to Lisa, Tory, and Robin,
our most successful joint
entrepreneurial ventures.

CHAPTER ONE

Facing yourself: finding the entrepreneur in you

There is a major sporting event in the United States that I have attended for years. I won't reveal its name; I don't want to ruin a good thing. This event attracts thousands of spectators, making it almost impossible to find a parking space. Alternative spots can only be found many blocks from the stadium and usually cost an arm and a leg. Unless you have a chauffeur.

Chauffeur-driven cars are given special treatment. They are assigned to a parking lot adjacent to the stadium and are allowed its use free of charge. This sort of elitism rankled me. I thought it was unfair for me or any other fan to be penalized for not having a driver. It also gave me the idea that an investment in a chauffeur's cap, a dark blue blazer, and a nondescript black tie would be money well spent. With these few items, I would strike a blow for the underdog.

The next time I attended the event, I donned my newly acquired finery and drove my wife Ellen and two friends to the stadium entrance. I had insisted that all three sit in the back.

When we reached the front gates we were stopped by a security guard. Peering into our Cadillac, he saw my three passengers, leisurely attired for a summer outing. Then he noticed me, decked out in chauffeur's finery and doing my best to pretend that I neither spoke nor understood English. The guard didn't give us a second look. He waved us through, allowing me to drop off my passengers in front of the stadium, drive the car into the elite lot, and park it. Then I did my impersonation of Clark Kent in a phone booth. Doffing the chauffeur's outfit, I put on a sweater, got out of the car, and approached a group of brother drivers.

When I asked them where a guy could grab a cup of coffee, I was directed to a refreshment stand located near the stadium entrance. Perfect. After strolling over and purchasing a cup of coffee, I continued walking until I was in the stadium.

An usher, having taken my ticket, escorted me to my group. Mission accomplished. I was so pleased with myself that I vowed never to pay to park my car here again. From now on, any time I came to this event, that chauffeur's cap was coming with me.

I've kept that promise. Of course, with my commercials being shown nationally this becomes more of a high risk venture each time. Every year that cap gets pulled down a little bit lower as I try to make myself less recognizable. Eventually, I'll probably augment the disguise with dark glasses and a false beard. I doubt that even Sherlock Holmes would think to look for the president of Remington under a bogus set of whiskers.

Reading this tale might lead you to believe that I was being pushy, even a little underhand. You would be wrong. I was being an entrepreneur.

What is an entrepreneur? The dictionary defines the word as someone who organizes or manages any enterprise, especially a business that involves considerable initiative or risk. For me, entrepreneurs are those who understand that there is little difference between obstacle and opportunity and are able to turn both to their advantage. Their willingness to seize the initiative sets them apart from their contemporaries. Entrepreneurs don't sit on their haunches, waiting for something to happen. They make things happen.

Entrepreneurs are risk-takers, willing to roll the dice with their money or reputations on the line in support of an idea or enterprise. They willingly assume responsibility for the success or failure of a venture and are answerable for all its facets. The buck not only stops at their desks, it starts there too.

They can be found anywhere. Most people think of them as mavericks, energetic guys running their own businesses. They certainly can be that. But entrepreneurs can also exist within the corporate mainstream as employees, injecting their companies with a dynamism they would otherwise lack.

Don King, the boxing promoter, is an entrepreneur. He has built an empire on the force of his personality and his salesmanship. If the Rumble in the Jungle, the climactic heavyweight title fight between Muhammad Ali and George Foreman, had turned out to be the Stumble in the Jungle, Ali still would have picked up his pay cheque (the money was already in the bank) and would have gone on to fight megabuck bouts for other promoters. King would have been the biggest loser. His reputation as the self-appointed 'greatest boxing promoter in the history of the world' would have taken a shellacking. He would have dropped a bucketful of dollars and would have been known as the man who screwed up the biggest boxing promotion of the century.

It's obvious that the woman owning and running the local hardware store is also an entrepreneur. But so is the fellow who owns the hot-dog stand parked outside her place. He has to decide how much to charge for that hot dog and coke. He must choose the location that will allow him the greatest flow of consumers interested in his product. Decisions on organizing a menu and how he should advertise his wares will be made by him. If bean sprouts replace double cheeseburgers as the craze of the moment, he'll have to recognize this and make an adjustment. He's investing time and money in this venture. Any mistake he makes could dig his hole a little bit deeper. If he makes enough errors, the only body that will be tossed into that hole will be his.

The daring executive, bringing innovation and drive to the products division of some large established company, is certainly an entrepreneur. His reputation is on the line. In many ways that's a more chancy thing than the risk of dollars and cents. If he succeeds, he's the blue-eyed boy. If he fails, he'll have a hard time selling his superiors on any innovative ideas he might have in the future. His bosses will think, 'The last time we listened to him we ended up stripped to our shorts.' If he is wrong often enough he'll soon be scanning the Help Wanted section of the newspaper.

The people I have just described have chosen not to have the courage of someone else's convictions. They're following their *own* vision and have decided to make any sacrifices necessary to achieve success.

1951. Having just graduated from Harvard Business School, I decided to join Lever Brothers as a management trainee. Money had nothing to do with the choice. I went with the company for two reasons. First, I was impressed with Keith Porter, an executive I met during the interview process and who would be my boss.

Second, Lever Brothers was a diversified and growing company. They were in an aggressive market. I was excited by the possibilities for growth and responsibility. I was also convinced that I could learn a great deal from Keith; he was a marketing genius.

For the next seventeen years I used the entrepreneurial skills outlined in this book to move up the corporate ladder, first at Lever Brothers, where I stayed for four years, and then at Playtex. I joined that company in 1955 as its Western regional sales manager. By 1968 I was president of its Sarong division and executive vice-president of International Latex.

I left the company that year; I was disenchanted with the direction it had taken after a recent takeover. I didn't feel any immediate financial pressures; there had been a healthy settlement with Playtex. I also had what I thought was a fairly impressive curriculum vitae. I didn't expect to have too much of a problem finding a job. The trouble was I didn't know what I wanted to do.

To get some direction, I called on an expert. George Haley was, and still is, the head of George Haley and Associates in New York, one of the most respected personnel search firms in the country. He was a headhunter, supplying high-powered executive talent in answer to the needs of big business. My meeting with him one February afternoon changed my life.

George, already aware of my background, suggested that I stop looking at myself as a potential employee for a large corporation. He said, 'Vic, you should go out on your own. Find a company you'd be interested in, buy it, and run it yourself. Or start a new company.' I told him that I doubted I had enough funds for either venture. George pooh-poohed that. 'If there's one thing I know,' he said, 'it's that there are an awful lot of investors in this town willing to back competent people with drive and ideas. The money will find you, or you will find it, without too much trouble. Let's look at your track record.' Picking up my CV, he continued, 'I see a fellow who has moved up the ranks quickly and in two major corporations. He has had excellent business and marketing training. He has also had managerial experience on every level. His rapid promotion would suggest a person with healthy ambition and someone who is not afraid of hard work. I don't think you'll have any trouble finding capital if you can find the right vehicle.'

I had long thought about doing something on my own; George had given me the push I needed. Shortly after our meeting, I went to the Yong President's Organization conference in Puerto Rico. The first day featured a seminar on entrepreneurship. Three legends were the main speakers: Al Lapin of International House of Pancakes, Sid Stanton of the international firm Laird and Company, and Nick Skalgo of the international conglomerate Bangor-Punta. Ironically, since that conference all three have gone bust. Lapin went bankrupt, Stanton went out of business, and Skalgo left his organization. No matter. Entrepreneurship does involve risks and, at the time of this gathering, you couldn't have been riding much higher than those three.

I listened to them talking about the thrill of doing their own thing. They seemed to indicate that you didn't have to be superhuman to be an entrepreneur. All you needed was a viable idea and the willingness to do everything necessary to make it go. Listening to them, I felt I was the only person in the room, that all three were speaking directly to me. I knew I couldn't always outthink or outplan my competitors. Who can? But I could sure as hell outwork them. I left the conference thinking, 'By God, I know I can do this.'

I believe the last eighteen years have proved me correct. Shortly after the conference, I bought into the Benrus Corporation and played a role in its turnaround. I acquired the Remington company in 1979 and put it back on its feet. How I made these acquisitions and revived these companies will be discussed later in the book. What is important to note here is the fact that I am not a genius. Far from it. I believe that any success I've had can be attributed to my adherence to the entrepreneurial principles I developed early in my career. By God, I *could* do it and so can you. The game is entrepreneurial tennis. While I can't guarantee that all of you will reach the same level of achievement, I can promise that, if you play to win, you will have more fun and excitement than you can imagine.

But, before you grab your racket and step out on to the court, you'd better make sure you're ready to play. Almost thirty-five years of participating in the ultimate contest have given me a good idea of what an entrepreneur's profile should resemble. I would like to help you find out if you have the stuff to make the team. If you're interested in knowing, all you have to do is look in the mirror and ask:

1. Do I have confidence in myself?

You have to believe in yourself. I've met hundreds of young executives who claim they would love to be on their own either running a company or assuming more responsibility within their present situation. I've had occasion to pick some of them up on it; not all were quick to seize the challenge.

Two gentlemen in particular come to mind. I had been trying to find someone who could head Remington's appliance division. I found two veteran executives. Both had been with General Electric. At GE, everything was done as a community effort. Plans were based on consensus opinion. No one executive could easily be singled out for praise, but neither could he become a convenient target.

At Remington, the head of this division would run the whole shooting match. He would have to get product, write presentations, devise campaigns, hire, fire, and a hundred other things. He would be answerable only to me and would reap financial rewards based on merit.

Both candidates were perfect for the position. Each knew more about the market than anyone I could find. It would have been hard to choose one over the other, but I didn't have to. Neither one of them wanted to get within ten feet of the job.

They didn't want to lose the security of the crowd. I thought I was giving them a chance to move up from the chorus line; they thought I was condemning them to stand in the middle of the firing line. Twenty years ago they were probably potential entrepreneurs. But, after all this time spent with a company that had refused to stoke their fires, whatever flame they'd had was dead. They didn't believe they could handle the responsibility I wanted to give them. They had become corporate drones.

It's a good thing neither accepted the position. Without self-confidence they wouldn't have survived. An entrepreneur must be able to motivate people, inspiring them to share in his commitment. In a corporation, you want the people working under you to follow your lead. You want your superiors to respect your judgement. If you're running your own company, you may want investors to place their money and trust behind you. You want your clients to catch your enthusiasm and to believe in your product or service. How can you inspire them if you don't believe in yourself?

This is especially true for the young entrepreneur. The entrepreneur at twenty-five is a different animal from the entrepreneur at fifty. If both executives walked into their boss's office with the same idea, the older one would get a fairer hearing simply by being the more experienced hand. A lot of respect is earned with that grey hair. The veteran's proposal would receive serious consideration.

But the younger dynamo, having made the same presentation, is more apt to hear, 'That's a nutty idea. Why did you waste my time with that one?' That sort of attitude is a problem in the traditional corporate structure. The corporate traditionalist is often guilty of thinking, 'She's only been with the company two years. She's twenty-five years old. What the hell does she know?' It takes a healthy ego to withstand that sort of buffeting.

As you will see, part of the entrepreneur's job is to stand out. You'll have a hard time doing that if you don't believe yourself worthy of the spotlight. There is a young fellow who has worked with me on occasion, for several years. Every time he opens his mouth to offer an idea he prefaces it with 'I'm not sure you're going to like this but . . .,' or 'Well, of course, this is only my opinion.' He says it in a sheepish voice that makes me believe he's apologizing for daring to have a thought. The irony is that every idea he has is first-rate. Absolutely brilliant. I continue to work with him because, as an entrepreneur, I don't give a hoot how a concept is wrapped. It doesn't matter if the gift-giver is young or old or if he's been with the company twenty years or twenty days. It's the thought I value. But though I still do business with him, I would never hire him to head a division of my company. His lack of confidence would make him a poor choice to lead my troops. I know it hurt him in his own field, costing him work he otherwise deserved. It's sad. He would be so much better off if he would only believe in his most important commodity: himself.

Allow me to be clearer. By confidence, I don't mean he has to think he's the centre of the universe. It doesn't require you to believe you are an expert in all the areas of your chosen field. I could no more make an electric shaver than I could swim the

English Channel. In fact, swimming the Channel might be the easier of the two propositions. But I am confident that I can pick the best people to make those shavers. I believe I'm the guy who can hold the venture together and make it soar.

What should you do if you don't have confidence? Find some. I'm sorry; I don't mean to be flippant. I wish I could wave a magic wand and give you the confidence you need. I can't. But I can suggest that you apply yourself seriously when drawing up the balance sheet described at the end of this chapter. After listing your liabilities, work on moving them into the assets column. Lack of confidence is not a disease; it's a symptom. Those self-perceived negatives are robbing you of a healthy ego. Working on them with any degree of success is bound to improve your self-image. Don't let the task overwhelm you. Remember, millions of people back horses, speculate on the stock market, and buy lottery tickets every day. All I'm asking you to do is to bet on yourself.

2. *Do I have confidence in my venture?*

I've been asked, 'If you make an investment, what are you really backing, the idea or the people behind it?' My answer? Both. No entrepreneur is a miracle-worker. I could not have turned Remington around if we didn't have a great shaver and a dedicated work force. You can bust a gut sixteen hours a day, seven days a week, but if your concept or product is lousy, you've wasted your time. Anything you become involved with must be worth your total commitment. Do you believe it has a chance to make it? Going into a venture with large doubts is writing a script for its failure. When the terrain gets rocky – and every entrepreneurial venture has its share of hard times – it's not likely that you will give the project the support it requires if you don't trust in its merits.

Late in my career at Lever Brothers, I was put under a new sales manager who came up with a programme I thought was absurd. It involved a new method for handling accounts. I knew it wouldn't work. After telling him so, I argued with him until we were both on the verge of apoplexy. I could not dissuade him. What could I do? I was one of the troops and had been handed my orders. Like the rest of the sales force, I went out and pitched it as best I could. It was no use. No matter where I went I kept hearing rejection: the sound of one door slamming.

After four or five turndowns, I was frustrated. This wasn't normal. My usual response to adversity is to dig down deeper to find a way to make things work. I didn't have my normal reserves to call upon in this instance because I had no faith in the new system.

The sales manager's methods failed, not just for me but for the entire sales force. They had been as dubious as I. The negative responses we received only substantiated our lack of confidence in the programme. Though you must always give your maximum effort, it is harder to do that when you believe you're backing a lost cause.

Your confidence in a product or venture must be strong. If your feelings are lukewarm, you need more information before deciding the extent of your involvement. At Remington, we recently developed a stop smoking device and I'm leery of it. It's a fine machine, but I've noticed that most of the similar devices already on the market give off a whiff of snake oil. Consumers have used them with little success and have felt ripped off by their manufacturers. I know this is a better instrument than its predecessors, but I'm afraid that if the public buys it and it fails to live up to its expectations, it will reflect badly on the entire Remington line. There's nothing worse than having your product tainted by the hint of fraud. Knowing this, I've decided to test market the device to get some answers. I'll be watching the results carefully. Terrific sales will do little to persuade me. If a large number of consumers, not necessarily a majority, questions its effectiveness, we won't go through with it, even though we could make a lot of money.

Another example of the need for faith in your product comes from a friend of mine, a fellow who worked in one of the better known New York shoe stores. He is a terrific salesman. I was in his place one afternoon when he sold $6,000 worth of merchandise to a lady from Brazil. He would have sold her more but he ran out of styles. He left that store for a year-long sabbatical and then returned. In his absence, management had changed hands and the quality of the stock dropped off. He didn't realize it at first. Then one afternoon a woman complained that the expensive evening shoes she was about to buy were a bit tight. He offered to put them on the shoe-stretcher in the back room. As he tells it, 'Of course, just as in most stores, the shoe-stretcher was nothing more than an old broom stick. I never liked to use it; it could damage the shoe. So I did what I always had done. I gripped the shoe with my hands and pulled. It tore in half. I couldn't believe it; I'm not exactly Charles Atlas. I tried tugging at several other pairs and met with pretty much the same result. What used to be a finely crafted shoe was now a worthless piece of junk held together by glue and hope. I took a closer look at the rest of our goods and realized that the shoes I had just ruined were probably the best of a bad lot. I went outside, told the customer the truth, and then found my supervisor. Then I did the only thing I could do. I resigned.' He made the right move. The lesson is simple: *you can't sell anything that you wouldn't buy yourself.*

3. *Am I willing to make sacrifices?*

How much should you be willing to sacrifice? As a salesman for Lever Brothers, I was so committed to doing the best job I could that I went to jail for it. I'd better explain the circumstances.

I didn't like to arrive in a town where I would be selling on the same morning I was due to start my rounds. I preferred to get there the night before. I'd check into a room, grab a good night's sleep, and get a head start on my competition first thing in the morning. If I couldn't find a hotel room, I'd sleep in the car.

That was the situation during one of my visits to Baton Rouge. I had arrived at 1 a.m. and found that there was no room at any inn. No problem. I parked on the side of a country road and flopped into the back seat. At about 3 a.m. I was woken by a knock on the window. It was a policeman. When he asked what I was doing, I told him I was a salesman and gave him my story. He was sympathetic. Smiling, he said, 'Well, you aren't doing anything illegal. But we really don't like to have people sleeping on the street down here. If anything happened to you I wouldn't forgive myself. I'll tell you what. Why don't you come down to the jailhouse and sleep in one of the cells? Now mind you, I'm not arresting you. We'll even leave the cell unlocked. You can get up and go as soon as you wake up.'

I didn't argue with him. I didn't want to get into any trouble, and to tell the truth, I was certain that even a jail bunk would be more comfortable than the back of my car. I spent the night in an unlocked cell. The next morning they woke me and served me coffee, ham and eggs, and a sweet roll. They ran a very nice establishment. I liked the place so much I wished I could have bought it.

I'm not asking you to do time in support of your enterprise. But understand that the life of an entrepreneur is full of sacrifice. Body-builders have a saying, 'No pain, no gain.' That should be the credo of every entrepreneur.

Forget watching the clock; nine-to-five doesn't exist for you. Business is a game and eight hours don't afford you enough time to score the deciding run. When I first hit the road as a salesman I noticed that none of my rivals worked at weekends. I had nothing particularly important to do on Saturdays; I was single at the time and unencumbered by the responsibilities of marriage. What was I going to do? Play tennis? Selling was my game and I intended to be a winner.

Saturday became part of my regular work schedule. Too often, I would visit a small store during the week only to find the owner was besieged by salesmen. I didn't think I could afford to wait for my turn; I had to move on to other accounts. Saturday was a busy day for these small shops. I knew the owners had to be in. When I called on them, they were willing to give me the time I needed to show them my line. They knew they weren't going to be bothered by any other salesmen that day. The owners were also more receptive to my Saturday pitch. A busy store and ringing cash register always put them in an excellent frame of mind. What's more, getting these small accounts out of the way on Saturday gave me more time to spend with my larger clients during the week. Look around you. Where can you find the edge that brings victory? Observation of the work habits of my competitors and a readiness to turn it to my advantage paid off.

My hunger to win the game allowed me to transform every negative into a positive. No sacrifice was too great. When a snowstorm hit my region it wasn't an obstacle; it was an opportunity! The idea that my rivals would be in their homes hiding from the elements, gave me the impetus to go from store to store, pushing my product. It was amazing how receptive a buyer could be when the snow outside his door was waist deep and climbing, and you were the only friendly face he had seen all day.

My tasks were made easier because I had a goal: to score more points than my competition by getting the order. I could have stayed at home just as they did, but that would have meant falling behind or settling for a tie. That wouldn't have been good enough for me and it shouldn't ever be good enough for you.

Once you've committed yourself to making the necessary sacrifices, be prepared for the effects this will have on your life-style. Time and sweat aren't the only prices demanded of the entrepreneur. Unless you're independently wealthy, your wallet could well get lighter during the initial phases of your career. As an entrepreneur starting out in a large corporation, you shouldn't worry about salary. It is a secondary consideration. Opt for the position that seems to have the greatest potential for growth. That may force you to accept low pay in the beginning, but, after you've proved yourself, the monetary rewards will be there. Since you have to be prepared for any opportunity, you may also be using a large portion of your salary to build a nest egg.

While at Playtex, I thought the company stock would be a sound investment so I kept buying shares on margin. I rarely went to the movies and I forgot what it was like to eat in a fancy restaurant. I became meticulous about hanging my clothes. I didn't want them wrinkled. Each dollar I kept out of the pocket of my dry cleaner was another dollar saved and another opportunity to acquire more stock. I'm sure some of my friends thought I had a screw loose during this period. It seemed to them that my life was all work and no play, but it wasn't. I was too involved with it to think or care about the things other people thought I was missing. By the time I left Playtex I was able to sell the stock I had acquired for $500,000, giving me a considerable profit. These were the funds that would help me to buy a piece of the Benrus Corporation.

If you're an entrepreneur opening your own business, the financial sacrifices will be even greater. You lose the security of a weekly pay cheque and those benefits you take for granted will disappear unless you pay for them.

Of course, dedicating yourself to carrying out your vision with such fervour is going to have an impact on your personal life. You're going to lose friends and not just because you don't have time for them any more. You're going to find that your interests have changed and that, unless your friends are of the same entrepreneurial bent as you, you no longer have much in common. There's no animosity involved; you just lose touch as a natural consequence of the maturing process. It can be painful.

If you're romantically involved with someone, a lover or spouse, you are well advised to warn them about the radical change that your life will undergo. There is going to be a disruption in the orderly flow of your existence. You might not be home at six for dinner; dinner will have to wait. Those quiet, relaxing weekends are going to become less frequent. You're too busy working. These things may not seem like much, but after five or six episodes of cancelled appointments and late dinners in a two-week period, the other half of this relationship might blow his or her top. You have to head off a potentially volatile situation. If the person you love is unable to go along with your new life-style, if you can't find compromises that suit both of you, it's best that you find out then and decide whether or not the sacrifice is too high.

By the way, if you expect the worst when you broach the subject, you may be surprised by the other person's reaction. I knew a woman who opened a bookstore. She phoned her boy friend on a Friday night, saying she had to finish the shop floor and asking if he would mind if she cancelled that evening's date. He asked if he could come over to help. It became a fun evening, heightened by the sense they both had that they had accomplished something together. In 1971, I entered upon an entrepreneurial venture, the jewellery business, with my wife. The experience helped an already solid rapport. It gave us one more common interest and provided our relationship with more glue. This is important. I've seen a number of entrepreneurs whose marriages fell apart. They go off hell-for-leather and forget about the needs of their most intimate partner. That's one sacrifice I don't recommend anyone to make.

4. Am I a decision maker?

You'd better be. As an entrepreneur you're pretty much on your own. You're responsible for your business or division and no one can make the tough decisions for you. I've always thought it would be good training, if you're in a corporation, to try to think as the president of the company would. I made it a habit, while at Lever Brothers and Playtex, to look at any decisions facing the company and then try to figure out what course of action I would recommend if the ultimate decision were mine. It's a habit you should cultivate and is a major step towards thinking entrepreneurially.

Unfortunately, all this theorizing wasn't much help when it was time for me to make my first hard decision. I was a recently promoted supervisor at Lever Brothers, responsible for eight salesmen assigned to my territory. This was my first managerial position. One of the salesmen was a fellow who had been with the company for nine years. Lately, his sales record had been dismal. He couldn't get an order.

I made a trip with him to find out what was wrong. You couldn't fault his work habits. He called on all his accounts and gave them a textbook presentation exactly as he had been trained. He followed up every lead. But he was dull as dish-water, unable to motivate or enthuse. I ended up going to most of his larger accounts and getting his orders for him. I was doing my best to cover for him. That wasn't charity. I was trying to avoid the issue that was hanging over both of us: eventually, I would have to let him go.

I was forced to confront this after another one of my salesmen took ill. I had to stand in for him until he got well and was no longer able to prop up my failing employee. He continued to sink and I was left without a choice. I went to my district manager and said, 'I've been supporting this guy for months, but there's no improvement. In fact, his situation has worsened. He just doesn't have it. We've got to let him go, but I don't have the heart to do it. Would you break the news to him?' My boss wouldn't hear of it. He said, 'Vic, you're a big boy now. This fellow works for you. He's part of your territory. You're going to have to make a decision and implement it.' When I protested that I didn't know how I could do it, he offered no solace other than the assurance, 'I'm sure you'll do the best you can.'

I knew he was right. This was my responsibility. For the next two days I steeled myself for the odious task.

I spent part of that time calling everyone I knew to see if I could find another job for him. No dice. There wasn't going to be any easy way out. When I finally met him, I gave it to him straight. I told him I valued him for his work ethic and his honesty, but that he was a poor salesman and I couldn't keep him with the company. I gave him a glowing letter of recommendation (which made no mention, pro or con, of his salesmanship) and told him I could get him six weeks' severance pay instead of the usual three. My heart was in my mouth the whole time. I was twenty-four years old and single. My work was my only responsibility. This chap was thirty-eight, married, and the father of three. I had met his family on several occasions. To make matters worse, protocol demanded that I confiscate his company car. I had to drive the poor guy home, collect his sample case and leave him without any transport. After it was over, I didn't like myself for days. But I had to do it. I wouldn't be doing my job if I couldn't fire someone for not doing his. This was one of my duties. It's the sort of thing you must become inured to if you are to function as an entrepreneur.

In a sense I was lucky; I had some time to make that decision. But you're going to encounter situations where time is not on your side. When a Lever Brothers salesman in Cleveland, Ohio broke his back, I was sent out to replace him. We were launching a major new product at the time called Ayer Magic. This was an iridescent material, developed by the chief make-up artist of Paramount Pictures. A woman could rub it into her wrinkles and it would supposedly eradicate the lines on her face. The company thought it would take years off her appearance. Of course, if she happened to walk under a neon light she would glow, but this didn't stop my superiors thinking that this was the greatest thing since popcorn.

My company decided to launch this wonder product in a major department store in Ohio. Cleveland's May Company was selected as the prime store. We arranged for Mr Hoffman, the creator of Ayer Magic, to appear for a week in its auditorium and to make up women in its salon. In addition, several stores in Akron and Youngstown in Ohio would host similar promotions. Alfredo Ferrara, a famous make-up man from New York, was to be flown in to apply the gook in these outlying areas.

I scheduled the promotion, placing full-page ads in the local papers of all three cities. I drove out to the airport to pick up Hoffman, Ferrara, and their secretaries. I only got half the package. Ferrara, ill with the 'flu, was unable to make the trip. I thought, 'What do I do now? I have major promotions scheduled for tomorrow and I can't cancel them. The ads have already been placed in the newspapers.'

I spent the trip back to the hotel devising a way to save my campaign. By the time we reached our destination, I had my solution. I had seen Hoffman work his magic before; it didn't seem an inordinately hard task. I asked him, 'Could you teach me to be a make-up man in twenty-four hours?' He replied, 'Possibly. But you don't have the air of a make-up man and you're too young.' I was undaunted. After having him put some silver in my hair, I spent the next twenty-four hours in a crash course of Basic Make-up 1. We used his secretary as a guinea pig. That poor woman. We practised on her until her face was raw.

On the morning of the promotion, Hoffman appeared as scheduled in Cleveland. Mr Ferrara's place was taken by me, wearing a touch of grey at my temples, sporting a French accent and answering to the name of Mr Omar. For the next six days, Mr Omar knocked them dead in Akron and Youngstown. That's not meant to say that any of these women resembled corpses when I got through with them. Actually, I wasn't doing a bad job. My moment of truth arrived when I took my act to O'Neil's department store in Akron. My first customer of the day was the wife of the store's president. I could hardly keep my hands from shaking and smearing the Ayer Magic all over her face. When I finished, she thanked me and left without comment. Oh boy – I figured the game was up. But, two days later, she came back. Her husband had liked the make-up so much she wanted me to repeat it, allowing her to follow the process step by step. Apart from the initial problem, the entire campaign went without a hitch. Developing a quick, positive response to adversity had saved an important promotion. Being able to think on my feet and assuming responsibility for what many thought a bold decision also helped me score points with my superiors.

5. *Do I recognize opportunity?*

This is vital. If you're the sort of person who often finds yourself smacking your forehead over some great deal you allowed to slip through your fingers, you have got to wipe off your bifocals. Get used to examining all the angles of every proposition. Approach each idea thinking, 'How can I make this work for me?'

You may have to learn the lesson the hard way. I did. I once knew a fellow who seemed to create a new invention every day. We had lunch one afternoon shortly after I had left Lever Brothers. Thinking I was still with the company, he tried to interest me in his latest gadget: a toothbrush with a hollow plastic handle, filled with liquid dentrifice. Squeezing it would soak the bristles, allowing you to brush your teeth without going through the ritual of dealing with a tube of toothpaste. After using up the dentrifice you threw the tube away.

I suggested he take it to someone I knew at Lever Brothers. That's when he realized I was no longer with the company. When he asked what I was doing, I told him I was with Playtex. The words were barely out of my mouth before he exclaimed, 'Have I got a product for you!' Reaching into his bag, he pulled out two innocuous looking pieces of fabric. One piece was nylon, the other was cotton. After sticking them together, he showed me how they adhered to each other without the use of hooks or zipper. I said, 'This is fantastic. I'm sure we'd be interested in this.' All I could think about was the implications this held for the brassiere business and what it could mean to Playtex.

I took it to the company president and he paid my friend $25,000 for a six-month option. Five months into the deal our research people rejected it. They didn't think it had a practical application for our products.

I still thought it was a hell of a product. I tried to put together a group of interested backers, but when we appeared before them it turned out that two of the people had been involved with the inventor before and had lost money. They weren't interested in backing him again. The deal fizzled. That product was Velcro and there's not a day that passes that I don't see it being used somewhere: curtains, surgical gowns, seat belts. It's a huge business, a thriving public company.

It didn't occur to me at first to try to take this product out on my own. Only after Playtex rejected it, did I see the possibilities it held for me. It was too late. I should have entered into a licensing agreement with my friend that would have allowed Playtex to use it for their products and permitted us to pursue other possibilities. I didn't see the opportunity. That was a tough lesson to learn. You can bet I didn't let many like that slip by me again.

6. Can I keep my cool?

The entrepreneur is generally captain of his ship. If that sloop is headed for a reef with a crew about to jump overboard, his mere presence must say, 'I still have the rudder and I know we can make it to clear water.' An unsteady hand will affirm his crew's worst fears. They'll assume the ship is about to be scuttled. Reveal a hint of trepidation and you will have no crew.

It's your money that is invested in the venture or, at the very least, your drive and energy that is keeping a project afloat. Everybody working for and with you will take their cue from you. If you're down, the company is down. You must maintain equanimity. I'm lucky; I can share my troubles with my young lady, my wife Ellen. But in the presence of my employees, all fear or sense of desperation must be suppressed. I've made it a practice not to let people know whether I'm up or down; I try to keep the same face in all circumstances.

In late 1984 my principal competitor was going introduce a new line of European shavers. In addition, another rival company was trying to drastically undersell me. I had to move fast to avert what could have been a disaster. I called a meeting of my executives and discussed possible responses. The Victor Kiam who held that meeting was calm, rational and honest. I didn't pull any punches. We all knew we had a problem, a critical one, and that decisions would have to be reached quickly. Was I worried? Right down to my socks, baby. But no one in the room knew it. They knew I had a deep concern and their experience told them the gravity of the situation. But since I wasn't reaching for the hemlock, neither was anyone else. The combination of tension and a disciplined calm gave us a necessary clarity, enabling us to deal with the problems in logical order.

There was nothing we could do about the new shaver line until it came out, other than anticipate what direction its marketing campaign would take. The threat of a price war with our other competitor was another matter. Here we had a limited number of options.

We couldn't match their price. Their shavers were imported. With the dollar flexing its muscles abroad they were able to buy low there and undercut us in the US. Remington, being Proudly Made In The USA, didn't have that advantage. When this rival company decided to cut eight dollars off the price of their best-selling shaver, I knew we couldn't match them. Eight dollars! We'd have gone broke if we went down that far. Midway through the meeting we decided our strategy would revolve around one of three choices. First, we could maintain the status quo. Second, we could drop the price of our best seller by a buck or two. Third, we could raise the price of our top shaver. What would you have done?

We decided to go with number three. The logic was improbable: we couldn't match our competitor's new price and, since it put us so far apart, a slight decrease by us wouldn't make a ripple. We were going to get hurt anyway, so we decided to maximize our return on each razor while hoping our superior quality would win out. This decision wasn't final. I promised to go into the field and meet with our leading distributors, giving me the chance to find out what the market would bear. One of my advertising people then suggested we increase the advertising on the shavers still comparably priced to our rivals'. That was the first splash of a wave of positive suggestions.

In grave situations – in any situation, really – the only thing worse than a wrong decision is no decision. It signals panic. Your employees figure, 'God, now we're really in trouble. He can't make up his mind. We've pooled our thoughts and we still have no direction.' Instead of a group of trained executives able to tackle a serious but resolvable problem, you're going to have a line of frantic employees heading for the nearest open window.

At home that evening, I gave a dinner party for a few close friends. I'm sure not one of them knew I had anything pressing on my mind. After they left, around midnight, I slipped into my den, put Julio Iglesias on the stereo, and indulged myself with a good half hour of the worries. Privately. I owed it to myself to let all the doubts dance across my face. By the time the album was finished, my troubles were behind me. I had allowed them their time; now I was ready to act.

The other side of the equanimity picture says you shouldn't get too high either. I knew a chief executive who was a chronic backslapper when things were going great. He'd give you his movie-star smile and smack you black and blue out of joy. However there were days when he couldn't maintain that level of euphoria. The reasons were often unrelated to business. During those times, he didn't seem depressed or even cold. He just lacked that extra zing everyone was used to. I can't tell you how much his normal, placid behaviour could send his office into a group depression. The contrast between his 'normal' behaviour and his unenthused (but certainly not down) mood was so striking that everyone familiar with him imagined there had to be something terribly wrong. There wasn't. But he was unknowingly sending out a new set of signals that were being misread.

You have to maintain balance. As an entrepreneur you command attention. Your swings in behaviour will affect others. To paraphrase Shakespeare: 'If one's company is to remain calm, then the chap at the top must give the appearance of being calm.'

7. Do I have high levels of energy and stamina?

Opportunity isn't a polite thing. It won't don white tie, tails, and a top hat and arrive at some mutually agreed time. It's a slippery streaker. You must be quick, grabbing it by any available part of its anatomy as it whooshes past you. You'll need stamina, allowing you to grab it without fear of its wrestling free.

It stands to reason: for an entrepreneur, 16-hour work days are not unusual. Not too long ago, I flew to Detroit on a Monday morning, rented a car and drove to Troy, Michigan for a meeting with buyers from K-Mart, one of the big supermarket chains. Returning to New York's LaGuardia Airport that evening, I was met by my driver and taken to Kennedy Airport. I arrived just in time for my flight to London. I did not get any sleep on the plane; we touched down at six in the morning. I went to my hotel, showered, and took a brief nap before rushing to a mid-morning meeting that lasted until 4 p.m. I assume most of those who were there went home for an early supper. I raced to the airport and caught the next plane out to Germany. That evening, I attended a sales meeting in Cologne. Eight o'clock the next morning I was on the stand at the Cologne Fair. By that afternoon I had a near-terminal case of jet lag.

I'll admit that is an atypical day in the life of an entrepreneur. But on a normal work day, it's not unusual for me to rise at 6 a.m., ready to call our companies in Europe. Two hours later I'm out of the house and heading for our factory in Bridgeport, Connecticut. Using a driver allows me to work on my mail and read reports during the trip. *Not a minute is wasted*. After arriving at work, I plunge into the day and often don't let up until 7 or 8 p.m. On the way home I review the events of the day and write memos to be issued the following morning.

My arrival home doesn't always mark the end of the work day. I can have any number of meetings scheduled for that evening. When I finally turn in, I can look back on a day filled *not with work but with accomplishment*. Just reading this section may cause some of you to reach for the pillow. Don't let it discourage you. I'll tell you something: though I'm tired at the end of the day, I'm not exhausted. If you don't have energy now, I guarantee you'll find it in your commitment. I'm 57 years old, but I feel as I did thirty years ago. I'm running from country to country. I eat on the run just as I did when I was on the road as a salesman. But I feel great. I have a zest for what I'm doing.

Have you ever noticed that when you're not busy you have a hard time getting up in the morning? How if you sit on the beach too long, watching the world go by, your brain starts to turn into an avocado salad? You begin to calcify. *Rigor mortis* sets in when you have no reason to get up.

That doesn't happen in an entrepreneurial life. I don't like to get too much sleep; I'm afraid I might miss something wonderful. Entrepreneurs have no shortage of energy. Why? Because we're involved. As far as I'm concerned I'm good for another 25 to 30 years. I don't even think about retirement. Look at Armand Hammer, the octogenarian industrialist. He still wheels and deals around the globe. Someone recently asked John Carradine when he would stop acting. He's over 80. He replied, 'To retire is to die.' That was a week before he opened in a Broadway play. Commit yourself to life and you'll find a reward you hadn't bargained for: the fountain of youth.

8. Are you willing to lead by example?

It's common sense really. You can't ask the troops to give their all if your idea of a rough day is two hours in the office and six on the golf course. I never ask any employee to do something I'm not willing to do. Because I'm completely involved in my ventures

I feel a responsibility to work even harder than they do. Your projects and companies will be your babies. If you don't care for them, who will?

Also, never use your employees as servants. If I'm travelling with one of my salesmen and he tries to take my bag, I won't give it to him. No way. This refusal isn't meant to make the chap feel better about himself or to convince him that Mr Kiam is a wonderful fellow. It lets him know that we are in this thing together. You have to be able to motivate the people around you. Leading by example is as good a way as any.

My next observation doesn't take the form of a question. It's merely a bit of advice. If you're going to be an entrepreneur, in a corporation or on your own, you should get a background in accounting. This may seem a small detail, but it's something I recommend to everyone no matter what their age. In so many ways, analysis of a profit and loss statement or cash flow can be useful. The most creative businesses are still businesses. Accounting is vital, even if it's used only to manage your home or personal affairs. Any bottom line profit or loss is reached by addition and subtraction and is read in dollar signs and decimal points.

My ability to read company statements helped me in my first office position. It gave me an edge over my less informed rivals. Also, being familiar with the ways of accounting meant I didn't have to trust to the kindness of strangers whenever I dealt with the financial end of a company or my personal budget. With all the night school courses available there is no excuse for not getting some sort of background in this area.

There is one element of accounting I have found to be a useful tool of self-examination: the balance sheet.

A balance sheet is a record, at some point in time, of the assets and liabilities of a company. At the Harvard Business School we would study the balance sheets of various companies and try to determine their value. We also worked on profit and loss accounts. A P&L is a company's scorecard. It reflects how the enterprise has utilized its assets and liabilities and covers the results for a specific period of time.

During the time corporations were sending representatives to Harvard to interview students as prospective employees, I wondered what I had to offer any of these companies. I decided to use a variation of the balance sheet to make an assessment of myself. I already had my P&L; that was represented by my exam results. The balance sheet required some work.

I didn't bother to do a financial statement on myself; that would have been a disaster. Whenever a corporation draws up a balance sheet it can leave open a line for goodwill. This represents an intangible value. It could mean the value of a trademark or the company name. It could also be the difference between what a company has paid for an item and its net asset value. Since my financial worth was almost zero, I figured I had better measure my goodwill. But besides my assets, I also wanted to get a handle on my 'bad will', my intangible liabilities.

Taking out a notebook, I drew a line down the middle of a page. On one side I listed everything I thought a company would find attractive. Being single with freedom to travel, having a second language (French), and possessing a sound business school background were among them. I also listed some personality characteristics that would not necessarily be a part of my business profile. I was the sort of chap people took strong positions on. They either loved me or hated me. I wasn't sure if that was an asset or a liability so I listed it in both columns. I had plenty of liabilities: I was shy; I was too disorganized. There were many others, but one stood out as the worst of the lot: I procrastinated. Given four days to complete a project at the Harvard Business School I would wait until the third day to start it and then work like a bloody tiger to get it in on time. For example, we were required to have our weekly papers in the school mailbox by nine o'clock, Saturday night. Most of the time I would get mine in just as the proctor was about to lock the box.

Confronting this negative attribute in black and white helped me overcome it. *I made it a point to tackle distasteful jobs first.* I hate trivial details; I'm an activist and nothing drives me crazier than having to go over and reprove someone's expense report. But I have to do it in order to maintain a budget. Whenever this was called for, it became the first thing I did. I would much rather have been studying orders or looking at volume, but I got the loathsome expense reports out of the way before turning my attention to those things I enjoyed doing. That became my reward for doing a tiresome chore. In a short time, procrastination disappeared from my list. Grappling with my other shortcomings in the same way, I was able to get them under control.

I continue to do a personal balance sheet, revising it every six months, keeping track of my progress. It's become a private confessional. Since I am the only one who will see it, I can be painfully honest. Facing my negatives, I begin to get a more positive sense of myself. I realize that there is nothing on this list I can't overcome if I am willing to make the effort.

Now it's your turn. Do a balance sheet of your own and then find ways to turn your minuses into pluses. In the entrepreneurial game that balance sheet is going to reflect your batting average. An upturn in assets should generate enthusiasm for further improvement. If the liabilities have crept ahead you'll be able to identify these areas of chronic weakness and take the necessary steps to keep them in check.

This first chapter has served as something of a balance sheet. You should now have a pretty good idea whether or not you have what it takes to play the game. I hope I didn't dissuade you; that was not my intention. I just didn't want you to leap on to the court without knowing what to expect. Now that you've been told, I would be remiss if I didn't mention some of the rewards you'll receive for the sacrifice you've been asked to make.

You're going to find satisfaction in creating something out of nothing. You will gain a positive sense of self, derived from tackling a job others shy away from. A spotlight, powered by the respect of your peers and bosses, will seek you out. Of course, don't forget there are also financial rewards. In 1951 I joined Lever Brothers as a management trainee. Seventeen years later, barely past my fortieth birthday, I bought a piece of the Benrus Corporation. It didn't take long. Successful entrepreneurs are unique individuals. They are as prized as rare art. Once you've made your reputation you're going to find it's a seller's market and you've got the goods.

It's not an easy life. Nothing worthwhile is ever easy. If David had slain a dwarf instead of a giant, who would have cared? Who would remember?

CHAPTER TWO

It's a jungle in there: the entrepreneur as corporate lion

Over the past decade companies eager to inject their flaccid divisions with a new, more dynamic spirit have embraced the entrepreneur as saviour. Despite the recent US economic upswing, there have never been greater opportunities for entrepreneurs working within the corporate structure than now. If you decide you want to play this particular version of the entrepreneurial game you must take care to pick a team which will properly display your talents.

If I had a background in high tech I would probably look for something in telecommunications. I read just recently of a cable TV company that sells products over the air, utilizing a telephone hookup that allows customers to charge various items. This is a growing company in an emerging industry and it's the sort of organization that should attract the entrepreneur.

The fast-food industry also has potential for growth, provided you hook up with the right company. I wouldn't look at McDonald's or Wendy's. They're both at the pinnacle and can expand only so much. Instead, I would look up the fellow in Chicago who's developing fast-food emporiums featuring Chinese cuisine. This represents a new frontier in franchising. If I were an entrepreneur with an interest in the food business, I would fly out, meet him, and try to get in on the ground floor.

You have to take a look at the nature of your prospective employer. In banking for instance, Citibank is huge and has been around for years but it's expansionist, always willing to try new things. They were the first to use automatic tellers. They bought their own credit card division. This is an operation run by trail blazers. Another well-known bank takes pride in being the leader in automobile loans. This doesn't seem to represent much of a growth market to me. If this is their only claim to fame, I doubt that I would want to work for them.

Some companies can change. Campbell Soups was a stereotyped marketer of a basic product. They had a division called Pepperidge Farm run by a chap named Gordon McGovern. He changed the entire focus of the division by developing a line of Prestigious Premium Cookies. Business went through the roof. When the chairman of Campbell's retired, McGovern was named as his successor. He did the same thing for Campbell's that he did for Pepperidge Farm. He put out a line of gourmet soups and approached and sold to new markets. McGovern has created an entrepreneurial attitude in what was once a stodgy company. Ten years ago, Campbell Soups was not a company I would want as my employer. It is a company I would want to work for today. It is on a growth kick and is looking for new ideas. It is no longer a plodder.

Once you've picked a company that seems right for you, you have to make sure you're right for it. This is a time for some more self-examination.

Use your balance sheet

That balance sheet you recently drew up is going to come in handy. Just before graduating from the Harvard Business School in 1951, I made an assessment of myself in order to determine what sort of company I should join. You should do the same thing, all the time remembering to *pick a company in which you can shine.* A glance at the assets column on my balance sheet showed that I had not only lived in Europe, but had also owned and operated a successful business there. I had listed my ability to speak French fluently, and that I could hold my own in Italian. Experience had taught me how to deal with many of the problems – taxes and insurance among them – encountered by Americans doing business abroad.

I also did a balance sheet on my top classmates and ascertained that most of them would be going into domestic businesses. Given this same information, what kind of company would you hope to join? If your balance sheet indicated a hefty knowledge of the inner workings of the stock market, wouldn't you head for Wall Street? If selling was a particular strength, how could you affiliate yourself with a company whose line to the top didn't cross through the sales division? With my background, I thought it wise to venture into foreign trade.

Having picked a field, I read everything I could on companies whose products seemed to have a world market. You have to do the same homework, making use of every possible research source: books, magazines, newspapers, trade journals, people already in the business, and anything else at your disposal. Armed with the necessary information, you should draw up a list of prospective employers and then prepare yourself for what some consider to be the worst of all possible ordeals: the interview. Rest easy. This can (and should) be a pleasant experience.

Into the lion's den

It boggles my mind how often someone will come to me for a job without knowing a thing about the company beyond the identity of its chief product. The common attitude towards interviews seems to be that you just show up. Absolutely wrong! I've never gone into an interview without having acquired as much intelligence on the company as I could.

When I went for my first interview at Lever Brothers, I walked in with both pistols drawn and loaded with facts. I knew they were a part of Unilever, a large international conglomerate that transformed basic commodities, such as coconut oil, into consumer products. I had found out the name of its chief executive officer and a few of its board members. I had an idea how much of its market was domestic and how much was foreign. A list of the company's wares, including some of the more obscure ones, had been part of my required reading.

Getting this information was easy; all it required was a bit of work. Trade journals and magazines are gold mines of facts, especially if you're dealing with one of the better-known corporations. If it's a publicly-held company, you would do well to get your hands on its latest financial or annual report. You should also find out who handles the company's advertising. In the UK, the advertising trade journal, *Campaign*, can give you this information. It may also be able to tell you how much of your prospective employer's advertising budget is spent on television, radio, and newspaper advertising. Take note of the company's ads and try to figure out what the company feels to be the major selling points of its products or services.

If you can, I think it is especially helpful to talk to those who deal with the company, its suppliers and clients, and find out what they think of the organization. They should have a dispassionate view of its strengths and weaknesses. You should do this for any business, but it is especially helpful when trying to gather information on privately-owned enterprises whose records are not readily available for public scrutiny.

These data have a purpose. Not only will they enable you to answer key questions about the company you are hoping to join, but they will also allow you to take control of the interview. When the personnel manager at Lever Brothers asked me if I knew anything about the company, I ran down a list of their products, mentioned some things I had read in their annual report, and told him what I knew about their advertising. Then I asked a question of my own. Pointing out that the company had just moved its headquarters from Boston to New York, I asked him how this would affect the company policy concerning promotions. I pointed out that a number of executives hadn't gone along with the move and asked if this had left the corporate hierarchy unsettled. One question led to another until finally I asked my interviewer if he liked working for Lever Brothers and what he thought the company's strong points were. You can see what happened. Our roles were reversed. I had become the interrogator. This gave at least the feeling that I was there to make a decision about the company, instead of its making one on me. Creating this atmosphere has to work to your advantage.

Revealing the scope of the research you've done to the interviewer also lets him know you care. Early on at Remington, I interviewed a young man for a position with the company. He seemed to know almost as much about the company as I did. This is rare. Some people come to us for jobs not even aware that we're a privately owned corporation. This fellow, however, was able to quote market shares, knew the names of all our products, and asked what new items we planned to bring out. He even asked how we were doing in the Japanese market in the light of the impact the strong dollar was having on international trade.

When he paused to take a breath, I asked him if he knew where our products were sold. He named several outlets, including drug stores, and added, 'but some drug stores don't like to carry the shavers. They have a hard time making a profit because discounters cut the price so much.' When I asked how he knew this, he replied, 'I dropped in on about twenty drug stores and talked with the owners.' I was flabbergasted. All I could think was, 'Wow, I'd better not let this beauty escape. If he cares enough about the company to research us this heavily before he gets a position, what will he be like after we hire him?!' You can bet he got the job.

There are some other questions you should be asking, none of which concern salary. Don't ask how much you're going to get paid; the interviewer will tell you that in good time. In an entry-level position the money isn't going to vary too greatly from one company to another. Do ask what the company position is concerning promotions. You want to know how quickly you can move up and you might want to let the interviewer know that you intend to go all the way to the top. Don't hide your ambitions. Most importantly, you should ask what your area of responsibility, if any, will be.

No matter how little responsibility you may have on the entry level, you at least want to make sure that your position is a line job. A person with a line job is someone who produces results that can be measured by a bottom line of profit, such as a salesman. You want to be able to make a measurable impact on the company.

I entered Lever Brothers as a management trainee in the marketing area and later became a salesman. My performance in these positions could be measured in dollars and cents and made it easy to stand out for a job well done. Remember, your salary – provided you're making enough to survive – is unimportant at this time. The chance to shine and move up is everything! I started at Lever Brothers at about the same time as another classmate from the Harvard Business School. He chose to join the company as a market researcher, a non-line position. His salary was slightly more than $5,000 a year – a handsome starting rate in the early 1950s. My job then paid about $3,000 per annum. My friend in market research was making two-thirds again what I was making, and wasn't shy about reminding me of it. That never bothered me; I knew where I was going. Three years after our launching, the market researcher was making $7,500. I was earning over $17,000. He had done well in his position, but it didn't offer any other opportunities. He could go only so far. I had taken a lower salaried spot, but one that was alive with possibilities for growth and recognition. I had opted for opportunity. That chance to advance was important to me. I knew I could make up anything I had missed in salary later. The entrepreneur must not confuse his priorities.

Having steeped yourself in the background of the organization and keeping in mind your own needs, you should be able to come up with your own set of questions for the interviewer. Learn how to present them. You can sharpen your skills with rehearsal. Grab a friend, preferably a fellow job-seeker, and run through several mock interviews. Keep switching roles. Practise, practise, practise until you feel completely at ease. Boxers spar hundreds of rounds before fight night. You should be just as diligent in training for your game.

During your rehearsal, keep in mind that the interviewer is going to probe you for weaknesses as well as strengths. You may very well be asked what your weak points are. Don't try to claim you don't have any. The interviewer will assume you're trying to fool him – or yourself. Have a negative ready, one that isn't too damning, but be prepared to demonstrate that you have it under control. If I were asked that question today, I would probably reply that I hate the drudgery of paperwork, but I make it a point to get it done before I attempt to do anything else.

If you've done your homework, the interviewer will be hard pressed to throw you with a question. You'll be able to dominate the interview and make your mark as a person who cares as much about the company as the company should care about you. I must warn you though, that there is one question that could undo all the good work you've done. Unless you're past middle age, do not, I repeat, do not, ask what your prospective employer's pension plan is. If you're in a position where you're trying to secure a position, you certainly don't want the company to think you're already dreaming about retirement. Not too long ago, a young man ended an interview by asking me what Remington's pension plan was. He was about 25 years old! I answered him, 'Son, you'll never find out.'

Standing out

Since I was looking for something in foreign trade, it may come as something of a surprise to learn that I joined Lever Brothers in a domestic division. The reason was simple: Keith Porter. Keith was the president of Harriet Hubbard Ayer cosmetics division and, as I mentioned before, a ball of fire. The personnel manager had suggested I meet him. Even though he knew of my predilection for foreign trade, he thought I would enjoy working with Keith and that I would fit into his department.

I was sold on joining Porter at our first meeting. He was only 33 and his rise in the corporation had been meteoric. I was especially drawn by some of the innovative plans he had for his branch. He wanted to sell his line door-to-door in marketing areas and ship the goods from the local department store. This had never been done before and, if it was successful, he planned to expand and add other products.

Talking to Keith, I learned that Harriet Hubbard Ayer was a small division. It accounted for only one per cent of the company's total sales. But, if it was successful – and with Porter at the helm I couldn't imagine how it could miss – the business could go bonkers. It could quadruple in the next year. Because of the division's tiny size, any improvement would stand out. Also, anyone connected with that improvement would shine as well. I decided to hitch myself to a fellow and a division I thought were rising stars.

Let me point out that I didn't think of myself as an entrepreneur when I first joined Lever Brothers. I was industrious, but I didn't have a grand plan. As a salesman, I just went out and sold. As a supervisor, I was too busy trying to manage my department to be concerned with whether or not my bosses noticed how good a job I was doing. I expected recognition to arrive as a natural companion to my efforts. Guess what I discovered? Life isn't always fair. It's not enough to do a good job; that's only half the battle. You also have to let the people who count, the ones who can advance your career in the organization, know that you've done a good job.

If you're in a small company, you don't have too much of a problem. For example, if you were one of only four sales people in a corporation, you'd have an easy time standing out. But if you're one of the faceless mass in a large, homogeneous enterprise, how the devil can you call attention to yourself?

In some positions, the bottom line can be your spotlight. As I told you earlier, selling on Saturdays gave me an advantage over my rivals inside and outside the company. I was putting in 75-hour work weeks while my peers were toiling for only 40 hours or less. The difference showed in my results and my bosses took note of it. It didn't matter that some of them were better salesmen than I am. It takes more than talent to come out on top. If you work 20, 30, or 40 hours per week more than your peers, you're bound to outperform them just on the sheer strength of the extra time you've invested.

After you've established yourself as someone who's not afraid to put in the hours, you can further impress your superiors by asking good questions. Remington recently went into the cologne business and one of the fellows working for me wanted to know why. What was our strategy? I loved it that he cared enough to ask, even though the decision had little impact on his department. If you don't know why your company is doing something, find out. Ask your boss and if he doesn't know, suggest that you both ask *his* boss. This accomplishes two tasks. First, like the fellow who asked me about the cologne business, you've called attention to yourself as an employee who is thinking about the company. You're not a puppet waiting to follow the latest edict without so much as a question. Second, if your boss doesn't know the answer to your query, for at least that moment he is no longer your superior. You're both equal to the extent of your common ignorance. You've pulled down another corporate barrier.

Your boss's reaction to the suggestion that you both speak to his superior is worth noting. If he says, 'That won't be necessary. I'll ask him and let you know,' or 'I don't know why we're doing it, just do it,' be wary. He's liable to be either a bad boss or an insecure one and afraid that you might steal some of his thunder. I once worked for a supervisor who didn't want me near his boss's office. He always gave me the 'I'll ask him' line. I tried to get around that by suggesting that I'd like to come along and ask a few more related questions. He replied that I should make out a list and that he would make sure all my questions were satisfied. I knew I was being stonewalled and that I would have to find ways to get around him.

One of the methods I devised came in handy at Playtex. As a regional sales manager, I noticed that one of the company's biggest problems was its employee turnover. Playtex was a great finishing school for people just entering the industry because we taught all the rudiments. Having learned these basics, the now well-trained professionals would quit the company and join the competitor. I couldn't blame them. They were paid a salary with a small overriding commission and they could get a better deal from our rivals.

It seemed an easy problem to solve. There were twelve salesmen and one manager assigned to each of my six districts. If we created twelve smaller districts and assigned six salesmen to each, we could offer twice as many managerial positions as an inducement for staying. A salesman could look forward to an early promotion and the larger pay cheque that went with it. Having implemented this plan, I could then tell a prospective employee, 'This sales job is only your first step. Your goal is management. If you want to be a salesman for the rest of your days, this is the wrong company to join. You won't last because you'll be up against some real go-getter who is looking for more than just a pay cheque. I want you to be district manager in two years. Are you up to it?' This approach would create an incentive programme that would cut down on the number of frustrated employees who were deserting the company.

I wrote up the programme and passed it on to my boss, Parker Drake, a fellow who was not interested in seeing Victor Kiam succeed. In fact, for reasons I'll go into later, he was hoping I would fail.

My suggestions never got past his desk. He refused to pass them on to his superiors. Discovering this, I made it a point to refer to the idea in my weekly report, copies of which went not only to Drake but also to Al Peterson. Peterson was vice-president of marketing and his permission would be needed to get this project out of the dream stage.

One of my reports to Drake finished with the comment, 'The more I think about the new sales organization that I submitted to you, the more I'm convinced that it will lead to less turnover of staff, greater productivity, and improved morale.' When Peterson noticed this, he went to Drake and asked him where my report was. Drake was livid. He took out a folder containing my proposal and slammed it on his desk. He told Peterson it was a lousy idea and that he didn't want to have anything to do with it. Peterson, after having looked the plan over, said, 'Fine, why don't we let Kiam try it in his region?' I was in. As the only one of three regional managers involved in a new programme, I would be reviewed by everyone in the corporate hierarchy. If it was successful, it would have repercussions throughout Playtex. When the experiment succeeded, the recognition I received was gratifying, especially since I'd had to overcome a formidable obstacle to get it off the ground. There was a certain risk involved in tangling with Drake, but it was something I had to do.

If your best ideas aren't reaching the powers that be, they're not going to bring you a victory. No matter how fabulous they may seem, they're not going to help you score any runs in the corporate game.

An insecure boss isn't the only person who will keep you from scoring. He or she might not allow you to pass your idea on if he doesn't share your enthusiasm for it. If that's the case, then you must decide whether or not to go over his head. If you believe in the concept and you think it will be good for the company, then you have to do your best to get a hearing. This requires a delicate touch. If you're on a firm footing with your boss, and if he's a secure individual, you might ask him to join you in presenting the pros and cons of an idea to his boss. If his opposition was half-hearted, you might want to write a memo outlining your proposal and send copies to both him and his superior. Don't be devious. Be sure to mention the objections already voiced by your own boss.

If your boss is body and soul opposed to your idea, your task becomes more difficult. In this case, I would forgo the memo and pick up the telephone. When I was still a marketing director at Playtex, I had become convinced that the company should market a three-quarter-length long-line brassiere. I was in the field and our retailers were telling me that many women found our regular long-line bra too long. They had to take them home and shear them down before they would fit comfortably. When I told Peterson, he said he wasn't interested in augmenting the line. He didn't want to clutter up our inventory. Al also pointed out that sales were up 30% with the product line we already had. 'I have a saying,' he told me, 'if it ain't broke, don't fix it.' I countered, 'But even if it's not broke now, it's wearing out and may break in six months. It might be too late by then to fix it.' I was fearful our competitors would bring out a three-quarter length long-line before we did. By doing so, they'd not only be cutting material from their bra, they'd also be cutting our share of the market. I suggested we take our disagreement to Wally Heinze, the president of Playtex. Al refused.

I did not sleep easy that night. Peterson had always been a fair man and had always encouraged his employees to be creative. If you brought him a worthy idea, he'd help push it upstairs and he always made sure you got full credit for it. But if he was adamantly against your plan – and he certainly was in this particular case – you were not supposed to go over his head. It was one of the things that was guaranteed to incur his rancour. Despite this, I elected to speak to Heinze on my own. I really had no choice. Believing strongly in my idea, I felt it had to be implemented for the welfare of our company.

When I met with Heinze over breakfast, I told him of Peterson's opposition to my plan. After hearing my proposal, Heinze agreed that Playtex *should* bring out a shorter long-line. He also assured me that he would see to it that Peterson's feathers went unruffled. He certainly did that. Wally was a consummate politician. When he suggested to Peterson that we develop another long-line bra, he made it seem as if the idea originated with him. I doubt that Al ever knew that I'd had breakfast with Heinze or that I'd had both hands in his decision. Knowing of Wally's diplomatic skills made it easier for me to approach him.

This knowledge was based on my having already established a relationship with Heinze. Once you've become comfortable in your corporate surroundings, you must do whatever you can in order to *get to know your boss's boss.* You want to establish a pipeline to the top.

I did this by working late hours. Most of Playtex's executives stayed in the office long after 5 p.m. With the pressures of the day behind them, they would gather in small, informal groups and talk shop.

There were six other men on my level. Come five o'clock, some of them seemed eager to win a line in the *Guinness Book of World Records*: 'Fastest Time in the Out-of-the-Building-Dash'. These were not lazy guys. When they got home, they probably put in another two hours working on ideas and finishing reports. I was putting in the same extra hours, but I chose to do it in the office. Remember, it's not enough to work hard, you need to get recognition for your labour. I wanted Heinze and Peterson to know I was burning the midnight oil.

I was aided in this endeavour by geography. My office was near the office exit and Heinze had to pass it whenever he left for home. He'd often find me ruminating at my desk. When he'd ask me what I was still doing in the office I might reply, 'I'm trying to figure out some promotions for next season. I have some ideas but I haven't got them nailed down yet.' Nine times out of ten, Wally would invite me out for dinner and a little brainstorming. During these sessions, we developed a rapport.

Peterson also knew of my fondness for late hours and he would call me in to kick around some ideas of his own. Before long, both men thought of me as part of their inner circle and as an executive to be watched. Let me make something clear: the pains I took to make certain that my bosses knew of my work and accomplishments were – they had to be – backed up by results. Without those results, anything I did to get closer to these two men would have been dismissed as a cheap political ploy. I wouldn't have been invited to repeated after-hours confabs if I didn't have something substantial to contribute.

I always made it a point to bring something to these meetings, even if it was just an informed ear. I looked everywhere for ideas. Some, such as the three-quarter length bra, were simply the result of observation. Unfortunately, these did not come as often as I would like. So I added to my creative arsenal by adapting the ideas of others.

I was a voracious reader of business literature. You can find little gems by reading what others are trying to do, not just in your business, but in related industries. Most of the people in Playtex read *Corset and Brassiere* or *Women's Wear Daily*. I did, too, but I also read *Forbes*, *Fortune*, *Business Week*, and *Sales Promotion Magazine*. In the UK, you'd probably read *The Financial Times*, *The Economist* and the weekend business supplements.

In one of those periodicals, I had read of how one company used Polaroid snapshots to keep records of their various displays in stores across the country. I thought this was a marvellous idea and wanted to take the concept a step further by making it the foundation of a contest.

I proposed that we give all our salesmen cameras, enabling them to take photographs of their clients' displays. These pictures would be entered in a competition. The best display would win a free trip for two to Paris for both the store owner or buyer and the salesman. There would also be ten second prizes. After finalists were chosen, we would send unannounced inspectors to the qualifying stores to make sure the displays were still up. This would prevent participants from hiring some junior-grade Walt Disney to create a 'Magic Kingdom' of a display, taking its picture, and then tearing it down before the public laid eyes on it. If the display wasn't out front for the full eight weeks of the promotion, the entry was invalidated.

The running of the contest guaranteed two months of eye-catching displays prominently positioned in all our major accounts. We ran it during November and December, our two best sales months, when we knew traffic would be heaviest. Our turnover skyrocketed. The bill for the entire promotion was less than $10,000 and the results more than justified the costs. More than anything I had done up to that point, this taught me that opportunity was everywhere if only I had the eyes to see it.

As you put together your own storehouse of ideas, don't limit yourself to addressing the needs of your own division or department. Broaden yourself. At Playtex, I was responsible for girdles and bras, but that didn't prevent me from looking at our other products. If I had an idea on how we could improve the Living Glove, I'd dash off a memo to Heinze. Some of my memos were well received; others not. Whether they were used or not, they were sound ideas and gave testimony that I was thinking for the benefit of the entire company. You want your superiors to know you're not narrow-minded. When a promotion comes up, you might have two candidates. One is the head of a division. He's done a good job, but has shown no interest in anything but his area. Then, you have another department head who has demonstrated concern for all facets of the company while maintaining a high standard in his own realm. Who do you think is going to be moved up? Isn't it obvious?

You must be careful not to inundate your bosses with every

wild idea that pops into your cranium. This doesn't mean all your hunches have to be successful; they just have to be well thought out. And even careful planning won't guarantee their success. I know. I've had my share of duds.

I once sold Playtex on the idea of a lightweight girdle for teenaged women. We dubbed it the 'Cloud 17'. It would give young women just enough control without subjecting them to discomfort. I thought it offered us a wonderful opportunity to grab an early lead with the next generation's girdle market. If we could get these women into the habit of buying Playtex at 17 or 18, I figured we'd have them for life.

The division conducted extensive research. Findings established that our test clients liked the product. When Playtex brought it out, we structured a huge promotion around it. The girdle died. Despite the comfortable, easy support it featured, teenagers wouldn't buy it. They associated girdles, any girdles, with advancing age. No matter how hard we tried, we couldn't create a demand for the product. The stigma was too great to overcome.

Another less-than-successful creation was a male girdle devised by me and called the 'Pot Holder'. This never got past in-house testing and I can understand why. Using myself as one of the guinea-pigs, I wore the undergarment for a week. I was never so miserable in my life. Though it was a bit less uncomfortable than being encased in an iron maiden, it did give me the most maddening itch. Whenever I took it off, I felt as though I had a severe case of poison ivy. I doubt anyone was happier to see that idea go by the board than I.

These two flops didn't deter me from coming up with more ideas. So long as they are the result of sound reasoning, you should keep those creative concepts coming.

You can safeguard against the possible harebrained scheme by putting all your ideas down on paper. I would always outline the steps which led me to my final plan of action. It's amazing how what you think is the idea of the age can suddenly disintegrate when you have to confront it in black and white. You can't hide the holes on paper. Your natural enthusiasm for a project is somewhat blunted by print; it forces you to view your plans objectively. If part of your proposal hinges on its ability to increase earnings by ten per cent, you're going to have to ask yourself the basis for this supposition. If it's purely guesswork on your part, with no tangible support, you will have to forage about for stronger evidence before your idea has a chance. Any questions that crop up in examining your thesis must be answered before you offer it for approval. The acid test of paper can prevent you from making a fool of yourself. It will make the difference between being renowned as one of the company's most creative forces, or being vilified as a corporate mad scientist.

This documentation will also protect you from thieves. Alas, they do exist and you have to be ready for them. An idea is an easy thing to steal. Particularly if you can't prove its source. I learned this early on at Lever Brothers. While working for a marketing manager, I came up with what I thought was a good idea for a promotion. It was a simple variation on an old sales play: the two-for-one sale. Everyone at the time was running one. I proposed we change the name of our version to, 'Buy one, get one free.' I thought it would have a greater psychological impact on the consumer.

I bounced this idea off my boss and he said he'd think about it and get back to me. A week went by. Nothing. Tracking him down, I asked him if he had given my idea any consideration. He claimed he had and had decided it wouldn't work. I was to forget about it. Fine. This wasn't exactly the invention of fire we were talking about, so I didn't pursue it any further. Three weeks later, I saw our new promotion schedule. The third entry down read 'Buy one, get one free.'

You may assume I was agitated. I confronted the marketing manager and demanded an explanation. He seemed bemused. 'I don't see your problem,' he said. 'Sure you brought me an idea, but it wasn't this. I changed it. You might have had the germ of a thought there, but it wasn't this promotion.'

I thought I was in the Twilight Zone but I knew there was nothing I could do about it. Why? Because I hadn't put anything down on paper. I had discussed the idea only with the marketing manager. I didn't know whether I should be angry or embarrassed. What made matters worse was the knowledge that I had been giving this fellow ideas for months. Every week or two I would call him up and pass on my latest brainchild. He said he would consider them, or suggest them to upper management, but he never followed up any of our conversations. Now I knew why.

I'm sure he thought I was quite a fish. Every time I phoned he probably took out his rod and began to reel me in. From that day forward, whenever I had the 'germ of a thought' I jotted it down, giving one copy to the marketing manager and another to Keith Porter. It's a practice I've continued and I haven't had an idea stolen from me since.

How much the maverick

In standing out, you can be as much of a maverick as you choose to be as long as you're successful. Unless your company is as rigid as a Victorian schoolmaster's spine, it will tolerate a lot if you deliver the goods.

While serving as regional sales manager at Playtex, I had two chaps working with me who had already flown over the cuckoo's nest. In fact, you'd have a hard time convincing me that they didn't stop in mid-flight and drop down for an extended stay. One of them was a district manager named Jack Carasomovich. He was a bit eccentric. Whenever he checked into a hotel he would ask the clerk the colour of the toilet. If it was blue, Jack would demand another room. Blue was his favourite colour and he couldn't bring himself to answer nature's call into a blue bowl. He left many a clerk scratching his head.

Jack made his eccentricities pay off in his dealings with his customers. He made an art of mangling their names. He called Henry Saltzberger, the president of one of our larger accounts, Mr Saltshaker. Jack wasn't being rude; he was just trying to stand out and he was likeable enough to pull it off. I must admit I was upset when he slugged an airline pilot who had kept him awake with a running travelogue during a flight to El Paso. I had to bail him out of jail over that incident. But I didn't fire him. He was too good at his job.

I did fire Stan Weaver. Weaver was a great salesman with enormous flair. He had business cards made up that read 'Stan the Man'. Weaver would, on occasion, take advantage of his position, but always in a creative manner. Before arriving in a city, he would take an ad in the local paper: 'Women Wanted to Model Playtex Bras and Girdles. If interested, call Stan the Man.' Added to this routine would be the name, address, and phone number of whatever hotel he was staying in. Stan would audition as many as half a dozen modelling hopefuls in his room. I never held that against him. I was willing to forgive him almost anything because of the way he produced.

Weaver did step out of bounds, ironically, after he got married. One afternoon, his wife called me and explained that Stan would have to take some time off; he was gravely ill with hepatitis. After expressing my concern, I told her he could take as much time off as he needed. His job would be waiting for him.

Two months passed. No Stan. In our now weekly chats, his wife assured me that he was making progress, albeit slowly. She was certain I'd be seeing him soon. She wasn't kidding.

The day after that conversation, I was having lunch in a caff. The popular game show, 'You Bet Your Life', was on the TV. You can imagine my shock when, midway through the show, the announcer said, 'And now, ladies and gentlemen, for the eighth week on our show, here is the contestant who has already won more than $15,000! The popular Stan the Man Weaver!' Weaver hadn't been ill. He had been cleaning up on a TV game show! The next morning I called him and gave him his notice. I could tolerate his highjinks, but I couldn't put up with a lie. That was overstepping the bounds. Looking back, I may have been too harsh. After all, how could Weaver resist risking his job for all that prize money? He was an entrepreneur.

Into the corporate war zone

Eccentric or straight arrow, there is a game going on within the corporate game, and it is often a dirty one. Inter-office politics have knocked out many a player before he knew the competition had even begun.

I got my first taste of the seamier side of company life at Playtex. Al Peterson had left Lever Brothers and had joined Playtex as vice-president of marketing in 1954. Under him was a national sales manager, Parker Drake, whom I have mentioned previously. As Drake had been with the company for twelve years, he resented Peterson's coming in from an outside company and assuming a position he himself had coveted. Drake formed an anti-Peterson clique with his two regional sales managers.

In 1955, Peterson persuaded me to leave Lever Brothers for a position at Playtex. He told me about the friction between himself and Drake. This was not done as a matter of courtesy, but as a warning. It was Al's intention to weaken the pro-Drake faction by forcing Drake to accept me as a third regional manager. I was placed in charge of the West and was responsible for all the territory west of the Mississippi from the Canadian border to the Rio Grande.

Drake and his cohorts were not pleased with my appointment. To them, I was Al's spy and a threat to their infrastructure. Drake decided that his best interests would be served if I failed. Nothing would have pleased him more than his being able to drag my prone body into Heinze's office and sadly announce, 'I tried to tell Peterson about this kid, but it was no good. He forced me to take him on and now look. He just can't make it.' Aware of this attitude, I was prepared for a cool reception from Drake and his clan. What I wasn't quite prepared for was how blatant their attacks on me would be.

At sales meetings, in front of the salesmen from all three regions, Drake would go out of his way to extol the virtues of his two cronies. He'd say, '. . . and Pat Murphy has done a magnificent job in the East. Volume is up and looking better all the time. I'm also happy to note that Al Lombardo is doing just as spectacularly in the Midwest.' Where was Victor Kiam in all of this? I was the Unknown Soldier. Worse. At least *he* got a memorial stone. No matter how good a job I had done – and often my region would lead the country – I never got a mention. Until I was forced to copy Peterson in my weekly reports, I could never float an idea past Drake's desk.

The attacks on me – and, indirectly, against Peterson – came from two sides. Not only was Drake doing a number on me, some of the older employees in my region were trying to give me a hard time.

One of them was especially belligerent. Jack Mills was the district manager in Seattle. Forty-four years old, he had been with the company for a long time and was an ally of Drake. When I first approached him about a plan I wanted to implement in his district, he growled, 'I don't have to listen to you. I've been here ten years. You tell me what you think you want done and I'll talk to Drake and see if I want to do it.'

I couldn't overlook this sort of insubordination. I called Peterson and told him I had to make an issue over this. I asked for his support. I was going to forbid Mills to call Drake. Then I wanted to tell Drake that I expected him to refuse to take Mills's call. Peterson backed me. He knew if he hadn't my effectiveness would be gone. Mills's one-man insurrection was temporarily quelled, but my problems with Drake were far from over. Things got so unsavoury that I called Al on at least two occasions and asked him why he had thrown me into this hornet's nest. He told me to tough it out and that eventually everything would turn out fine. I decided to stay, but I also chose to go on the offensive.

If you get caught up in this sort of corporate skirmish, you have a number of options. You can give up. You can fight back with the same dirty tactics. Or, you can outperform your enemies to such a degree that their weapons are rendered useless. I chose the third option.

First, I had to cut some of the ground from under Drake. The first chance I had, I fired Mills. That was easy. I was building a powerful sales armada, peopled by dynamos. Mills stood out among them. He was so lazy you couldn't miss him.

I had asked him to accompany his salesmen when they called on key accounts. He claimed he was more effective staying at home and directing the field force by telephone. Analysis, he liked to claim, was his strength. Nonsense. He just didn't want to do any work. Having ordered him to meet those major clients, I made it a point to call his home every morning to make sure he had gone. Then I would have his salesmen call me just before their meeting. I'd always ask to speak to Jack. When he came on, I always had some fabricated reason to talk with him. Despite the thin masquerade, I'm sure he knew I was checking up on him. These conditions proved intolerable to Mills. The more work he was responsible for, the more he shirked. Eventually, his natural laziness caught up with him. He started to skip those meetings and take other shortcuts. When I found out, I put him on the carpet. After repeated transgressions – all of which were carefully documented – I was able to let him go. Drake didn't like this, but there was nothing he could do. The evidence against his man was overwhelming.

This was only the first volley of a long battle. The reports I was getting through to Peterson were winning recognition for me and my sales force. Our numbers were soaring to such an extent that Drake could no longer ignore us. With my region leading the company in performance, the Drake clique was running out of ammunition.

With their position weakening, I picked an ideal time for a frontal assault. I decided the best way for my region to stand out was to have it make history. We were going to have the greatest sales week in the history of the company.

I had a strong promotion to build around: the 'Mould 'n' Hold Girdle'. For the first time, women would be able to buy a latex girdle with a zipper. That may not sound like much of a breakthrough, but in 1956 this was something of a technological advance. Instead of wasting minutes wrestling themselves into the girdle, women would now be able to slip it on and zip it up in seconds. When I first saw the design, I knew what it could mean to the industry. I had been to the mountain, now I had to bring the word to the faithful.

To give the girdle the launching it deserved, I took a risk and called a secret meeting of all the salesmen and managers in my region. This was no small gamble. The airfares and hotel bills for the eighty-plus salesmen would come close to $20,000. My budget didn't have room for that expense, but I had already justified it with my Risk-Reward Ratio.

The Risk-Reward Ratio is a weighing of all the aspects, pro and con, of an endeavour. If it were written as a mathematical equation, it would probably look like this:

Possible Benefits of a Project of Investment
Time Expended + Money Spent + Reputation Risked

You won't find the result on any computer: all the figuring must be done in your gut. Using the Risk-Reward Ratio, my strategy for the 'Mould 'n' Hold' seemed sound. I was going to spend $20,000 of the company funds to call an unauthorized sales meeting. That would place me in some jeopardy. But I knew that by the time the bills reached Playtex, our promotion would be over. If it was as successful as I hoped, no one would care about the expenditure. If we fell short, I knew we would increase the volume at least enough to cover the extra monies spent. My reputation would have suffered a setback, but with the numbers my region had been turning in, I was confident I would be forgiven a 'first offence'. The one thing I was leery of was Drake's vengeance. If I failed and he was hungry, I was going to be lunch.

Guarding against that possibility made me doubly meticulous in my planning. I documented my strategy, knowing that if we fumbled the ball, I would need it. My carefully drawn-up plan would give powerful evidence that I hadn't gone into this programme half-cock. Whatever negatives my superiors could draw from my violation of company policy would, I hoped, be neutralized by our show of initiative and creativity.

I met my sales force in Denver in late August. All the troops had been sworn to secrecy; it was as if we were preparing for D-day.

In July, I had written to the general merchandise managers of every major store in our region, telling them that we were presenting an unbelievable promotion in September. I swore it was so big that we had to have the merchandise manager, the buyer, and the advertising manager present at our pitch. I even suggested the store president might want to attend.

In preparing for our onslaught, I had our salesmen break off into teams and practise their pitches for three days. I had picked Denver because there was so little nightlife there at the time. I wanted the entire sales force to think about nothing but the 'Mould 'n' Hold' and how it was going to sweep the nation.

We attacked during the first week of September. Everyone was on alert; this was not going to be a five-day week. It would be a six-day week. Also, no one was putting in a nine-to-five day. The salesmen were on the job at 8 a.m. and often didn't finish until after nine o'clock that evening. I wanted everyone to put in a 75-hour week in order to get sales that would be earth-shattering.

I put in the same time as the salesmen. Having made a list of the largest accounts, I called on all of them. At each stop, we pushed the zippered girdle as if it were a new wonder drug. 'A zippered girdle,' we would tell the buyers; 'can you imagine it? Think how easy it will be to put on. It will revolutionize the industry!' From there, we would go into the advertising campaign, the display, how the client's volume would increase, and other niceties. We would always finish where we began: the innovative feature of the girdle.

When I finished with the pitch, I would tell the buyer, 'I want to get your order first so we can ship to you first. I don't want to see this thing break across the country before you have a chance to get your stock off the floor. This is going to be so damned huge, it's scary.' Then I took out a pre-written order. We bowled the storepeople over so thoroughly that many of them bought the girdle without ever actually seeing it.

After the first two selling days, I knew we had a smash. Normally, I would have phoned in a midweek tally on Wednesday. This time I didn't call. Playtex couldn't read me. I was moving around the country and had neglected to give them my itinerary. Neither Drake nor Peterson knew where I was. I took calls from my salesmen every night. This was another change from the norm; usually, they would report their sales to the district manager. I let everyone know how well they were doing and how we were topping ourselves each night. This kept everyone motivated. They felt they were part of an important event, and they wanted to make it as big as possible.

Friday night, we got ready for the final push. I asked the salesmen to spend Saturday visiting whatever stores they couldn't close during the week. Calling these outlets, I would give them the pitch on the phone before the troops arrived. That night, too exhilarated to be tired, I stayed up until dawn preparing my results for the week.

The numbers were staggering. In an average week, our volume was a healthy $80,000. This six-day period, however, yielded a slightly higher figure: $800,000. Early Sunday morning, I sent this tally to Playtex via the usual telegram. Then I went out to the hotel pool and collapsed. I was a basket case. I couldn't move a muscle, but I had such a glow. We had pulled it off. My anticipation of Monday was sweet. I couldn't wait for Monday!

I reached Parker on Tuesday morning. Before I had a chance to say hello, he screamed, 'What the hell are you pulling out there? You sent two telegrams that don't make any sense. You show your week's volume at $800,000. That's 20% of your year in a single week! These numbers are off the wall.' Noting his chagrin, I asked, 'Well, do you want the business or not, because that's what we wrote last week.' He couldn't believe it, so I told him, 'Fine. Don't take my word for it. But get ready for those orders. They should be coming in already.' This good news did little to cool him off. He said, 'What the hell did you do? You get on a goddam plane and get your ass in here. You've got some explaining to do!'

I was in his office the next day. By the time I arrived, everyone knew what had happened. The order department had been deluged. Our production schedule was thrown off course for the next eight weeks. As I walked through the building, I was greeted by nothing but smiles. A meeting was convened with Heinze, Peterson, Drake and myself. The first thing Wally said was, 'Well, you had a fairly good week. Would you mind telling me how you did it?' My plan was typed up and ready for presentation. There wasn't a crack in it. No one, not even Drake, bothered to bring up my unauthorized expenditures. Three months later, I was promoted to marketing director of girdles and bras and Drake had to report to me. Peterson and I had been vindicated.

Drake and I ended up working quite well together. I met with him shortly after my promotion and signed a truce over lunch. I told him, 'If you choose to stay, your position is secure. I can't do the job you do. Wouldn't want to try. As long as you keep doing a good job, I won't interfere with you. I won't tell you who to promote or who to fire. You run the show. This company is growing and we can both make a lot of money while having a lot of fun. I want us to work together, building the business.' He agreed, and for the next two years we had a very good relationship. Despite our differences, I liked Drake. He was the greatest salesman I had ever seen: Parker could have customers eating out of his hand. He could motivate his people and they loved him for his sense of humour. Talent such as this is so precious you can't afford to lose it over personal squabbles. Drake could be a hardnosed SOB, but he got results. He was exactly the type of player I wanted on my team.

The sort of guy I *don't* want on my side is the back-stabber. You'll run into your share of those as you climb up the corporate ladder. You must be aware of them, because the more adept ones will clap you on the back with one hand and fillet your innards with the other. If you receive word that some rival is sharpening his knife on your backbone, whether the blade is formed of lies or innuendo, you must take immediate action. I hate to say this, but you might have to do unto others. Try to avoid this by confronting the person. You don't want to get into a slugging match; that might open the door for a third party who isn't busy thrusting and parrying. Let the ripper know that a peace pact is in both your interests. I once told a particularly obnoxious merchant of slander that I knew exactly what he was doing and said, 'I'm not interested in knowing the reasons why. If you keep this up, I'm going to do the biggest hatchet job on you this company has ever seen. Now we can cut each other up, or we can compete on merit, letting the chips fall where they may.' This usually ends the attacks. A ripper generally fears his victim, or he wouldn't have reason to ambush him. He certainly doesn't want to be the rippee. Insecure about his own record, he knows what a potent weapon it would be if turned against him. If you're able to persuade your rival to desist, great. If not, take your knife out of its sheath and go to town. *Don't*, however, sink to his level. Nail him on something authentic, attacking each of his failures. The ripper usually has a closet full of them. Never let the world forget his smallest screw-up. And make sure your flank is covered by the shield of your own solid performance.

Getting further ahead

Not every rival will try to mug you in your sleep. If the company you work for is worthy of you, it shouldn't be any problem finding a number of talented people willing to hustle as hard as you in an effort to reach the top. You have to watch for these dynamos and be able to assess their strengths and weaknesses.

I used to do a balance sheet of all the key executives at Playtex, paying particular attention to those who had climbed to the same rung as I had.

One chap, Leo Richards, was the head of the family products division at Playtex. This fellow was the direct opposite of me; he could squeeze a gallon of orange juice out of a mummified orange. He scrutinized every nickel his division spent. That department wasn't expansive, but its bottom line profit was brilliant.

My division had a healthy interest in keeping expenses down, but not at the cost of growth. The balance sheet I did on Richards told that I could never match him in the area of cost-cutting: it just wasn't in my nature. The best I could do was hold my own and hope that the difference between us in that measurement wasn't too glaring.

Richards's obvious weakness was that he never created a new

product, service, or idea. That was where I could shine. In trying to expand the business, I might have some failures, but my hits were memorable. Richards never had any failures – he was too cautious – but he never had any spectacular successes, either.

I tried to exploit his Achilles' heel and he returned the compliment. Any chance he got, he would point out the difference in our bottom lines to Peterson. Mine went up and down, because I was building the business. Richards's always showed a steady upward climb, but reflected no growth. Richards also would highlight any problems my more daring concepts encountered, to imply I was 'off the wall'.

I countered Richards by listing all the innovative things we had tried and spotlighting any new ideas we had generated in our division or others. Then, I would subtract the failures from the successes. The monetary result was always a plus. This would allow me to get my digs in: my division was one of tremendous potential. While some other divisions of the corporation might be more profitable (now who could I be referring to by that?) they were not displaying any ingenuity or growth. I agreed we would make some mistakes, but they would pale next to our triumphs. Therefore, I suggested, any investment in the future should come to our division. We were the ones building the company. And I was right! After three years, sales for Richards's division increased ten per cent. Mine climbed almost 300%!

Making my point in this manner did two things. First, I muted Leo's criticism of what he perceived to be my reckless ways, by minimizing the impact of my mistakes and heightening the importance of our successes. Second, I hinted that Richards could not build the company. He could maximize profits, but without expansion he would only bring us to a dead end. Our methods were geared for the long haul, and were the type that won wars.

We duelled for two years and Peterson made the most of it, playing us off against each other. He'd drop by my office and say, 'Boy, you know the family products division's sales aren't up, but they made one million dollars more this year than last!' Then he'd tell Richards, 'Did you see that promotion for the new product Kiam came up with last week? Wow, what a zinger!' This competition engendered by his prodding was good for the company and especially good for us. It spurred us on. We were always finding ways to top each other, and this brought out the best in both of us during our struggle for the top seat at Playtex. When we started this tussle, I was at a disadvantage. Leo was several years older than I and had been with the company longer. When we departed, I would have to admit that he was still slightly ahead of me in the line of succession. But I was gaining on him all the time.

The balance sheet will do more than just allow you to probe your opponent's weaknesses. It will let you take note of talented individuals within the company, people you can utilize as your position grows stronger. It may also acquaint you with a reality: you may not be the best person to sit on top of your particular company. Going up the corporate ladder, the rungs get smaller in width and the competition intensifies. You will be pitted against two, three, or four people who are every bit as good as you are. All of you are competing to reach the highest spot. What are your chances? In one case, you may have a boss due for retirement in five years. If you wait that long and don't get his job, has that time been wasted? Do a balance sheet on yourself and your rivals and make a point-by-point comparison. If it becomes obvious that someone else is better suited for the presidency than you, then you must make a decision. Can you catch and pass the frontrunner in five years? If you can't reach the pinnacle, are you willing to continue with the company on a high level, or should you look for a new frontier to conquer? Being entrepreneurial *doesn't* necessarily mean you have to be top dog. In any given situation, there may be an entrepreneur who is better than you. Your job is to be the best you can be: your ultimate satisfaction will come from that.

Of course, you may want to leave the company long before you're in a position to compete for the top spot. A word of advice: stay with the organization until you reach the first level of management. That first supervisory position gives you a background and proves to yourself and to others that you're executive material. It's easy to leave a company for a higher-salaried position with another corporation. The increase in pay may be tempting, but you'll set yourself back if you've never managed before. Don't lose sight of your priorities: get on the scoreboard. Getting over that first managerial hump in your first corporation makes a wonderful impression and it gives you the credibility you'll need if you want to go after a managerial position elsewhere.

There is one reason why you should leave a company, no matter how long you've been there. If you find you can't function as an entrepreneur, if the atmosphere is too restrictive, you've got to leave. Start sending out CVs. A restrictive company doesn't encourage you to grow, is run on consensus opinion, and is averse to new ideas. If you've blundered into such an organization, one that you thought was run by a go-getter but is actually a local chapter of the 'Guardians of the Status Quo', you won't have a chance to stand out. If you stay, your adventurer's soul will die a lonely death.

If you're not interested in standing out, you don't have to play the game and it won't matter what company you join. If all you want to do is hang on until you're eligible for that pension, allowing you to sit on the beach for the rest of your days, then don't take any risks. Sink into the background. Don't get noticed for anything good and by all means don't get noticed for anything bad. Hold tight. In twenty, thirty, or forty years your sentence will be up. You can deposit your nearly lifeless form on to the beach blanket and congratulate yourself for reaching paradise. Of course, you'll probably be too bored or too structured to enjoy any of it. You'll execute your retirement the same way you executed your job. You'll merely exist, not live.

It doesn't have to be that way. You can live in paradise *now*. Take the gambles and explore the depths of your potential. As a corporate entrepreneur, your Shangri-La isn't forever bathed in sunlight; it will have its share of tempests. But its atmosphere will always be crackling with the electricity that emanates from its centre: your own rich and vibrant life.

CHAPTER THREE

Putting your best foot forward

In 1954, though only a salesman, I was asked by Lever Brothers to represent the company at a meeting of sales managers from McKesson & Robbins, the largest chain of wholesalers in the United States. This was an important task; McKesson & Robbins dealt with most of the major drugstores and supermarkets in our regions. They could easily make or break a product. My job was to convince this group of forty thousand businessmen to push Pepsodent with their accounts. The assignment came at a crucial time in the toothpaste's life.

Pepsodent was the number two toothpaste in the country, just behind Colgate. We were pleased with that lofty position, but we wanted to be number one. Colgate had held the top spot for what seemed like an eternity. However, in 1954, with the implementation of an aggressive marketing campaign, Pepsodent had made sizeable gains and appeared ready to dethrone the champion. Then a new product, Gleem, entered the fray and quickly established itself as a formidable contender. It jumped to number three in a few short months and was soon drawing nearly even with us in the ratings. This rapid rise concerned Lever Brothers. We now not only had to think of ways to cut further into Colgate's share of the market, but we had to fend off the challenge of Gleem.

Getting McKesson & Robbins to support Pepsodent aggressively was going to be a tough sell. As far as most of these fellows were concerned, there was little to choose among the major toothpaste brands. Most of them were made from essentially the same ingredients, though each featured its own distinctive flavour. Some claimed an advantage over their competitors in their ability to prevent cavities or to whiten teeth. Others featured a colour other than the traditional white. Despite the claims and appearance of the product, the dissimilarities were slight. Toothpaste was toothpaste.

With so little to work on, I was expected to come up with a presentation that would capture the wholesalers' imaginations and kindle their enthusiasm for Pepsodent. This would have to be accomplished quickly. On the day I was scheduled to appear before them, they were also going to meet with thirty-five other sales representatives from rival companies. Each of us would have no more than ten minutes to knock their socks off. During my flight down to Florida, I wondered what on earth I could do in this brief time that would make me and Pepsodent stand out in the crowd.

I racked my brain for hours, trying to come up with a solution. Nothing. It wasn't until I walked past a pet shop that I found what I was seeking. Deciding on a radical course of action, I turned into the store and purchased a monkey.

I showed up for my presentation at 9 a.m. on a Saturday morning. Having been greeted by a receptionist, I was ushered into a small room where I was expected to wait my turn with the other 35 hopefuls. Though none of them realized it, the monkey had accompanied me. Hidden from view by a purple velvet cover draped around his cage, he slept quietly and gave no hint of his presence or identity.

Fourteen salesmen made their pitches before I did. When my turn arrived, I reached into the cage, took out King Kong's grandson, and perched him on my shoulder. Ignoring the startled looks of my rivals, I strode into the conference room. I acted as if nothing out of the ordinary was transpiring. Placing my samples on a table, I turned to the assemblage and announced, 'Gentlemen, I'm here for Pepsodent and I have a monkey on my back. It's time I got him off!' With that, I tossed the monkey on to the meeting table and watched as he proceeded to run amok. He raced the length of the table, knocking over glasses and disrupting papers along the way. The McKesson & Robbins people went wild! Some of them were overcome by fits of laughter; a few of them turned pale out of sheer terror. There wasn't one who didn't evince some sort of reaction.

Oblivious to the commotion he had caused, the monkey transformed the room into his private playground. After about five minutes, I had to climb up on a chair and pull him down from the top of the venetian blinds. His capture was the signal for something resembling order to be restored. Claiming the monkey, I turned to this now thoroughly stunned group of executives and announced, 'Thank you for your time, gentlemen. Push Pepsodent.' I offered no explanation for what had just taken place. I simply left before they had an opportunity to call either the police or a psychiatrist.

On the day following my monkey-shines, I visited a supermarket in my region. It had never been a particularly large customer of ours. The moment the owner saw me, he started chuckling. 'Kiam,' he said, 'I just have to ask you something: what the hell did you do at that meeting the other day? The McKesson & Robbins guy was just in and the first thing he talked about was you and your monkey. He said he realized it might sound crazy, but it was the most exciting sales pitch he had ever seen. It left everyone speechless!' While I was glad that it was received with such good humour, I was a bit concerned. It hadn't been my intention merely to provide the wholesalers with an afternoon's entertainment. I didn't want the purpose of my mission – the selling of Pepsodent – to be obscured by the hoopla. Any fears I had vanished when the store owner continued, 'I sure wish I could have been there. It must have been something to see. The McKesson & Robbins salesman talked more about Pepsodent today than he has in the last year. He went on about it so much that I felt obliged to double my usual order.'

That's what I'd wanted to hear. Visiting other stores, I received this same reaction from almost every buyer and owner I spoke with. With a little help from a simian friend, the drive to make Pepsodent the number one toothpaste in the country was off to a flying start.

Despite this success, I don't necessarily advise my readers to run out and buy monkeys before they give a presentation. Just as I didn't want my point obscured by a stunt back then, I wouldn't want the thrust of my message buried by an anecdote now. What I hope will be noted is what I discovered that day: in making any sort of pitch, the entrepreneur mustn't be afraid to stand out.

Throughout your entrepreneurial life, no matter what course it takes, you are going to be called on to convince others to accept a product or a concept. You will have to be able to write memos and reports that are clear, concise and persuasive. You may also have to become something of a public speaker, expected to address large audiences.

Before you make your presentation, you must be sure of your facts and believe in your product or idea. Nothing is more easily read than false enthusiasm. It is an instant turn-off. Let's assume that, since you are an entrepreneur, you wouldn't be associated with anything you didn't believe in. Let's also assume that your work ethic demands that you come prepared at all times. You're two-thirds of the way home. Now all you have to do is figure out how to make your presentation live in the memory of your audience. As you can gather, there are different strategies for every situation. If you follow the proper steps, you won't make a monkey of yourself in any of them.

Getting the appointment

You can't put your best foot forward unless you first get it stuck in the door. Before you can persuade anyone to consider anything you have to offer, you must first get to see them. Gaining an audience with a busy individual is often difficult.

I've always found that the best way to get an appointment is to show up without warning. Whenever I did this, the goal of my game plan was to score points by either seeing the party I wished to do business with or securing a firm date for another time.

I tried the conventional methods. Phone calls were hit and miss. Often, when I was calling on behalf of Playtex or Lever Brothers, I would be shunted off by the person on the other end of the line before I even got a chance to explain fully the reason for my call. They would hear the name of my company and announce they had no interest in any of our merchandise. It didn't matter that I might have been calling about a product they were unfamiliar with; they had already made up their minds that I wasn't going to get near first base.

That they could shrug me off so easily shouldn't come as a surprise. *A faceless voice over the telephone wire is never hard to dismiss.*

A letter requesting an initial meeting is even less effective than a phone call. I must receive fifty letters a day from various firms, agencies and individuals, all requesting meetings or interviews. My morning mail is filled with the damning evidence that large segments of the business world are meeting-crazy. Much of this correspondence comes accompanied by colourful brochures. A lot of them are attractive and show creativity. But, after a while, they tend to blur into one another until I can't tell them apart. Unless these letters are really outstanding – and too few are – the postman will be taking the writers a courteous but firm 'no' in a matter of days. If the letter is mundane, one that barely steps above the level of junk mail, it will probably end up in the waste-paper basket.

A physical presence is an entirely different matter. You can hang up on a person, but only if he has telephoned. You can toss a letter into a wastepaper basket without straining a muscle. But, unless you're Arnold Schwarzenegger, you can't easily toss a person into the same receptacle. When you show up, asking to be received, you are generally not going to be ignored.

When I was a salesman with Lever Brothers I made a habit of calling on potential new accounts without warning. I would present my card to the receptionist and say, 'I don't have an appointment with Mr Jones, but I *do* have several accounts in the area. Since I was in town I was wondering if Mr Jones could see me for five or ten minutes.' Sometimes I would be ushered in quickly. On other occasions I would be told that the boss was tied up and couldn't see me now. I always had a reply for that excuse. I would say, 'That's fine. I have no pressing engagements scheduled for the rest of the afternoon. If Mr Jones can squeeze me in during the next few hours, I'd be glad to go out, grab a bite to eat, and come back.' The majority of the time, I got to meet my quarry that day. At the very least, I came away with a commitment for a session in the not-too-distant future. I think you'll find most executives are impressed with this action. I know I am. If someone risks taking the time to try to see me without any guarantee that he will be successful, I will certainly try to find the time to see him.

If your attempts to make an uninvited personal appearance fail, use the telephone. Your phone conversation should resemble a good memo. Make it concise. Don't waste valuable time on pleasantries. I can't stand it when a person with whom I've never spoken before calls me and the first words out of his mouth are, 'How are you?' He doesn't care how I am. If I said I felt fine or was two toes in the grave, it would be all the same to him. Nine times out of ten, the caller would have the same reaction to either reply. His reactions are canned, just like the pitch he's about to make. A friend of mine was nearly driven mad by a salesman who always called and asked about his health and that of his family. No matter what my friend replied, the salesman would say, 'Great, great, glad to hear it,' and then proceed with the real purpose of his call. One day, as an experiment, my friend replied, 'Well, my wife was just killed by an axe-murderer and my children were kidnapped and then sold to gypsies.' The salesman didn't drop a beat. He replied with his customary, 'Great, great,' and went into his spiel. The caller was committing a double sin. Not only was he wasting valuable time on claptrap, but he wasn't listening. If you're going to use the phone, take full advantage of it. Listen fully, not just for words, but for moods. Judge the tone of the other person, and respond to it. You're trying to establish a relationship and you can't do that if you're on automatic. I especially hate a caller to start a conversation with, 'Mr Kiam, I know you're a busy man and I don't want to waste your time.' Why, then, is the caller wasting my time by saying that? He should get to the point. I'd much rather he say, 'Mr Kiam, I'm Ron Blum and my communications service can cut your phone and telex bills in half and deliver better with the same quality you're already enjoying.' Bingo. He's got my attention and I'm dying to hear more. Whenever you make a call, keep in mind that you and the person you've reached have other things to do besides chatting about the weather. Don't kill time. Even in this age of miracles, time can't be recreated.

You don't seem to be making any headway on the telephone. What should you do? You might want to send a letter, but I believe a telemessage is a better option. It doesn't come in with the rest of the mail and it has a sense of urgency. Like the entrepreneur, it stands out.

If you'd rather be more conventional and decide to send a letter, strive for economy in your writing. I've always found a one-page letter to be at least 50% more effective than a two-page communiqué. Many people are too busy to give lengthy letters their full attention. Often, they will skim the correspondence, hoping to discover a paragraph that summarizes the letter's contents. If you must write a long letter, accompany it with a note outlining the topics it covers and emphasizing your request for a meeting.

If all else fails, and the appointment means enough to you, use any means imaginable to gain your objective. By this time, you have nothing to lose. My wife and I are in the jewellery business. When we first started, we tried to arrange a showing of our merchandise to the buyers of many of the major stores in the United States. One buyer with a famous emporium in New York was particularly resistant to our request for an appointment. She claimed to have no interest in seeing the line. No matter what we tried – we made at least a dozen phone calls – she wouldn't budge. Since the mountain refused stoutly to come to Mohammed, we went out and purchased a dozen roses, a mammoth box of chocolates, and one hundred balloons. These were attached to a sample of our jewellery. Accompanying the package was a note: 'Please, may we show you the rest of the line?' A delivery man was hired to take the gift to her office. One hour after its arrival, she called us. I'm happy to say we did end up showing her the range and her store became one of our largest accounts. As in the case of the monkey, this was an extreme measure and we took it only as a last resort. The bottom line, in this case, was that we needed to score. In that circumstance, in order to have a chance to get to home plate, you must find a way to get to first base.

Once you've got your appointment, make the most of it. Don't waste time with small talk; you might have only five minutes to present your case. Get off the mark right away. You're not going to have time to exhibit charts or graphs. If you're good in this initial shot, that opportunity will come later. Right now, you have to engender interest. You have to excite the person you're meeting as quickly as possible. Let's suppose you're with an ad agency. If you were to come into my office and say, 'Mr Kiam, I think my company could do a job for you in advertising,' I'm going to ask why and how. Anticipate those questions and answer them before they are asked. Be specific. Come in and say, 'Mr Kiam, I've seen your commercials on TV. You obviously believe in using that medium as an advertising tool. What would you say if I told you we had a way to save you millions of dollars against your current advertising expenditures while doubling your air time?' You have to know this sort of pitch is going to grab my attention. You're playing up to my needs. Now that you have me hooked, go into the particulars of your proposal. Before you know it, I'm either going to cancel my appointments for the next hour, or I'm going to arrange to meet you again at your earliest convenience.

After you've met an individual several times and you've developed a relationship with him, you can set up future meetings over the phone. There will be times, however, when a phone call might not be enough. If I'm going to meet someone with whom I'm already acquainted, but plan to discuss something out of the ordinary, I'll send him a letter beforehand, explaining the topic I want to discuss. It's important that I don't spring any surprises.

Recently, I went to Washington to meet Senator Dodd of Connecticut and Vice-President George Bush. I'd had some slight prior contact with Senator Dodd, but didn't really know him. I was certain he wouldn't know why I wanted to speak to him. Was I going to tell him that Remington was pulling out of Bridgeport? Would the conversation centre around the job-training programme in Connecticut, the subject of our last meeting? What exactly did this fellow Kiam want?

Neither did the Vice-President know why I was dropping in on him. Unlike my acquaintance with Senator Dodd, George and I go back a long way. The last time we'd spoken, some eight months prior to this occasion, Bush told me to visit him the next time I was in Washington. It's probable that he thought I was taking him up on the invitation and that my visit was mainly a social call. It wasn't.

I wanted to engage both men in a discussion on the impact the strong dollar was having on Remington's business overseas. As I said earlier, we were getting hurt and I wanted to know what the government could do to help the only shaver company based in the United States. Had I hit either Bush or Dodd with this out of the blue, each would probably have said, 'Gee, give me a couple of weeks to examine the issues and I'll get back to you.' I didn't think we could afford that kind of delay, so I sent letters to both of them, outlining the subject of our meeting and listing some of the alternatives open to the company. I made sure my letter was in the hands of both men a week before we were due to meet. When I got to Washington, neither of them needed time for additional research. We addressed the pertinent issues immediately.

I did the same thing before I met the president of one of the country's leading chain stores. I wanted to discuss some of the marketing ideas I had for the book you're now reading. I was certain he would think I wanted to talk about the shavers or some of the other Remington products his stores have carried. He had no idea I was doing a book. I sent him a letter in order to make sure that, as in the case of Dodd and Bush, he would be predisposed to the subject at hand before I arrived. When I got to his office, he had his vice-president in charge of marketing, his book buyer, and two of his advertising people sit in with us. The meeting couldn't have gone more smoothly and part of the reason was that we were all prepared.

The speech

Do you have any idea what, according to a recent survey, was the thing Americans fear most? It wasn't death, aeroplanes, nuclear war, or an audit by the IRS. It was public speaking. I'm only mildly surprised. No one has to tell me how hard it is to talk in front of an audience. When I was younger I was something of a wallflower; I was terribly shy. Talking to people in a social situation was akin to undergoing the Chinese water torture. Speaking in front of a whole group was worse than the rack.

I often tell the story about the first time I gave a speech. I recall how I was so nervous that I kept my eyes closed throughout most of the monologue. I kept hoping that if I didn't look at them they would quietly go away. When I had finished, I opened my eyes and discovered that, unfortunately, my wish had been granted. There was only one person left in the audience. He was a bookish-looking fellow wearing a sour expression. Hoping to find some solace in this catastrophe, I asked him why he had stayed. Still frowning, he replied, 'I'm the next speaker.'

The story is apocryphal, but I think it describes, to some small degree, the sheer terror many of us go through when called upon to make an address in public. It also isn't too much of a stretch from what I actually went through in my first couple of appearances. I had a case of the jitters during my first two speeches and it was unfortunate. Had I been more calm, I could have raised the level of my performance on both of those occasions from absolutely awful to simply bad.

You see my nervousness was only a small part of the problem. In direct contradiction to my entrepreneurial philosophy, I was ill-prepared to give either of these talks. I rambled and referred to notes too frequently. My phrasing was redundant. My nervousness constricted my energy, causing me to deliver the vital points of my address without sufficient punch. Worst of all, I was long-winded. This murdered the attention of my audience. That the length of my speech exceeded all the boundaries of human tolerance was evident in both cases. In the first episode, I appeared before a group of high school freshmen. By the time I finished rambling, they all looked old enough to graduate.

The second gathering consisted of selected members of the Yale Club. The youngest of these gentlemen was perhaps 75 years old. Midway through my speech, I noticed an inordinate number of heads nodding forward. It also seemed that the room was alive with the steady drone of snoring. It seems my audience was trying to tell me something. They didn't have to say it twice.

Disturbed by both these experiences, I did some self-examination and came to the conclusion that my nervousness was the first problem to be overcome. Since I thought my case of the jitters was a reaction to the intimidating number of people I might have to address – 'intimidating' here being defined as more than one – I felt it necessary to discover a method of dealing with them. Having become less shy, I noted that I rarely had trouble speaking in a one-to-one situation. I therefore reasoned that I would feel much more comfortable if I stopped thinking of the audience as a faceless mob. I personalized them and thought of each assembly as a friendly individual who had invited me into his living room for an informal chat. I would create a mental image of my friend, taking care in each instance to be specific about his appearance. If the area where the audience was seated was darkened, I placed him in the centre of it. If I could see the group I was addressing, I would pick out what seemed to be a sympathetic face and transform it into that of my friend. This exercise enabled me to cut the crowd down to a manageable size and gave the speeches a more personal quality. I felt as if I were talking *to* someone rather than *at* a human wall. This method allowed for ease of concentration, letting me divert my attention from my nervousness.

I also reminded myself that whenever I gave a speech, the audience was there to see me. I had information they wanted to hear. Realizing this and mastering the substitution technique soon saw to it that the jitters and I were no longer on speaking terms.

The problem of my lack of brevity was tackled next. Going over both talks, I found they were too detailed. A preponderance of facts in a verbal presentation can represent a quagmire that can bog down even the most skilled public speaker. President Reagan is known as the Great Communicator, but do you remember what happened when he squared off against Walter Mondale in the first presidential debate of 1984? Before this confrontation, Reagan had taken a lot of criticism from opponents who charged he was a candidate of little substance, lacking a grasp of important facts. On the evening of the debate, you got the impression that the President had thought, 'I'll show 'em.' He whipped out a basketful of facts and figures in an obvious attempt to show how well he paid attention to detail. He wound up losing a large segment of his audience in an avalanche of numbers and, after a while, tripping over his own decimal points.

Mondale, on the other hand, touched only on the broad numerical parameters of his points. He used some figures, but he knew these weren't important. It was the message, supported by the numbers, that was the key. Polls taken in the days following their clash showed that Mondale came out the better by a wide margin. In their next meeting, however, Reagan avoided the mistake he'd made in the first debate. He didn't allow himself to be snared in a web of minutiae. As a result, he gave a much better account of himself.

The President learned the same lesson in that initial debate that I was taught by my first two talks: a speech is not an oral examination. The speaker is not at the podium to prove that he understands higher maths. The purpose of any talk is to sway the audience. In future speeches, I tried to exorcize the unimportant details that tended to stem the flow of my monologue. Instead of saying, 'Over the last year we sold over 1,567,347 units,' I would now say, 'We've had sales of over a million and a half.' If our volume had risen in each of the last four quarters, I wouldn't give exact percentages for every period. I would merely say, 'Sales have gone up steadily over the past year.' The exact dates and figures are wonderful garnishes, but are best left for an annual report, where they can be examined at the convenience of the reader. The fact that business is booming is the meat and potatoes, the main course, and is what the audience wants to be served.

Referring too often to notes can be fatal, too. After giving that first speech to the freshman assembly, I asked a friend who had attended how I had done. To my astonishment, he termed my performance memorable. When I asked if he was joking, he replied, 'No. Of course not all of it was memorable, just certain parts. For instance, your hair. I doubt anyone will ever forget what a nice full head of hair you have. You certainly gave us enough opportunities to look at it. First, we had a frontal view of your hairline. Then, every minute or so, you'd give us a lovely aerial shot of the top of your head. The only thing you neglected to show us was the back. Perhaps you should have pirouetted once or twice in mid-speech to make sure we saw all the angles. The speech certainly made your point. Throughout your talk, I kept thinking, "Who's his barber?"' That, I'm afraid, was not the message I had hoped to impart. My constant reference to notes had distracted my audience and, as I would learn from others later, helped build the impression that I wasn't on top of my facts.

I saw a graphic illustration of this during the vice-presidential debates between George Bush and Geraldine Ferraro. I couldn't tell you who won that evening, but I do know Congresswoman Ferraro injured her cause whenever she glanced down towards the podium. She did this much too frequently. I don't know if she was looking at notes, but it seemed as if she was. I have found that audiences doubt the sincerity of a speaker who uses excessive notes. They don't believe the words are coming from the heart.

I don't use notes and I don't try to memorize speeches word for word. I do draw up and commit to memory a specific outline for my speech and refer to it whenever I feel I'm starting to stray from the subject. I approach the speech as I would a conversation. If I asked you to come into my office in fifteen minutes and discuss your ideas for improving the shaver business, I doubt you would come in with a prepared statement. You'd organize your thoughts, making sure to cover the key areas of your case, and then speak extemporaneously. Your pitch wouldn't sound as if it were coming from a cassette. It would sound as if it were the carefully drawn-up plan of a thinking, feeling human being. You'd also give the impression of having a working knowledge of the subject you're addressing. Furthermore, once you've cast off the shackles of the neatly typed speech, you'll find that your natural enthusiasm for the subject is given free rein and will lend an energy to your words that might otherwise be lost.

If your speech is 99% fat-free, you shouldn't be concerned with its length unless you have only a brief time to deliver it. Then you have to pare it down. On the other hand, if you've been given too much time, let the organizers of the event at which you're appearing know of this, and make sure they compensate for your brevity. Don't try to bull your way through by fluffing your speech with a lot of marshmallow. If the person in charge can't accommodate you, don't be intimidated. Give your speech as planned.

I was once asked to give a speech before a local political club. The chairman said I would be the last speaker and would have an hour to air my views. When I protested that I needed only one-third of this time he said, 'Fine. We'll schedule you for twenty minutes.' When I got to the dais that evening, I looked at the programme and saw: 'Guest Speaker – Victor Kiam – 10–11 p.m.' I turned to the chairman and said, 'But I told you I needed only twenty minutes!' He gave me his most charming smile and said, 'Yes, yes, but that was far too short. I'm sure you'll do your best with the time I've given you.' I certainly did. Exactly twenty minutes after I started my speech, I was finished. Then, I resorted to the old standby: 'Does anyone have any questions?' The audience's queries killed another fifteen minutes. Having answered the last question, I thanked the club for its attentiveness and added, 'Now I know you're all anxious to hear from the man who brought me here. I know your chairman will be able to expand further on my thoughts.' Before polite applause, I led the chairman up to the podium and then returned to my seat, where I had the pleasure of watching him tap-dance for the final 25 minutes of the evening. I suppose I should have felt sorry for him. I didn't.

The more subtle skills of speech-making can be acquired only through experience. You have to learn how to build the peaks and valleys of your talk and how to read the ebb and flow of your audience. Watch other speakers and observe how they work an audience. It requires a delicate sense of timing which can be acquired only through practice. Rehearsal can help. After my first two speeches, I practised in front of my mirror and then in front of a small group of friends. Afterwards, they would criticize my performance. This helped me to eliminate the weak links in my verbal chain and facilitated the development of my own style. I learned to keep my anecdotes short and uncomplicated and never to use a funny story unless it made a point. I also learned not to use an anecdote that was *too* funny in the middle of a talk. It would stop the speech dead in its tracks and leave me with nowhere to go. That could be as bad as ending the speech on a downbeat. Even if the bulk of the news you bring is grim and the future looks gloomy, you want your audience to know that hope is not lost. End the speech as an optimist – always – however you feel.

Reports and memos

At Playtex, Wally Heinze insisted that our reports be no more than four pages long. I've carried this philosophy over to every division and business with which I've been involved. The monthly reports filed by my employees all have a similar format. Apart from content, you'd think they were written by the same person. Each starts with a summary of the last month, a recap of how we did versus our projections, and a rundown on the significant events of the period. The next section deals with the current month. What had we planned, and what strategy is in place now? What are our current projections and how might they have to be altered? The third page focuses on the coming months and addresses the direction the company or division is taking and our plans for that period. The report is rounded off with a forecast of the year to come. Four pages and I have the entire business at my fingertips.

I learned to write memos at the Harvard Business School. I adopted their method for doing case studies. We were taught to start the case study of a company with the conclusion, followed by our recommendations. The body of the study, in outline form, would be the analysis that led us to our conclusion: past history, present situation and future projections. The first paragraph would contain the reason for our conclusion followed by a summary reiterating that conclusion and our recommendation.

I chose to do memos in a similar manner. I want the reader to absorb the rest of the information contained in the body of the memo in context with the conclusion. I want them to know where they are headed. *A memo is a work of non-fiction but it is not a mystery*. The readers shouldn't have to wade through endless lines of analysis before finding out whether or not the butler did it. As an entrepreneur, you must be conclusion-oriented. *In your world, no one wants to hear about the labour pains, they just want to see the baby.*

I love a memo I received recently. It started out with a recommendation of what we should be doing with our jewellery business, the Friendship Collection. This was followed by a paragraph on each of the various aspects of the company. Everything from inventory to Friendship's distribution channels was covered. The entire memo took up all of two pages and outlined ten hours of meetings and what steps were being taken to implement the decisions reached at those meetings. It gave us the whole direction of the company without any fat. This was the sort of lean and mean memo an entrepreneur has to love.

No matter how well they are written, though, memos should be kept to a minimum. Any correspondence that raises an issue which can be responded to immediately should be answered by telephone. Try not to get involved in a game of Duelling Memos. It's wasteful. I had some questions about the Friendship Collection memo and I knew they couldn't be answered without some research, so I didn't bother phoning. Rather than squander my secretary's time and my own dictating a reply memo, I wrote my query on the side of his paragraph on inventories. My question asked, 'Are these inventories being done every quarter or semi-annually?' Then I sent it back to him. If there's still enough space left on the page, he'll write his answer beneath my query, or else he'll telephone me. There won't be minutes lost drafting yet another memo and we won't bury our operation in a sea of worthless paper.

The oral presentation

Any time you have to make an oral presentation, whether it be at a business conference or when you're selling to a client, you, as the entrepreneur, must control the meeting.

If you're going to use slides, present your audience with a notebook detailing the information found on the slides, so they don't take unnecessary notes during the course of your pitch. Remind them that they don't have to put anything down on paper, because it's already explained to them in the books you've just given them. You may also take this time to present them with an outline of your presentation and a summary of the information contained in the charts and graphs you use, if any. Restrict their note-taking: you want to be the centre of their attention.

Before starting, make an announcement about questions. I usually tell my audience, 'It's fine to ask questions as we go along, but it will serve everyone better if you wait until we have finished. Of course, if we lose you at any point, feel free to ask for a clarification.' If a question is asked, answer it in general terms and move on with the show. The worst sin you can commit is to allow a question to sidetrack the purpose of your meeting.

We would give classes in sales meetings at Lever Brothers. Various groups of salesmen would practise for a day and participate in a contest. Each squad would make a presentation for the same product. The best performance would earn the winning team a $500 prize. This was a valuable experience for our sales force. Its members would not only have a chance to pick up some extra cash, they would also be able to evaluate their performance against that of their peers. One fellow in particular gave a marvellous presentation, but his group always missed the top spot because he was too easily led astray by questions. For example, during his pitch he might be asked, 'Didn't Colgate do something like this?' Instead of saying, as he should have, 'Yes, but it didn't work out and after the presentation I'll tell you why,' he went into the entire history of the Colgate campaign. Having been asked the time, he proceeded to tell us how to make a watch. When he was finished, we had forgotten everything that had preceded the question. He had lost both his audience and the $500.

Before making your presentation, you have to decide whether you want to give your conclusion first, as in the memo, or if you want to opt for a dramatic build-up to a final climax. There are no hard and fast rules for making that choice. Generally, I like to save the conclusion for the end, but that could be because I'm gun-shy. I once gave a presentation before a new account in which I gave the conclusion at the start. The chief executive of the company agreed with it but he hadn't alerted me to that fact. Ten minutes into the presentation he stood up and said, 'Call me back when this thing is over.' Then he left, throwing a bucket of cold water on my enthusiasm. Fortunately, the only reason he walked out was because he had already made up his mind to do business with us.

Giving your conclusion at the beginning of your presentation is especially helpful when you are constrained by time. If you have only 20 minutes to make your pitch, you have to give your conclusion first and then make your audience buy it. I always ask how much time I have to make my presentation. If I don't think it's enough, I'll say, 'That's no good. When can you give me more time?' Then I'll state how much more time I need. You have to take control. Of course, if all you can get is ten minutes, then you have to do the best you can with that.

No matter how often you repeat the same pitch, make sure it gives the appearance of being tailor-made for its audience. Slip in something that enhances that illusion. For instance, a fellow recently gave a presentation at Remington and midway through it he said, 'Now I know Remington has gone into the apparel business, so I'm sure you'll find this next part interesting.' We felt that performance was geared to us. That is important. You don't want your pitch to sound as if memorized by rote.

Some companies may have a presentation pre-designed for you, and will insist that you use it. By all means, follow company policy but don't be afraid to abandon it if the situation demands it. At Playtex, we had a presentation book that all our salesmen were supposed to use whenever they called on an account. Al Peterson was adamant about this. Shortly after I came in as regional sales manager, I had to appoint someone to head one of my districts. There were three candidates. I spent three days in the field with each of them. One of them, Peter Palizolla, stood head and shoulders above the other two. I knew he was the man for the slot, but when I told Peterson, he rebelled. He claimed, 'The guy's no good, I don't care how well he did. He doesn't use the presentation book.' Apparently, Al had been on the road with Peter several times and noted this defect in his work habits. I had seen the same thing, but I realized Peter wasn't using the book only because the majority of his clients didn't want to see it. They had all told him they weren't interested in hearing a form letter. Rather than antagonize the account, Peter closed the book and played it by ear. Quite successfully, I would add. Naturally, I thought Peter was doing the right thing. I didn't care what method he used to get the order, as long as he got it. I stood firm with

Peterson, reminding him that he had promised me a free hand in the area of promotions. He gave in after I promised to take full responsibility if Peter fouled it up. Eight months later, I was promoted to vice-president in charge of girdles and bras. I'll give you three guesses at the name of the brilliant district manager whom Peterson moved up into my vacant position.

CHAPTER FOUR

Closing the deal: the art of selling

In 1958, while still a marketing director of bras and girdles at Playtex, I was asked by Wally Heinze to help the company out of a jam. He came over to my office one evening and said, 'Vic, we have a little problem. Playtex has a television contract and it's just about to drop the ball. Our company has to be in the cosmetics business by midnight tomorrow. We have developed a product that could be sensational, but we need someone to sell it. Can you go out on the road tomorrow and get orders for the product by 5 p.m.? That will give you time to call in the orders before the deadline. It would be a tremendous help to the company. I'd ask one of the salesmen to do it, but I know you're the man for the job.' That last piece of flattery didn't turn my head. Of course I was the only man for the job. I was working my usual late hours and, outside of Wally and a few janitors, I was the only person left in the building.

I agreed to do it. The entrepreneur never passes up a chance to shine, particularly when it's at the behest of the president of the company. Since I had to sell the product, I asked him to tell me everything he could about it. He replied, 'It's called Living Cleansing Cream. It moisturizes while it cleanses, but its chief selling point is that it doesn't contain any mineral oil.' When I asked him what was so special about that, he explained, 'Don't you know? Mineral oil causes cancer.' I must admit I had never heard that claim before, and I rather doubt that any reputable member of the medical profession was aware of the grave dangers posed by this sinister lubricant. I tried not to appear too sceptical when I asked, 'Can we actually say that to our accounts?' Heinze insisted we could. Before I could raise another objection to this unlikely claim, Wally cut me off by saying, 'Of course, if you don't feel comfortable saying that, you don't have to. Just get Living Cream sold to someone.' I told Wally not to worry, I'd get the job done. When I asked him for a sample case he said, 'We're so far behind on this product that all I have are the jars. Give us about half an hour and we'll have them filled with cream. Just wait till you see this product. It will practically sell itself.'

Having picked up my samples of wonder cream, I went home and mapped out my strategy. I thought it would be fruitless to try to sell the product to one of our accounts in New York City. The next day would be Friday and it would be almost impossible to see a buyer at such short notice on the final business day of the week. I might spend the whole day calling on accounts and still manage to see only two or three of them. I needed to go to a less busy area, where I could see the maximum number of clients in the shortest period of time. I called the airlines and booked an early morning flight to Binghampton, New York. Reaching my destination at 8.30 a.m., I rented a car and drove out to a department store that represented one of our largest accounts in the city. Its buyer had a name I'll never forget: Henrietta Zipp. Meeting her and the store's merchandise manager, I extolled the virtues of the cream as a moisturizer and promised the store top billing in a full page ad on Sunday. The clincher came when Henrietta sampled the stuff and pronounced it 'as good as Ponds Cold Cream, maybe better'.

After getting the order from Ms Zipp, I raced out and called on a number of the smaller accounts in the area. I sold to nine of them. Then I went to the local newspaper and took out an ad for the Sunday edition. Once I made sure the ad was in place, I was able to call our office in Delaware and give them the order. We had beaten the deadline. They had already been alerted by Wally Heinze and were prepared to ship the Living Cream immediately. It arrived at our accounts on Saturday afternoon. I flew back home that evening and I couldn't have been more pleased. I had done everything that had been asked of me. Our television contract was no longer in jeopardy.

When I showed up for work on Monday morning, I went straight to Wally's office and told him of our success. He thanked me for pulling the company out of its mess and asked me to keep him abreast of how the cream sold.

I had planned to call Ms Zipp sometime that afternoon. That

wasn't necessary. About an hour after I had made my report to the president, Ms Zipp called me. She did not sound happy. When I asked her how the promotion was going, she replied, 'Not too well, I'm afraid. We have a problem.' What could possibly have gone wrong? I saw the orders delivered, so I knew the product was in stock. She assured me that the ad had run. Puzzled, I asked, 'Well, are you calling me to say the cream isn't moving?' 'No,' she replied, 'it's moving. It's just not selling. You see, when this stuff arrived on Saturday, we had no place to store it. So whoever was planning its display for this morning took it into the cosmetics department and stacked it in three neat rows. On the radiator! The cream overheated and the jars exploded sometime last night. When I said the stuff was moving I meant it was moving from the ceiling to the floor. In large, greasy, white plops! The gook is all over the place. It's like the Blob!' 'Well,' I ventured brightly, 'now you know why we call it Living Cream!' Thank heavens she had a sense of humour. I apologized for the accident (though I certainly didn't have to – after all, I wasn't the yo-yo who put the tightly-lidded jars on the radiator) and agreed to give her store a credit for the ruined goods.

Apart from the adventure of Ms Zipp and her exploding cream, the promotion went well. We fulfilled the terms of our contract and the other stores did a brisk business. This was, however, the product's one brief moment of glory. To the president's dismay, the public never quite bought the mineral oil claim. It wasn't long before the Living Cream was dead.

Flushed with the small success of that weekend, I rediscovered something about myself that I had always known: I loved selling. If business was indeed a game, I decided that selling was its grandest competition. Much as a singles tennis match does, selling features a one-to-one confrontation, requiring both participants to possess a high level of concentration and a sensitivity to the subtle changes in the tempo of play. A degree of brinksmanship is involved. An account who wants to dicker over terms can show as many slinky moves behind the desk as Bobby Riggs, tennis's all-time super hustler, exhibits on court. The ability to perform under pressure, the stamina to give your all no matter how long the match, and the resilience to bounce back from a gruelling defeat are the attributes that will serve a salesperson in a client's office just as well as Bjorn Borg on centre court at Wimbledon.

Most importantly, selling is a contest where the score is easily kept. Whenever you leave an account, you have only to look at your order forms to learn whether you won or lost. This was a game I enjoyed playing.

After the Living Cream episode, Heinze and Peterson would come to me whenever Playtex had to squeeze out of some hole. Once I had four days to sell five million aspirin for the company's drug division. I welcomed these challenges because I knew they helped me to stand out in the company. I also relished the kick I got from making the sale.

Much as I love the thrill of getting the order, I found out early in my career that I hated having my goods rejected. I've always had a problem: I have a hard time selling something if I don't believe in it. Living Cream was an exception, but in that instance I was aided by the rush of adrenalin that is the common experience of most rookie salespersons. On the whole, whenever I tried to sell anything of dubious value I would flop.

The reason for the failure is easily understood. For the entrepreneur, selling is an almost zen-like experience. The product or service you're offering should become an extension of yourself. You develop a personal pride in your merchandise and this allows you to generate the infectious enthusiasm you need to get the order. I've been lucky. I've been with companies which always sold morally acceptable products that were top of the line in quality. I had no qualms about placing my confidence in them and, in fact, would get so involved with the merchandise that I took any knocks against them as personal insults. They are a part of me! This has never been more true than with the shaver. If I run into someone who uses a Remington and he tells me how much he loves it, he had better be wearing sunglasses because he won't be able to see me for the glow. But if he rejects it, he's rejecting me. I'm going to grill him to find out what his objections are and then I'm going to do my damnedest to convince him he's wrong. Maybe I'll change his thinking, maybe I won't. But I am going to give it my best shot. *The pride you take in your product or service will give you the strength to deal with rejection in a positive manner.* That's why, as I said in Chapter One, entrepreneurs have to believe in the enterprises they become involved with as much as they believe in themselves.

One of my first experiences with rejection occurred shortly

after the Living Cream episode. It took a generous helping of entrepreneurial confidence to persevere during this incident; I was literally swept out of a store.

My travels for Playtex had brought me to Tupelo, Tennessee, where I spent the day calling on our accounts. One of these was a small clothing store located in the middle of town. The owner of the store was sweeping his floor when I walked in. Extending my hand, I told him I was from Playtex. He ignored me. I started to open my sample case. He responded by pushing his broom towards my feet, forcing me towards the doorway. When I inquired what was wrong, he swept me closer to the exit. I was about to lodge a formal protest but, with one last sweep of his broom, I found myself on my derriere outside the shop.

Was I dejected? No. A bit sore, perhaps, and slightly bemused. But not depressed. Before my samples and I had tumbled out, the drugstore owner had said, 'I don't ever want to see you or your samples around my store again.' His hostility challenged me to discover its cause.

After speaking to some other salesmen and store owners in the area, I discovered that this broomstick cowboy had a legitimate beef. The Playtex salesman who had worked this region before me had made it a practice to overstock the drugstore. He had left it with more merchandise than it could sell. This sort of oversell is sinful. A salesperson, especially an entrepreneurial one, isn't calling on an account merely to get an order. The purpose is to build a long-term relationship that will serve both parties. You want your accounts to know that you have their best interests at heart as well as your own. The two concerns must be one and the same.

I knew something had to be done to put this situation right. Without telling Playtex, I arranged to have one of my larger accounts purchase the excess stock from the druggist at cost. The next time I visited the store there wasn't a broom in sight. The owner gave me a warm reception and he became a loyal Playtex customer. If I had let his initial rejection defeat me, we would have lost the account.

Keeping the customer satisfied was always my main objective. I knew it would pay off on the bottom line. I'd seen what could happen if you cared little for the welfare of your accounts. When I first went on the road for Lever Brothers, I was assigned to a district manager named Barry Ruff. I always felt he had been aptly christened because this was one rough customer. He was an old time vendor who didn't care what lengths he had to go to to make a deal; Barry was the sort of guy who gave salesmen a bad name.

Ruff had a huge beer belly and he always reeked of last night's drink. His sense of humour was no more attractive than he was. He had a foul mouth and a penchant for crudity. Once while we were touring my region we had to spend the night in a motel. Ruff told me to park the car while he went in and registered for both of us. By the time I was finished, he had checked us in, taken his key, and retired to his room. When I asked the clerk for my room key, he gave it to me with a leer. I couldn't understand why. Having reached my quarters, I was about to make a phone call when the maid popped in and started to take my bed apart. This was strange; it seemed perfectly fine when I got there. After stripping it, she covered the mattress with a rubber mat that looked as if it had barely survived the last World War. She then placed several flannel sheets on top of that. When I asked her what on earth she was doing, she replied, 'Mr Ruff told us about your problem, so I'm fixing your bed.' She must have seen that I was puzzled because she continued, 'He told us you can't hold your water at night.' Ruff had told the motel clerk that I was a bed-wetter! That was his idea of a joke.

This lack of finesse carried over into his dealings with customers. He was a notorious overstocker; he even bragged about his ability to coerce clients into ordering twice as much merchandise as they really needed.

He also believed in selling through intimidation. Using his beer belly as a battering ram, he would push a client into a corner. With his victim cowed, Ruff would make his pitch. He would ask the store owner if he was still buying Colgate, our biggest competitor. When the client confirmed that he was, Ruff would retort, 'Don't. They've found leprosy in the Colgate factory. They're going to have lawsuits coming out of their ears. Buy Pepsodent.' It was embarrassing.

Whenever he pulled his act on one of my customers, I would invariably call them up and apologize for his behaviour. I would also do anything I could to turn his negative into a positive. By extending the courtesy of a phone call to my clients, I was building a personal relationship with them. None of them held Ruff's behaviour against me. In fact, many sympathized with me for having to put up with such a neanderthal of a boss. They went out of their way to treat me well.

Observing Ruff taught me the liabilities of his hard-sell methods and convinced me that a good-news approach was the way to build a loyal clientele.

For example, I can remember calling on a small account for Playtex. The stock just wasn't moving as well as it should and the owner was getting discouraged. Our biggest selling size was the 34B, but he didn't seem able to give any of them away. I didn't dwell on this bad news when I called on him. I did focus on the number of 42D bras he had sold in the last four weeks: one. That might not seem like much of an accomplishment but it allowed me to say, 'You sold this 42D? This is fabulous! Do you have any idea how hard it is to sell that size! You're off to a great start. 42D is the worst-selling size in the line. Now if you can do this well with the worst-selling size we have, it should be easy for us to figure out how we can boost the business on the 34B because that's the best-selling size we have. I suggest we take the bras out from behind the counter and put them on display where the public will be able to see them. If you can sell a 42D without having the bras displayed, you should be able to sell a truckload of 34Bs and other sizes once your customers are aware you carry them.'

It had been obvious from the start that the reason the line wasn't moving was because no one knew it was being carried. It's true, there was no excuse for the owner not to know this. But if I had chastized him for this slip or in any way implied he didn't know how to run his shop, I would have lost him and his business. Only after building him up did I point out what he was doing wrong, and, even then, I used a manner that was not accusatory. I also tried to build an atmosphere of co-operation by asking what *we* could do to boost up the business. The owner ended up keeping and displaying the line and sales for all sizes improved dramatically.

This experience and others taught me the value of the good-news approach. I began to use it even in my initial contact with a potential client. No matter how badly things might be going, I always found something good to talk about. Even if it was something as mundane as a merger that had occurred in the industry,

I'd play it for all it was worth. You have to. You want the people you're calling on to buy. You want them to be receptive. If all they hear is bad news, how receptive will they be? You want to control the atmosphere of the meeting and create an air of optimism. Any negative thoughts your potential customer might have are a danger to the order. They can easily latch on to you or your product.

Information is the key to building a relationship with an account. You should try to learn as much as you can about the person you're dealing with. Before I would call on major buyers, I would visit their individual stores to check their rate of sale. Talking to the salespeople on the floor, I would find out how our product was selling compared with the competition. Then I would ask them what sort of problems they were having selling our merchandise. I wanted to have solutions to those problems *before* they were brought up in my meeting with the buyer or store owner.

I expected to sell to everyone I called on, even in the very first meeting. Naturally, I wasn't always able to. But, at the very least, I always came away from the initial meeting with information that could help land the order down the road. One fellow in Chicago, the buyer for a large department store chain, was a football fanatic. I learned this during our first contact. He spent the first ten minutes of that meeting lamenting some narrow loss the Chicago Bears had suffered the weekend before. Noting this, I made it a point to buy the *Sporting News*, the famous sports weekly, whenever I was about to call on him again. The evening before the meeting, I would pore over its football coverage looking for titbits about football in general and his beloved Bears in particular. If the opportunity presented itself, I wanted to be able to discuss something that interested him outside the realm of business. Football became our common ground.

Any information I could glean while with a client was filed away for future use. I'd write it all down on my call sheet after the meeting and transfer it to a notebook later that evening. This requires intense listening, but it pays off. There was a buyer for the May Company who was forced to work on Saturdays. He hated it. Every time I visited him he had some sort of comment to make about his missing a full weekend off and how it was especially galling to be cooped up in the office on a day when most of the country was enjoying leisure time. Noting this, I always made sure we had a lunch meeting on Saturday. I gave him a reason to get out of the office at least one Saturday out of every four. When we did get together, we didn't actually discuss business until the last half of the lunch. Instead, we talked about his family. His wife was a horticulturist, his daughter was studying animal husbandry, and his son was a physics major and a star on his college basketball team. All the data I had picked up over the months was brought into play to create an empathy between us. This introduced a human factor that raised our business relationship above the ordinary. It wasn't long before he was looking forward to seeing me (and, of course, the merchandise) whenever I came to town. This is precisely the exchange you want to take place. You want the account to feel you're as interested in him as you would like him to be in you and, more importantly, your products.

Besides helping you build a relationship, the intelligence you gather serves another purpose. It can save you the sort of embarrassment I once suffered early in my career at Lever Brothers. I had called on a small drugstore in Sharon, Pennsylvania and had found them unusually receptive to my pitch. They were ready to buy anything I showed them. The larger the order got, the more I romanced them. By the time I left I had a three-thousand-dollar order. That was enormous for such a small pharmacy. I was thrilled. I called the order clerk the next day and told him what I had done. Instead of congratulating me, he put me on hold. When he got back on the line he said, 'You did a hell of a job. Too bad we can't ship them.' Stunned, I sputtered, 'What do you mean you can't ship them? I got the order. They signed it.' The order clerk chuckled and said, 'Oh, I bet they did. I would also wager that you didn't check that little book of credit we gave you. If you had you would have discovered they have the lowest credit rating in the territory. Of course they were happy to buy from you. Nobody else will ship them merchandise because they don't pay their bills. Why, if you had stayed there long enough you probably could have got an order ten times this one. It wouldn't have made any difference. No matter what the size it still wouldn't have been worth the paper it was written on.'

Was my face red! I had the information at my fingertips and hadn't used it. My lack of preparation had cost me most of the day and had left me with nothing to show for it. It was a painful lesson, one I never forgot.

Once you've set the tone of a meeting with your client, you must be able to focus that person's attention on the product or service you want to sell. At Playtex, we were required to make presentations that appealed to as many of the five senses as possible. If you could occupy a buyer's sense of sight, sound, taste, touch, and smell, he would be less likely to have his attention distracted from your sales pitch. If your product features a fabric of unusual texture, place a sample in the buyer's hands. Let him run his fingers over it. If it is something that has a particular odour to it, make sure the odour is present.

The elastic contained in the Playtex girdle was an exclusive feature that set us apart from our competition. I would always hand a buyer a swatch of that material and ask him to examine it closely. He would tug at it to test its elasticity. Then I would rub my fingers over it and ask him to listen for the velvet swish of this elegant material. All his attention would be fixed on that swatch.

In doing this, I was careful never to handle the product as though it were just another trite commodity. I would hold it as if it were a piece of rare crystal, as beautiful as it was fragile. In speaking of it, I tried to caress it with my words. I was creating an impression and, with it, a need on the part of the buyer.

I would never knock the competition directly. There was no need to introduce the name of a rival product into a conversation that was supposed to be focusing on my own merchandise. Instead, I would call attention to my product's virtues, especially those that set it apart from its rivals. If our bra contained more elastic than any other bra on the market, you can bet I didn't miss the opportunity to introduce that piece of information during my pitch.

No matter how much of a wave you seem to be on, it's important not to become so absorbed by your own presentation that you stop noting the reactions of the people you are trying to sell to. Read their body language. Are their eyes wandering or are they drumming the desk with their fingers? You're starting to lose them and should get to the meat of your presentation as quickly as possible. Are they checking their watch every few minutes or have they just yawned? You're in trouble. They are as good as gone and the only way to get them back is to change the strategy in mid-pitch. The first time I encountered a yawner I immediately slammed the ball into his court by asking, 'How do you like what

I've shown you so far? Is there anything here that interests you or something that you find particularly unappealing?' Of course, there was a lot he found unappealing and he made no bones about telling me about it. That was fine. But at least I had involved him in the presentation and given him a chance to air his objections to the merchandise. Once I knew what the turn-offs were I had something to work with. I could address problems that specifically applied to him. I had won back his attention. As it turned out, this fellow didn't think he could carry any of the Lever Brothers lines because he didn't have any floor room. Having already visited his store, I was able to suggest how he could display the merchandise without cutting into space reserved for existing stock. I left his office with an order.

You won't always be able to handle every objection on the spot. Make a note of what the obstacles are and promise to come back with a way around them. In 1957, I called on the merchandise manager of Macy's. His store wouldn't carry the Playtex line because our mark-up policy was at odds with his store's policy for the department. The foundation department required a higher mark-up than we could allow. I told the merchandise manager that I understood his problem. He couldn't buck store policy. I also told him, however, that the policy was costing him as much as it was costing us. Playtex held 20% of the market and Macy's wasn't getting any of it. I didn't have a quick solution to our problem, so I asked him to give me a week to think of something.

Naturally, he was intrigued. Not only had I appealed to his bottom line, I had also showed genuine interest in doing business with his company. Macy's was an important account, perhaps the largest single account we could have dealt with at the time. I wanted him to know how much it meant to us. One week later, I came back with a plan I had already cleared with Al Peterson. I suggested that Macy's create a Playtex department that would be completely apart from the foundation department. It would be operated as a separate entity and have its own mark-up and financial policy. Macy's merchandise manager liked the idea and, after consulting with his buyers, gave it his approval. The Playtex department was a huge success for all concerned. In its first year, it racked up a volume in excess of one million dollars. If I hadn't bothered to address Macy's problem, if I hadn't questioned the reasons behind the decision not to buy, who knows when we would have got into the store?

After you've overcome the objections raised by your prospective account, you can entice the client further by establishing goals for the product and describing how those goals can be achieved. At Playtex, this was known as 'painting the vista', and was a valuable tool in maximizing the size of your order.

One of the ways to paint the vista was to discuss market share. When I called on a store in Kansas City, I asked the store's president what percentage of the city's Playtex volume he thought the store should have. This was one of the largest department stores in town. The store president replied, 'Last year we had 15% of the market for the area, but I think we could step that up this year. I think we're looking at 20%.' Without realizing it, the president had already applied the opening strokes to the canvas. I now had an idea of the picture he wanted to see. I told him we had done $700,000 in Kansas City the year before, but were aiming to top the million dollar mark this year. Then I described the great advertising campaign we had planned and how we were going to spend more money on local promotion than ever before. I showed him how well similar campaigns had done throughout the country. He got so excited that it wasn't long before we were taking equal turns with the brush. When we finished, I said, 'You see what we can do together. You want 20% of the market. I just proved that the market should go over a million. You want $200,000 for the year at four turns a year. That means you need to start off with inventory worth $50,000 retail. The cost of the order will be $30,000 and we'll put one-tenth of that amount back into advertising. That's the order you'll need. When would you like us to ship it?' We decided on a date and then he dropped the paint brush, picked up his pen, and prepared to sign on the dotted line.

Notice that the vista we created was not one of pie in the sky. You can't dip your brush in hyperbole and expect to build a lasting relationship with an account. He picked the colours to be used when he told me what his needs were. I chose the site to be immortalized when I told him how much volume we expected Kansas City to do that year. The paint we decided on had a base of numbers (last year's numbers) and logic (an increase in advertising has to lead to an increase in sales). Together we painted the vista of opportunity that he wanted to view. This was a picture of his dream. Once he was absorbed by it, I brought him back to reality by telling him exactly what he needed ($30,000 at cost in inventory) to reach that dream. By the time I told him this, the numbers weren't an obstacle. They were superfluous. All he could see was the vista.

Once you're certain you've made the sale, take out your order form and write it up. Don't let the customer get so much as a peek at the purchase order before you've agreed on a deal. The order form is a gun. It should always be loaded and should be pulled only when you're ready to use it.

Receiving the order means you've reached your goal. Don't mess things up by staying past your welcome. If you keep selling past the closing of the deal, you stand a chance of talking yourself out of the order. This was a chronic problem for a salesman who worked for me at Playtex. He drove me crazy. Once he had a buyer with the May Company ready to put his monicker on a huge order. Before pen met paper, the salesman blurted, 'And if you think this long-line bra is good, wait till you see the new three-quarter long line we're bringing out next month. It's terrific!' The moment he heard that, the buyer dropped the pen and said, 'Is that so? Well then, maybe I'd better wait until I get a look at that new bra before I order too many of the old ones. I want to see what sort of impact the new bra will have on the market. I don't want to get stuck with any obsolete merchandise. Let's cut this order by 75%. That will give me enough inventory to last until the new models come in.' This was a costly error. The salesman saw a large portion of his commission go out the window and, I assume, had quite a medical bill to pay. It took a team of surgeons to extract this fellow's foot from his mouth.

You've taken your best shot. You've answered all the objections voiced against your product, but you still can't get the order. Don't despair. Go back and try again. I've learned that persistence can be its own reward.

In 1954, I was selling Harriet Hubbard Ayer cosmetics for Lever Brothers. Most of July was spent pushing our Christmas line in our southern territory. The line consisted of different cosmetics, including lipsticks, that were packaged together in festive wrapping.

I pulled into York, Alabama and called on the proprietor of

the local Rexall drugstore. Having lugged my bulky samples into the pharmacy, I told the girl behind the counter that I had come to call on Doctor Bill. Almost every druggist in this section of the South was known as doctor though I imagine few of them had any serious medical training. Doctors were scarce in these parts, so the local pharmacists usually attended to the minor medical complaints of their neighbours.

Dr Bill was downstairs mixing up a version of Hadacol, an elixir that went down like cherry cough syrup and had the kick of low-grade bourbon. It was supposed to be good for whatever ailed you. I'll say this, it might not have cured anyone but, if they drank enough of it, they sure would forget whatever was bothering them.

Joining the good doctor in the basement, I introduced myself and told him I was with the Harriet Hubbard Ayer division of Lever Brothers. Dr Bill remembered the line from when it was an independent company in the thirties. When he asked what I wanted I went into my pitch, explaining how Lever Brothers had acquired the Ayer company and how we were going to back the line with a powerful Christmas promotion. I gave him an idea of the national campaign we were going to run in major magazines and newspapers across the nation. He seemed unimpressed. Peering at me over his rimless spectacles, he said, 'I don't know, son. I've got Elizabeth Arden in stock and I do just fine with that. I don't know why I would want anything else. Why don't you show me what you've got and I'll think it over?' I trotted out the samples. They were a mess. It must have been 110 degrees in the shade that afternoon and the cosmetics were wilting faster than I was. That's saying something because I was only two steps away from heat prostration.

Dr Bill, apparently impervious to the heat, took his time about examining the merchandise. With the cosmetics in such sorry condition, I tried to direct his attention to the wrapping. Holding it up to the light I said, 'Look at this package. Doesn't it sing?' Dr Bill said, 'Yes, it does. But it's not any song I want to hear. I don't think I can use this. I'm happy with what I've got, but if you do a good job with your advertising and I get some calls for it, I'll put it in. I wouldn't count on it though. I haven't had anybody ask for this stuff in years.' When I attempted to make another pitch, Dr Bill let me know his answer was final. I packed up my samples and dragged my body up the stairs and out of the drugstore. The last words I heard were the salesgirl's. As I drove off she called, 'Nice seeing you. You-all hurry back and see us soon.' I thought, 'You can bet your last dollar on it.'

I returned four times in the next three months. I received the same negative response on the first three of those visits. I still didn't quit. On the fourth try, I walked in and started my pitch, but Dr Bill cut me off less than half a minute into it. He said, 'Son, I've watched you come in and out of my store with that damned gook more times than I care to count. I keep turning you down and you keep coming back. You don't take no for an answer. Hell, if you believe in the stuff so much that you'd keep tramping out here to sell it, then I guess I have to take a flyer on it. Take out your order form and let's do some business.' His order couldn't have totalled more than $200, but I couldn't have been happier if it had been for ten times that amount. You can't place a monetary value on the satisfaction you get when your persistence finally pays dividends.

I enjoyed calling on small stores like Dr Bill's. Everybody wanted to sell to Macy's and the other big accounts. So did I, but I also knew that if I strung together sixty little stores the volume would equal a Macy's. Besides giving me an opportunity to score points in the selling game, those smaller stores let me practise my presentation, allowing me to hone it before I approached the larger accounts. They provided an excellent training ground. By the time I got around to the Macy's and the Gimbel's, I had a fair idea what to expect in the way of questions about my merchandise. I had already heard them all in little towns from Tupelo to Kalamazoo.

Working those smaller accounts also taught me a valuable lesson: *business is where you are.* No matter what the size of the store or company you're calling on, during the time you are there it is the most important account in the world. You are totally committed to it from the moment you walk into it to the moment you leave. You don't rush through a shoddy presentation at the mom-and-pop drugstore simply because you're in a hurry to run off and pitch Bloomingdale's. For one thing, the small store owner wasn't born yesterday. He knows if you're sticking him with the short end and he's going to resent it. In a business where time is such a precious commodity you're wasting yours, because that shopkeeper is probably so offended you could promise him the moon and he still wouldn't buy. Also, the shoddy work habits you develop in these instances are not easily dropped. They will carry over in your presentations to the larger accounts.

I've always made sure that I had plenty of time to complete my business. If it took longer than I had planned, I stayed until I was finished. This goes back to the time that I scheduled a presentation at a small gift shop in St Louis. Playtex bras and girdles had been doing well there and the owner wanted to expand his inventory. I planned to meet him three hours before I was supposed to call on the buyer for Famous Barr, the largest department store in the city. The meeting went well, so well in fact that after two hours we still hadn't finished. I knew there was no way I was going to get to my other meeting on time unless I left immediately. Did I make my excuses and go? No. Instead, I told the shop owner about my other appointment – making sure to let him know who the appointment was with – and then asked if I could use his phone. Having reached the department store buyer, I apologized and explained that I had been delayed. We scheduled our meeting for the following morning. With that out of the way, I turned back to the shop owner and continued with my pitch. That gentleman, having been receptive to my merchandise to begin with, was twice as ready to do business with me by the time I got off the phone. With that single call, I had let him know that he and his shop were valued. I've seen so many salespeople who will stop in mid-presentation and say, 'I'm sorry, I have to get to another appointment. Can I come back and finish this tomorrow?' If I'm the buyer in that situation, I have to think, 'To hell with you. You have another appointment and it's more important than this one? Great. Do business with them. If you have better things to do than to sell to me, I have better things to do than to buy from you.'

Time should be the salesperson's greatest ally. It will become your enemy only if you mistreat it. One of the faults common to novice salespeople is their ability to waste time. I've already told you how, as a salesman with Lever Brothers, I refused to watch the clock. Besides working Saturdays, I made a habit of putting in twelve-hour days. I was up at seven o'clock each morning. I wanted to be dressed and on the road by eight, enabling me to call on my first account of the day by 8.30. Breakfast was a cup of coffee and a glass of orange juice. If I suffered severe hunger pangs, I would munch half a buttered roll before shooting out the door.

Working straight through the day, I paused only to grab my usual lunch: a milkshake on the run. If I called on a client and found a large number of salesmen in front of me, I didn't hesitate to ask them how long they thought they would need for their pitches. This information let me formulate my Risk-Reward Ratio. I wanted to know if it was worth my time to wait to see the account. If I was going to spend ninety minutes cooling my heels, I had to be darned confident that I was going to come away with a substantial order. This sort of thing happened frequently when I was selling cosmetics for Lever Brothers. It was a very competitive business. I remember calling on a buyer for one of the largest chain stores in the South. When I arrived to see her, I found six other salesmen waiting. The receptionist apologized for the delay, explaining that it had been a hectic day and that all the appointments had been delayed. She did say, however, that everybody scheduled would be seen and that we would each get fifteen minutes to make our pitch.

I didn't have to be a maths genius to realize that I was facing at least a ninety-minute delay. I sat down and did some fast figuring. Though this was an admittedly attractive account, it was already carrying five rival cosmetic lines. The buyer was going to be resistant to introducing a sixth. The odds were high that I would be unable to sell to her on this initial visit. More than anything else, this was really a let's-get-acquainted call. I would do my best to sell to her, but even if I did, the most I could hope for was one-sixth of her cosmetics market. My computations made for an easy decision. After arranging with the receptionist to come back at a more opportune time, I moved on to another account.

The time spent between appointments should be put to use. This can be a period of opportunity! Say I finished with an account earlier than I had anticipated. My next call, one that might be only ten minutes away, might not be for another hour. Many rival salesmen used this lull in their day to treat themselves to a good meal. I always felt it should be spent researching stores in the surrounding area. I'd walk into a shop and see how our merchandise was being displayed. How did its presentation compare with that of our competitors? Then I'd strike up a conversation with the sales staff, the people who were in the trenches, and find out how the public was reacting to our products. What did they like about the merchandise and, more importantly, what didn't they like about it?

This research served at least three purposes. First, it gave me a dispassionate first-hand assessment of the strengths and weaknesses of any product I was representing. Second, I could keep tabs on the competition. By asking pertinent questions about their merchandise, I could do an informal balance sheet on my rivals' products and my own. Whatever strengths were found to be peculiar to my product would be built up in my presentation. Third, it gave me the semblance of a personal relationship with the people who were selling my merchandise to the general public. This gave me an advantage over my competition. If a customer wandered into the store looking for toothpaste, but was uncertain of which brand he wanted to buy, there was a good chance he would ask the sales staff for help with his selection. Since there was little difference in price and quality between the leading brands, whose toothpaste do you think they would recommend? The fellow who drops in on a regular basis and is interested enough in their opinion to ask them questions about his product or the relative stranger whose concern for the business ends once he's got an order?

I also used my spare time to look for outlets that weren't carrying my line. An entrepreneur has to be an expansionist. Part of his business is the creation of new business. If I walked into a drugstore that wasn't carrying Harriet Hubbard Ayer, I'd make a note of it. I might not have the opportunity to see the shopkeeper right at that moment, but you can bet I'd be back with my samples on my next swing through town. Building your volume is a sure way to stand out in your company. When I was selling, I never bothered to figure out how much commission I was earning with each order. I always felt that I was working for the company and that the volume I sold and its success for the retailer was my major priority. We had a salesman at Playtex who had inherited a very large account when he took over his territory. He lived off that one department store. His figures looked good every year, but that wasn't surprising. With that giant propping up the rest of his territory, he would have had to mess things up completely to deliver numbers that were anything short of sensational.

Many of his peers glanced at his bottom line and thought, 'Gosh, this guy must be some salesman!' I had my doubts. They hadn't noticed that this boy wonder had opened hardly any new accounts in two years. On the other hand, there was another salesman who had a territory consisting of fifty small stores. His biggest account did less than $10,000 a year. He went out and opened up fifty more stores in his territory. In less than ten months he had doubled the number of his accounts. As soon as I could, I moved him into a bigger territory. He did the same thing there. His rise at Playtex was rapid. The other fellow, being content merely to be carried by the business that had been handed to him, didn't go very far. His laziness kept him away from the management level. He was passed over in favour of go-getters who weren't afraid to use some sweat to help the company grow. Before long, the numbers declined at his big account. Other than showing up and writing out an order, he had never had to do very much to maintain the bottom line. When the crunch came, as it inevitably does in selling, he didn't have a clue as to how he could get the numbers back. Six months after their fall, he was transferred to a smaller territory. Nothing could have been more disastrous for a person of so little ambition. Three months after the move, he left the company.

No matter how successful my day had been, it didn't end until the last store was closed. That usually occurred around 9 p.m. At Lever Brothers, I was required to write up my orders each evening and send them in to the order clerk. I'm afraid I didn't choose to obey this particular company rule. Instead, I rewarded myself for my labours with the best meal I could afford. Then I either went back to my hotel room to get some sleep or I drove off to the next town. My reasoning was simple. If business required me to stay put, I wanted to be fresh for the next day of selling. If I had to move on, I wanted to leave immediately so I could get a head start on tomorrow. The order writing could wait until Sunday.

This approach to selling helped me to make my mark. I didn't have to be very good to be successful. Most of my accomplishments came as the result of sheer doggedness rather than talent. After all, I was working twelve-hour days, six days a week. Many of my peers were working less than half that. The time I invested made the difference between me and the rest of the pack.

I've tried to draw some guidelines for successful selling in this chapter. None of this advice is carved in concrete. Selling is an art and the entrepreneurs who try their hands at it shouldn't suppress their own creativity. The method that is best for you is the method that works. You might not believe some of the imaginative approaches I saw while I was working the road for Lever Brothers and Playtex.

One fellow, John Henry James, worked for a rival cosmetics company. He was six-foot six and weighed 245 pounds. He was also the only salesman I knew who had his own chauffeur and limousine. James would sit in the back of the limo and sip mint juleps while his chauffeur drove him from store to store. At each stop, the driver would get out of the limousine and roll out a red carpet from the car door to the store entrance. Then he would walk inside the store and announce, 'Ladies and gentlemen, Mr John Henry James has arrived!' James would stroll in looking as if he were a character in a Noël Coward play. He would be dressed to the nines. The chauffeur would dash out and return a few moments later with John Henry's samples. With this sort of introduction, buyers and store owners would be overwhelmed before John Henry had uttered a word. Opening his sample case with a theatrical flourish, James would turn to his prospective client and croon in a rich baritone, 'I do believe we're going to do some business today.' Nine times out of ten, he was right. James was a living legend in the South. It was said that the product hadn't been made that James couldn't sell. More than anything else, that was a tribute to his magnetic personality. People liked doing business with him. He was an honest tradesman and an engaging fellow who could sweet-talk a rose into blooming early. Of course, that dramatic entrance which became his trademark didn't do his mythic quality any harm. Once you saw, you never forgot it and you couldn't wait for him to come back so you could see it again.

James had a counterpart in the Midwest. His name was Bob Englud but he was better known as 'The Fur Coat'. He wore a raccoon coat whenever he called on a customer. Time of year or climate had no influence on his fashion sense. Your shop could have been in the middle of the Sahara, but Englud would still show up wrapped in his fur. For some unexplained reason, though, no matter how hot it would get, Englud never seemed to perspire.

Whenever anybody quizzed him about this oddity he would reply, 'You know old Bob. I'm just a cool customer.'

I had occasion to meet him at a convention. The first thing I asked him was why he always wore the coat. He chuckled and said, 'So you think this is a fur coat, huh? Let me tell you, it's not that at all. This is an ice-breaker. How many times have you called on a new client and been unable to think of anything to say to get the conversation rolling? No one likes to start talking business from the off. When I walk in with this raccoon draped around me, I don't have to wonder whether we're going to discuss sports, the latest movies, or the state of the Union. I know what the centre of the opening conversation is going to be because I'm wearing it. I'll tell you something else: there are about nine billion salesmen in this country. Almost every buyer we call on sees so many of us on any given day that they can't tell us apart unless we have numbers on our backs and they have a scorecard. This coat is my number and when I wear it they don't need a scorecard. They know it's Bob Englud coming to call and they know what I want to talk about. When they see the coat, they're ready for business.' I admired Bob's nerve, but I was sceptical when he told me the coat helped him to get orders. I casually asked him what sort of year he was having. The numbers that rolled off his tongue ended my doubts and moved me to ask Bob for the name of his tailor.

Flashy garb, limousines, and chauffeurs weren't exactly my style, but men such as John Henry James and Bob Englud taught me that I could afford to be daring in my approach to a customer. The entrepreneur mustn't suppress his creativity. You don't want your presentation to be merely good. With practice, any salesperson can give a good textbook presentation. You want your pitch to be memorable.

When we made the big push to sell the zippered girdle during that historic selling week discussed in Chapter Two, we pulled out all the stops. We came in with charts and graphs and an entire advertising campaign. We had orders filled out before they were made. Our request that the presentation be attended not only by the buyer but the marketing manager and store president as well announced to everyone that this was not just another item we were selling. During that week, I was painting vistas with both hands. I told you that many of the buyers were so captivated by our pitch that they gave us orders without bothering to see the girdle. We brought it with us, but we tried to achieve the sale without having to show it to them. This was true concept selling. Our Playtex girdles came packed in tubes. The reason for that was well thought out. Tubes could not be stored on shelves or counters; they would roll off. The shape of the packaging forced store owners to feature our merchandise in special racks called 'Fountains of Youth'. This meant the Playtex girdle was virtually guaranteed a prominent display in any corset department or store that carried it. Whenever a buyer asked to see the new zippered girdle, we would take out the tube, walk over to the wastepaper basket and empty its contents. Instead of a girdle plopping out, the tube would discharge nothing but sand. Turning to the buyer and the rest of the assembled group, we would say, 'You haven't bought a girdle. You've bought a concept. The girdle and the zipper are almost unimportant. If it wasn't any good, we wouldn't sell it.' This may sound like a crazy move, but you know something? No one was offended by it. In fact, it made them feel they were part of a happening and raised their already heated enthusiasm to a feverish level.

People admire those who take risks. One day, a fellow came to the Remington factory and asked if I could spare a few minutes to see him. Minutes into the meeting, I realized he wasn't here to sell me a product or a service as I originally suspected. He was there to sell me on the idea of hiring him. I looked over his résumé, chatted with him a few minutes, and then told him that I didn't have anything available at the moment. I also told him to keep in touch and that I would keep him in mind if a position opened up. Normally this would signal the end of the interview, but this man was not so easily put off. Instead of getting up to leave, he continued to sit and make one of the most incredible offers I have ever heard. He said, 'I think there is a position for me here, but you're not aware of it. The reason you're not aware of it is that it hasn't been created yet. I'll make you a deal. Let me work here for one month without salary or expenses. I'm willing to wager my free labour that I'll find a niche for myself with your company in thirty days.'

What could I say? This was the sort of entrepreneurial proposition that could not be easily ignored. I agreed to his terms. Thirty days later he presented me with a report outlining deficiencies in a particular area of my company and detailing how he would correct them. He concluded his report by saying, 'I think you'll agree that I've targeted an area that needs someone's attention. I believe I'm the man for the job.' He didn't have to sell me any more. In the parlance of the salesperson, he got the order. I hired him immediately and I have to admit that if he hadn't created the position, I would have considered him for employment as soon as a slot opened. Creativity such as his is rare. When you find it, you latch on to it for all you're worth.

If you're selling on the road, you'll have plenty of time to dream up creative pitches. You'll also have an opportunity to broaden your horizons. I wasn't crazy about being on the road, though I loved the challenges it offered. I'm a family man and I didn't like to be apart from my wife and children for too long a period of time. That's one of the reasons I filled every minute with work. I wanted to take my mind off my loneliness and I wanted to make sure I had everything out of the way so that I could enjoy some leisure time when I went back home.

The road is not a pretty place. You spend a lot of time going from one strange room to another, eating food of dubious origin, and living out of a suitcase. You deal with rejection every day. I tried to make the best of the situation by studying the culture of every town or country I visited. I was fascinated by the history and customs of the different people who did business with me. I think learning something about their tradition made me a better salesman. When I visited China for the jewellery business in the mid-1970s, I read everything I could on the Great Wall and the ancient dynasties that had ruled over China. I stood at the Wall and I visited temples and communes. I drenched myself in the country. It was an unforgettable experience.

The distractions in the States weren't always quite as exotic. In North Dakota I used to carry a shotgun with me in the car. Every now and again, I'd break the monotony by pulling to the side of the road and getting out to hunt a pheasant. In a good week, I'd bag one or two. Bringing them to whatever hotel I might be staying at, I'd pay the cook to prepare them for me. They made for delicious eating and the chase kept me from being bored.

I also eased the tedium by picking up hitchhikers. I'd give a person a ride to have someone to swap travel stories with. I got out of that habit in a hurry. I picked up two guys in the backwoods of Louisiana. There was nothing unusual about their appearance. They looked like two clean-cut college kids, but as soon as they got into the car one of them took out a hunting knife and started cleaning his nails with it. He had the same wild-eyed look that Richard Widmark wore in the movie *Kiss of Death*. He started talking about how well he handled his knife and how it was great if you had to skin something. I got the distinct impression that he wasn't talking about deer, antelope, or any other four-legged animal. Every time he looked at me I felt he was wondering how I would look stuffed and mounted on his wall. I laugh about it now but it was a bit hairy then. There wasn't anyone around for miles. I was relieved when I was finally able to drop them off. I don't know if they were just trying to have some fun with me, but I can assure you they were the last hitchhikers I ever picked up. After that, I contented myself with listening to the car radio and talking to myself.

During those inner dialogues, there were moments when I would ask why I was subjecting myself to the rigours of this life. The answer was never long in coming. It was because, as an entrepreneur, I consider selling to be one of the noblest of professions. You're dealing one-to-one with a person and you're trying to motivate him to become as enthusiastic about your product or service as you are. You have no help in this. You are in very much the same situation as the boxer, standing alone in the naked glare of the klieg lights as he waits to face the vindication or repudiation of the career he's chosen. Joe Louis, the former heavyweight champion, once said of the elusive Billy Conn, 'He can run, but he can't hide.' Neither can the salesperson. No amount of excuses can disguise your failure. The method of scorekeeping is too simple. You either got the order or you didn't. The defeats are many and they are painful. But, with championship spirit, you fight back and triumph. It is a win that belongs only to you. It is that victory that makes it all worthwhile.

CHAPTER FIVE

Start-ups

Those of you who are familiar with the plays of Tennessee Williams might be interested to know that the streetcar named Desire does exist. One of its stops was only four blocks from my home in New Orleans, Louisiana. Steamy Louisiana nights and the sounds of eager Desire racing through its runs did not inspire me to spin lurid tales of Stanley Kowalski and Blanche DuBois. Instead it provided the setting that invited the entrepreneurial muse to perch on my shoulder and whisper the suggestions that guided me to the path I'm still travelling today.

I was eight years old when I became involved with my first company. My grandfather had given me five dollars and I used the money to buy one hundred bottles of Coke. Normally, if an eight-year-old buys one hundred bottles of soda (albeit that's not something that occurs too often), the result is the Frankenstein of stomach-aches. But these soft drinks were not for sipping, not by me anyway. They were used to launch my first business.

I noticed people coming home from work at the end of the day and looking as if they would pass out if they had to take another step without the pleasure of a cool drink. I certainly didn't realize it then, but looking back I see that I recognized a need. My neighbours were desperate for refreshment. If I could supply it, they would be willing to pay for it.

Having had my grandfather help me bring my sweet inventory home, I raided the ice box for as many ice cubes as my grandmother's wash tub would hold. This chilled tub provided the perfect resting place for the bottles of dark caramel-tinted liquid that represented my first foray into the world of high finance. Before I could take my next step, however, I had to settle on a price for my goods. I was unused to the vagaries of the retailer's world and had no idea what I should charge. With naïve boldness,

I settled on a mark-up of 100%. The cokes cost a nickel apiece; I sold each for a dime.

Business was brisk on the first day and it got even better as the week progressed. You would think I was on my way to becoming a pint-sized John D. Rockefeller. My grandfather was of that opinion. So you can imagine his shock when I, having sold my entire stock, had only four dollars to show for my efforts. I had operated at a loss! At first he assumed I had drunk all the profits, but I assured him that this wasn't so. Instead, I had given my merchandise away to whatever poor souls couldn't scratch up the price of a drink. Only some of my customers could afford to pay ten cents for a bottle of Coke. Many couldn't even afford the nickel I needed in order to break even. It was so hot that I couldn't bear to let anyone go away empty-handed. Operated in this manner, it was no wonder that my first business was a financial failure. But it sure did build up a lot of goodwill.

My next venture met with more success. In my first year at high school I had a model aeroplane that was the envy of the other students. Every boy who saw it wanted one for himself. However, this particular plane was sold in only one store in the immediate area. It was an out of the way hobby shop I discovered while out on a jaunt. Knowing the store's location made me the only source in the school for this highly coveted toy. This was an ideal entrepreneurial situation. Taking orders on Fridays, I would purchase similar model planes over the weekend and bring them to my fellow students on Monday. The planes cost fifty cents. Considering time spent on pick-up and delivery and the law of supply and demand, I put on a mark-up that brought the price up to ninety cents. I was making forty cents a plane. As more students bought them, they became something of a status symbol. Some boys bought as many as three or four. I must have sold over one hundred planes before the demand died.

Pardon an obvious pun, but those first two businesses of mine were kid's stuff compared to my next undertaking. In 1948, I was studying French at the Sorbonne in Paris. A previous two-year stint in the US Navy had made me eligible for the benefits of the GI Bill, letting me attend the prestigious French university as a guest of Uncle Sam. I was in Paris on a lark. When I got out of the service in 1947, I had gone back to Yale and put in the final year I needed to graduate.

1948 was not a good year to be seeking employment. Veterans, having gradually returned from war-time service, had glutted the job market and industries that had been going full-tilt during the fighting had to cut back in peace time. Having just come through the rigours of the Navy and Yale, I was in no mood to knock my brains out looking for work that didn't exist. I also needed a vacation. Several like-minded friends and I decided to go to Europe and seek adventure while trying to figure out what to do with the rest of our lives.

Three of us flew to Paris as part of the Youth Hostel Organization programme. I had my savings from the service and would also receive $75 a month as part of my benefits as a veteran student at the Sorbonne. That was a generous stipend in 1948 and, with the help of a devalued franc, I was able to live quite well. In fact, by pooling some of our money, the three of us were able to afford to buy a car. Scouring the city, we came up with a serviceable Simca Huit, a four-door saloon that was very similar to a Fiat. I don't believe that car cost us more than one thousand dollars in US currency.

My two buddies left for the States after only two months. I decided to stay in Paris. Before their departure, I arranged to buy the car from them. They agreed to let me pay them the balance of their investment over the next six months. It turned out to be one of the best business deals I've ever made.

Paris was an exciting place in 1948. Trying desperately to forget a war that had left it scarred, all of France seemed to be celebrating the life it had come so close to losing. With my friends gone, I joined four other American youths I had met at the Sorbonne and moved into a garret on the Left Bank. We had hardly a stick of furniture between us. We slept in sleeping bags on the floor. No one minded. The flat was little more than a place to store our belongings and bed down at night. With a pulsating Paris on our doorstep, no one wanted to spend too much time inside.

Living the life of an American expatriate, I grew a beard and frequented the cafés and art museums. My friends and I would lunch at the Deux Magots, a marvellous bistro that was a hang-out for poets and artists. I was introduced to the writings of Jean-Paul Sartre and found his work so fascinating that I attended many of the lectures he gave in and around Paris. The Vieux Colombier, a private social club, opened while I was there. It was the forerunner of the discotheque and it featured such artists as Sidney Bechet, the innovative jazz musician who had become a legend throughout Europe. Membership of the club cost only a few francs and Americans were especially encouraged to join.

Kept busy with school and the distractions of city life, I had little time to think about such things as work or what the future held for me. I was the willing prisoner of the present. So it is only fair to say that I did not rush into my first major business venture. I stumbled over it.

I was getting my mail at the American Express office on Rue Scribe in downtown Paris. While picking it up one day, I overheard an English couple objecting to the high prices American Express charged for their chauffeur-driven cars. The company demanded thirty-five dollars a day and the couple didn't want to pay it. I thought nothing of their plight, but Max Chenier did.

Max was one of the city's more colourful characters. He ran a newspaper stand outside the American Express office, but he was also known as a man who could get you almost anything you needed. If you wanted silk stockings, chocolate, an electrical appliance or any other hard to get item, all you had to do was ask Max and he would make it appear magically. He was an interesting fellow. He always had two days' growth of beard and he dressed with a shabby neatness. I discovered later that this was his public face. Invited to his home for dinner, I was met at the door by the private Max, a clean-shaven man with the sartorial flair of a member of the French diplomatic corps. He lived with his wife and children in an elegant apartment in the city. Though no one who encountered his worn appearance at his newsstand would believe it, Max was one successful entrepreneur.

Always quick to seize opportunity, Max approached the harried English couple and asked where they wanted to go. They explained that they wanted to see Versailles, Fontainebleau and any other places of interest in the area. Turning to me, Max said, 'Victor, you are doing nothing today, yes? You have your Simca and you know the country. Why don't you be a good fellow and drive these people around? You don't mind earning some money, do you?' I sure didn't. After assuring the couple that I spoke both English and French and would be able to act as a translator as well, he told them they should pay me fifteen dollars for the day plus expenses. They accepted the deal.

That day went very quickly. I took them to every historic spot I could think of and even gave them a tour of some of the vineyards in the French countryside. They had a wonderful time and so did I. After dropping them off and getting paid, I hurried back to Max and said, 'This was a great idea! I had so much fun and I made fifteen dollars. I'll tell you what I'm going to do. I'll give you 10% of what they paid me and that's just the start. I think we have the makings of a good business here. If you continue to steer chauffeur-seeking tourists in my direction, I'll give you 10% of whatever I make.' Max was used to this sort of arrangement; it was one of the reasons he was able to afford that lovely apartment. He agreed to the terms. The following day the European Touring Service, Incorporated was officially launched.

I had business cards printed and I passed them out to the concierges of many of the hotels in Paris. I made the same deal with them that I made with Max. Whenever a guest needed a driver and car, the concierge inevitably recommended me.

The business snowballed. Within a year, I owned a fleet of six cars and had my room-mates working with me. By then I was charging twenty dollars a day. The drivers got half of that. After paying for insurance and other incidentals, I was making about seven dollars a day from each of the other five cars and twenty a day from my own. That was quite a bit of money then. In 1951, having been accepted at the Harvard Business School, I had to leave Paris and the car business. I did not go empty-handed. I sold the business to my drivers, making enough on the deal to pay off what I owed on the cars and still realize a healthy profit.

Diverse as the three start-ups I have just described were, they still had at least one thing in common: each filled a need that wasn't being satisfied. Too often, would-be entrepreneurs refuse even to think about going into their own business because they believe they have nothing to offer the marketplace. They seem to think they need an idea worthy of an Einstein before they can hang out their shingles. Brothers and sisters, I'm here to tell you it's just not true. You don't have to redesign the wheel or be the new wizard of software to have a viable enterprise. All you have to do is offer a product or service that people need and are willing to buy. You must be alive to opportunity!

I discovered opportunity as an eight-year-old when I stopped looking at the people who walked past my house as hot, thirsty neighbours and started seeing them as hot, thirsty customers. By looking at the model plane as a valuable product that only I could supply, instead of a treasured toy, I unearthed another source of income.

Where are your openings? I knew a young man named Robert who worked in a department store cafeteria. He hated it. He didn't like working indoors, the routine was stifling, the food tasted awful, and the paycheque had him wondering if Abraham Lincoln had indeed signed the Emancipation Proclamation. He drove to work every day and would spend most of the thirty-minute journey wondering how he could improve his lot.

The answer came to him in a petrol station. It was the only one he passed en route to work and it did an incredible business. One day, seized by morning hunger pangs, Robert pulled into the station and made a beeline for the chocolate vending machine. No luck. The machine was empty. Robert found the cold drink machine in the same condition. When he asked the station owner if he had any refills, the owner replied, 'I'm afraid I don't. I can't stock enough snacks and drinks to keep those machines full. You know there aren't many stores around here, especially along this road. A lot of people who come to fill up their cars also want to put some fuel into their bodies. They keep those machines busy.'

Visions of hundreds of hungry travellers passing by that petrol station every day haunted my friend into the evening and gave him an idea. One week after their conversation, the young man went back to offer the station owner a proposition. If the owner allowed him to open up a takeaway on the side of the station, he would give the owner 15% of whatever profits he realized from the venture. During the previous seven days, Robert had cleaned out his savings account, secured a loan from his dad, and priced the necessary equipment. His experience in the cafeteria had taught him where he could buy the food he needed wholesale. He knew he could make the business work. The owner wasn't so sure, but he knew he had little to lose by agreeing to Robert's plan. If Robert failed, it wouldn't cost the owner a cent. If the takeaway succeeded, the owner would receive an income from a small plot of ground that didn't now add a nickel to his bankroll. They drew up an agreement, outlining terms and absolving the station owner of any liability.

Robert opened his stand two weeks after they signed their

agreement. The takeaway was a smash from day one. Not only did the owner reap the rewards from his share of the profits, he benefited from the increase in traffic engendered by Robert's business. Robert put the money he made back into the business. He bought more stands and hired people to run them throughout the state. Eventually Robert expanded, developing a hot lunch service delivered to factories and offices. Fifteen years after his stomach growled, Robert is the head of a thriving business. He has the satisfaction of seeing his dream become a reality and the material rewards that go with an income that passes six figures. All of this because he wasn't blind to possibility and was willing to put himself at the mercy of his own skills.

Robert is cut from the same entrepreneurial cloth as George Morris. George was a doorman in a luxury building located in mid-Manhattan. He liked people and enjoyed his work, but he wanted to make more money. His opportunities were scarce. George was thirty-five years old and had dropped out of high school. His lack of a diploma, however, did nothing to quell his powers of observation. He noticed that many of the tenants in his building needed to have the windows in their apartments cleaned as often as once a month. The superintendent wasn't responsible for this work, so the tenants were forced to hire window-cleaning services. Many of these companies charged ten dollars or more for each window.

George had been cleaning the windows of his own flat for years. On the few occasions when he performed this service for a friend his work got rave reviews. Since he already had the necessary equipment, he wondered why he couldn't do the tenants' windows in his spare time.

The idea was a compelling one. Each apartment had at least five windows in it. By undercutting the professional services and charging six bucks a window, George stood to make thirty dollars per flat. Experience had taught him that he could do five windows in less than an hour. If he could get the business, George would be able to make almost as much in an hour as he was currently earning in a day.

After first getting permission from his landlord, George had leaflets printed announcing his venture and his low prices. He slipped these under the doors of every apartment in the building. The response was slow at first, but he did manage to do four apartments in the first two weeks. He did a first-rate job. The pleased tenants began their own word-of-mouth campaign and before long George had so many window-cleaning assignments he had to quit his position as doorman. This did not sadden him. The building was a large one and had an extraordinary number of dirty windows. After paying for soap and utensils, George was able to clear over five hundred dollars a week.

Spurred on by this triumph, he had more leaflets printed. He paid his doorman buddies to pass them out in their buildings. As the demand for his services increased, George hired two friends to assist him. He expanded the business to include painting and general cleaning services. Today, that business employs over fifty people. George, having picked up a high school diploma and a degree in business administration, runs the whole ship with the aid of an accountant.

These two stories are solid evidence that opportunity is everywhere if you're able to recognize it. Take stock of yourself and your surroundings. What talents aren't you exploiting to their fullest potential? Don't take any of your gifts for granted. A woman I've known for years had a marvellous eye for art and decoration. She didn't have any special training, just the intuitive knack of being able to pick the right painting for the right space. Instead of ignoring this talent, she nurtured it with study and launched her own business. She became a buyer of art for corporations. Her selections hang in the lobbies of many of the most reputable banks and companies in the world.

As an entrepreneur, you should be exploring the possibilities of every situation. Max Chenier taught me this when he suggested I chauffeur that English couple for the day. I saw two people complaining about the high cost of doing business with American Express; he saw an opportunity to earn some money. The eventual success of the business that was spawned that day fine-tuned my entrepreneurial antennae.

One reason to remain alert to entrepreneurial prospects is that you can never be positive when or how an opportunity may be thrust upon you. I became part of a start-up business in Europe under most unusual circumstances.

My wife Ellen and I were married in 1956. This was not an entrepreneurial venture, though I imagine there are times Ellen wishes she had figured out her Risk-Reward Ratio before saying

'I do.' At the time of the wedding, I had just been promoted from regional sales manager at Playtex to marketing director in charge of girdles and bras. Because of the move I could get only one week off for our honeymoon. That wasn't fair to Ellen. I made it up to her by arranging to take off all of October the following year. We would spend all four weeks in Europe.

Our belated honeymoon was something of a homecoming for me. I still had acquaintances in Europe and we called on them shortly after our arrival. One of them was a fellow named Roberto Cessini Jr., whose father owned a jewellery business. Roberto was a bit of a wild man and he kept some pretty exotic company. He was a shade over five feet tall and must have weighed over 200 pounds. He thought his corpulence gave him the appearance of Aly Khan; I thought he resembled a human netball. He was sensitive about his height and was the only man I ever knew who wore elevated tennis shoes. This handicapped his game. He was slow as a tortoise and the lifts made him unable to move a step to his left or right with anything approaching grace.

Roberto had a habit of dating chorus girls from Billy Rose's night club. The women were all six feet tall or more and were known as Billy Rose's Long-stemmed Roses. Talk about odd couples. Every time Roberto took one of them out he'd ask her to marry him on the first date. Whether the girl accepted or not was immaterial; Roberto also had a habit of forgetting his proposals very quickly.

One of Roberto's close friends was the actor Errol Flynn. I went out with them on several occasions and count myself lucky that I survived to tell the tale. Flynn was a charming fellow, still handsome though dissipated, and always eager to have a good time. If he had been drinking heavily, however, he could be a problem. He broke the nose of a good friend of mine over some minor dispute, and he was always trying to move in on some other man's date.

Roberto and I had once attended a homecoming party with Flynn in New York. He had just completed shooting some Z movie in the Caribbean. I think it was called 'Rebel Girl with Castro', or some other awful title. This was at the very end of his career, and I'm not sure the movie was even released. No matter. Errol was back in New York, and he had a fat pay cheque to celebrate with.

We had arranged to meet him at the airport. When Flynn arrived he was sloshed out of his head. Despite this, he insisted on driving the car. Roberto, to my horror, handed Flynn the keys and let him take the wheel. The ride into the city wasn't too bad, but when we reached the hotel where Flynn's party was being held Errol made a serious miscalculation. While trying to park the car, he slammed into a fireplug, knocking it over and causing considerable damage. That hydrant spewed a tidal wave of water all over the avenue. Flynn hardly took notice of the catastrophe he had caused. Strolling into the hotel, he signed a few autographs and went upstairs to his party. Once there, he greeted some well-wishers and passed out. Roberto and I were left downstairs to make our explanations to the authorities.

Perhaps it was the game side of Roberto that was most appealing. Whatever it was, we got along well despite being oil and water. He seemed glad to hear from us when we telephoned from Monte Carlo. We arranged to get together when our trip took us to Rome.

Reaching the Eternal City, Ellen and I first stopped at Buccelatti's, the store owned by a family whose name had been synonymous with fine jewellery for centuries. There had been a brooch in their New York store that had caught Ellen's eye, but had been too expensive to buy. It cost over 350 dollars, and I just couldn't afford it at the time. Friends had told us to see if we couldn't get a better price at Buccelatti's in Rome. Just as they suspected, we did. The brooch that cost 350 dollars in the United States was selling for 165 dollars in Italy. It was a bargain I could not let pass.

Later that evening, Ellen and I joined Roberto at his father's villa for dinner. During the meal, Roberto Sr. complimented Ellen several times on her brooch. When he asked her where she had found it, she told him, and I chimed in, 'And boy what a steal this was. We saw the same brooch back in New York for almost twice the price.' That comment stirred the elder Cessini's curiosity. He said, 'Would you mind if I asked how much you paid for it?' Hearing the price, he let out a polite chuckle. 'My dear friends,' he said, 'I'm afraid you've been taken. I could get you the same pretty item for around forty dollars.' I asked him where he could get such a price. He replied, 'There is a small town just outside of Milan where all this jewellery is produced.' I was flabbergasted.

I said, 'If you can get this kind of jewellery at that price, we could have a wonderful business back in the States.' Mr Cessini thought about it for a minute and said, 'Okay, we'll go into business. We'll split everything fifty-fifty. I'll acquire the jewellery and ship it to you in America. You'll sell it to the various stores and boutiques and manage the accounts.' It sounded like a fine idea, so I told him I was interested.

During the rest of the time we spent in Rome, Mr Cessini never once mentioned his proposition. He didn't bring it up again until the day we were due to depart. Taking me aside before we left for the airport, Cessini said, 'Don't forget, we're going into business. You'll hear from me very soon.' There wasn't a word from him for almost two months. I completely forgot about his proposition. It was apparent that he had lost interest.

One week before Christmas, I discovered this wasn't so. Twenty-five thousand dollars' worth of Italian jewellery was delivered to my apartment in New York City. I couldn't believe it! Ellen and I spent the holidays with the pieces spread out on the living-room floor while I went over the prices and checked out the inventory. The stuff was just as impressive as the brooch I had bought Ellen; the prices were everything Signor Cessini had promised. By the time I finished going through the consignment, I felt we had an opportunity.

Ellen and I took the pieces to a friend who had become the merchandise manager of Saks Fifth Avenue. He gave us our first order. In February 1958, Saks ran a full-page ad in the *New York Times*, announcing the arrival of the Comte de Cessini Fine Jewellery Collection on our shores. The fancy title turned out to be apt. The subsequent success of this promotion gave our new company a royal launching.

As with any start-up venture, we had to keep our costs down. *Cash is king during a company's early stages of development.* Nothing is more precious. In an attempt to hold on to ours, we ran the business from our apartment. Our den was turned into a shipping and receiving area. I would come home from Playtex at about 7.30. Ellen and I would have dinner and then spend the rest of the evening going over orders, preparing invoices, and packing whatever merchandise had to be sent out. It was a real cottage industry. Our only employees were a salesman who called on customers during the day and an Italian-born secretary. The secretary would come two or three times a week. I would dictate letters to her in English, and she would translate them into Italian. These communiqués formed the weekly reports that kept Signor Cessini abreast of the business.

Operating in this manner, we went from a tiny company based in my home to the second largest importer of Italian jewellery in the United States. Things couldn't have been running more smoothly. Then Signor Cessini came over for a visit and unleashed a hurricane on our parade.

He told me that he was pleased with the company's success, but that he couldn't enjoy it fully. He was troubled by the lifestyle of his son Roberto. He had hoped that his namesake would have settled down by now and would have shown something resembling serious ambition. The only things Roberto seemed interested in were chasing show girls and having a good time. Hoping to alter the course of his son's life, Signor Cessini suggested that I ask Roberto to come to the States to assist me with the company. I refused. I liked Roberto and I was appreciative of the vital role his father had played in the formation of the company. But I was running a business, not the American branch of Ne'er Do Wells Anonymous. Signor Cessini considered my position and replied, 'When I got involved with this business it was with the idea that it would be for my family. That is how I want it. If it can't be that way, perhaps we should end our arrangement.'

This was a terrible blow. The company had made a profit but I had put most of it back into the business, hiring additional sales help and covering our operating expenses. I had so much faith in the enterprise, I had mortgaged 50% of my apartment and had used that capital to build up the business further. I had no cash. Cessini was cutting my legs off at the hip just as we were about to see our greatest rewards.

With Cessini out of the picture, I had to get financing. We didn't need a lot of money. Five thousand dollars would have been adequate. But I soon learned that money is hard to get when you really need it. Five banks turned down my loan requests. I eventually got the money through an entrepreneurial venture. While in Europe on business, I turned an investment of one hundred dollars into 4,000 dollars at a casino in Cannes. I did it as a lark and it was one of the few times I ever gambled on anything other than my own ability. Had I blown the hundred, I wouldn't have bet another penny. But I kept winning and I finished the evening with enough cash to finance a buying trip to Italy.

Resurrecting the jewellery business wasn't that difficult. We had established and maintained the accounts in the States. Cessini's strength had been his contact with the sources of supply. Losing them would have been more crippling than the loss of financial support. However, I had letters from most of the people Cessini had dealt with. I knew who they were, though I had never met them. When Ellen and I returned to Italy, we reached agreements with the same merchants who had dealt with Cessini. They sold us merchandise. With this stock, I was able to get some money from Standard Financial, a financing company in the US that was willing to give me seventy-five cents on the dollar based on my receivables. We used that money to finance the rest of our venture.

Meeting the dealers, we found that Cessini hadn't treated us fairly. Signor Cessini was supposed to be supplying us at cost. We would sell at a profit and divide whatever money we made with him. Ellen and I discovered that he was putting on a 15% mark-up before sending the pieces over. If a ring cost eighty-five dollars, he would sell it to us for one hundred bucks and then still share in the profits after we sold it.

When I found out how he had profited at our expense, I became more determined than ever to build the business back to what it had been. I hired Cessini's top salesman away from him. He was a fellow who had worked with me before Cessini had forced me out. He wasn't fond of the Signor and when I told him what Cessini had pulled on us he decided to throw in his lot with me. Two weeks after I returned from Europe, we were ready to operate.

The salesman, Ellen and I hit all the stores we had dealt with before. They knew we had quality merchandise so there was no problem getting an appointment to see the buyers. They were hungry for what we had to offer. We whetted their appetites further by offering the pieces at reduced prices. With Cessini's hidden mark-up eliminated, we could lower the price without cutting into our profit margin. In a short time the company was more successful than ever.

I kept my part in the company until the winter of 1960. Business had grown so dramatically we had to move it out of the apartment and into an office on 46th Street off Madison Avenue. The demands on my time increased with each new account. When Playtex named me president of Sarong, Inc., I knew I had to give up the jewellery business. It was too much of a load. Ellen had just given birth to our son Tony and I was about to assume a position that could have helped me realize a goal I'd held since my first day at Playtex: the presidency of the company. That was too tempting a bauble to ignore. I sold the jewellery business to the Moba company, our biggest competitor. The deal was not unpalatable. I came away with a reasonable return on my investment of time and money. I also left with a sense of triumph over having been able to make a business fly not once but twice.

There were other rewards. I learned a great deal about running my own business. My experience with Cessini taught me never to take a partner unless it's absolutely necessary. Having a partner is almost contrary to entrepreneurial philosophy. Entrepreneurs don't look to share their responsibility or their equity with anyone.

There are three exceptions to this observation. If you don't have the funding necessary to launch your endeavour and you can't acquire it from any other source, you may be forced to turn over part of your company in exchange for the capital you need. The inverse of this occurs when you have nothing but money. You want to do something on your own but you don't have a sellable idea. Get together with the creative person who's looking for a backer and combine your strengths.

Lack of experience in a chosen field may also compel you to seek a partner. A writer wanted to start a small publishing company. He did all the necessary research and realized he didn't need very much start-up money. A little-used den in his flat could be converted into an office. The writers he hired would work on a commission and, initially, he would do most of the selling himself. This part of the operation presented no problems. However, though he had been a successful writer for almost ten years, he knew little of the publishing end of his business. He had no idea how to assess paper prices, what were the different print sizes, how a choice of book jacket could radically affect his costs, what printers were right for what jobs, or what impact over a hundred other variables might have on his enterprise.

He also knew that although he didn't need a lot of money at the beginning, he might soon. Acquiring it could be difficult. A bank might be hesitant to lend money for a venture headed by someone with so little expertise. Aware of his shortcomings, the writer joined forces with a printing broker, a fellow who knew all the ins and outs of the industry. The writer shouldered the editorial responsibility for the alliance. He initiated projects, wrote proposals, hired other authors, and edited their work. The broker dealt with printers, designers, typesetters and shippers.

Both men acted as salesmen and kept track of the sales and costs. As with any successful relationship, this was not an arrangement in which the right hand didn't know what the left hand was doing. The broker taught the writer the rudiments of the printing process. The writer took some of the mystery out of the creative process for the broker. Both men had a healthy respect for the work ethic and, through their efforts, the company thrived. Theirs was the perfect partnership: a marriage of convenience.

My situation with Cessini was similar to that of the writer and broker. I had the idea, Cessini had the sources and the expertise. One aspect of the arrangement I did not care for: I didn't have any direct contact with his side of the business. He would never have been able to put on the extra mark-up if I had. At least I was lucky enough to have a record of the merchants he had dealt with. If you're involved in a partnership, insist on knowing who are your sources of supply. Meet them if you can. If something happens to your partner or if your alliance is dissolved, you don't want to be wasting time re-establishing vital relationships. If I hadn't some idea of which companies Cessini was buying from, resuscitating the jewellery business might have been impossible.

I mentioned earlier in the chapter that cash is king during a company's early stages of development. Let me amend that statement: *cash is always king*. As we found out after Cessini pulled out, if you don't have money, it's very hard to find. I couldn't get a loan when I needed it. The banks didn't want anything to do with me. I didn't have anything to offer as collateral. If I had any collateral, the banks would have offered their money at terms that would have been stacked against me. Some of the fellows I met might have been too squeamish to hold the debtor down while Shylock hacked off his pound of flesh. But they would gladly have sharpened his knives.

Using your savings is the ideal way to fund a venture. You have no interest costs and you retain all the equity in the company. But how many can afford to do that? If you're not one of the lucky few, there are several options available to you. The ones that come most quickly to mind are banks, business mortgages, the government, bodies such as the Industrial and Commercial Finance Corporation (ICFC) in the UK, and sometimes local councils. Banks are the obvious first choice if you want a sort-term loan – that is, one for anything up to a year. The best and cheapest way of borrowing from a bank is to have an overdraft facility which you can use how and when you want, so long as you keep within the given limits. And so long as your business prospects look promising it is usually fairly easy to renew your overdraft at the end of the fixed period.

For longer-term finance, banks will make a 'term loan' at a fixed rate of interest for a fixed period of time, which helps you to avoid the overdraft trap of borrowing money at low rates of interest and having to ask for an extension when they are high. The clearing banks have been moving into medium- and long-term loans in a big way over the past five years, and small businesses can now get loans specially tailored to suit their needs. Anything from £2,000 to £25,000, repayable in up to ten years, is available for those who can show they are a good business proposition and know how to run things well.

Going in cold and seeking an appointment at your chosen bank or with any other prospective lender is fine, but your path will be smoother if you have a friend who can introduce you to a high-ranking official. The introduction is invaluable. Starting at a low level forces you to deal with someone whose work will have to be reviewed and approved by a superior. This takes time. If you get a no, you'll have to start all over again with another bank, and you'll be that much further from getting your project started.

For finance on a much larger scale, a business mortgage will enable you to raise up to 75% of your assets, repayable over a lengthy period of time. Insurance companies and pension funds, rather than building societies, are the best source of these, but you may find it difficult to raise less than £50,000.

Government loans are another possibility, though these are relatively expensive. Your application will be scrutinized by a bank and passed on to the Department of Industry if it holds water: again, you will have to prove in detail that you are credit-worthy. If you succeed, grants of up to £75,000 are available, repayable in two to seven years.

Still further up the scale, the Industrial and Commercial Finance Corporation (ICFC) is the major source of loans. Set up in 1945 and owned 15% by the Bank of England and 85% by the English and Scottish clearing banks, it will lend anything from £5,000 to £2 million to small businesses. Most of its loans are for around £100,000 but don't be put off by the fact that they are so large: the ICFC will consider all applications. Get help from an accountant in presenting your business in the best possible light; the ICFC has a great deal of experience and could provide you with just the financial package you need.

These are by no means all the sources of finance; there are funds available from central and local government and from certain agencies and the EEC; there are arrangements such as trade credit, factoring, hire purchase, and sale and lease-back which may all help to give you the cash you need at the time you need it. To help you find out more, there is a Small Firms Centre in most towns in the UK now and there are many excellent books on the subject; the most practical starting point, however, is your bank manager.

In order to get money from anyone, you're going to have to sell them on your idea. This will require an in-depth game plan. Nothing is more important to the creation of that plan than field research. Anything you can't document from your experience or the experience of others is theory and has little value.

If you were going to open a greengrocer's stall, you would learn everything you could about the business. You would talk to other greengrocers, getting an idea of their costs and the problems that crop up in their industry. What are your sources of produce? What sort of insurance are you going to need? Find out if there are any trade journals or other literature available for study. You want the answers to any questions you have pertaining to your venture.

That field research will include weeks of intensive observation. The entrepreneur opening a greengrocer's stall has to pick a location. How close to the spot being considered is the nearest competition? If another stand is near-by, can the area support another market? What is the area's population? He can clock the traffic that runs past his selected site and determine the size of his universe of potential customers. If there is a supermarket in town, he will have to decide whether or not he can compete with it. It might be able to undersell him; he may be able to nullify that disadvantage by offering a wider variety of produce and more personalized service. The entrepreneur needs the answers to these and other questions long before he sets up shop. It doesn't matter if you're opening a fruit stall or a market research company, you have to determine your venture's chances of success. Research is the only way to do this.

Armed with this information, you draw up a best case and a worst case balance sheet and then calculate your cash flow projections. This will determine your budget. It should be based on your worst projections and should reflect your fiscal expectations for the enterprise. This is a measure of your future liquidity. Done as a weekly or monthly analysis, it is arrived at by adding your available cash to your projected income and then subtracting your fixed and anticipated expenses.

Your research will be time-consuming. If you're working at a steady job, don't leave it until you've got all the information you need to launch your enterprise. Conduct the investigation in your spare time. By cutting the umbilical cord from a weekly pay cheque, you would place unnecessary pressure on yourself to open the business as quickly as possible. This means the danger of your using sloppy preparation as a short cut. Capital that could be invested in the undertaking would be spent to support yourself. However, by continuing to work nine-to-five and using your leisure time to prepare a game plan, you're going to get the first taste of the rigours of entrepreneurial life. Everything will be sacrificed for the sake of the project. This is a marvellous testing period. You may go a month without seeing a film or dining out. Instead of going to a concert, you stay home to read industry statistics and commerce reports. If you go to bed full of complaint ('What a wasted evening!') and bleary-eyed, maybe you should hang on to that job. You might lack what it takes to make it on your own. On the other hand, if you go to bed enthused ('Boy, did I learn something tonight. I can't wait to get this business started!') and fall asleep with a smile on your face, you've probably got the stamina to go the distance.

Now that you're fully aware of the gamble attached to your venture, you can assess whether or not you want to go through with it by calculating your Risk-Reward Ratio. Will the remuneration be worth the time, energy, and money invested?

My barber Jack has been cutting my hair for years. At first he was working for someone else, but, after a while, he decided to strike out on his own. When he first opened his shop he didn't have any grey hair. Now the snow is creeping in around his temples, and the circles have congregated beneath his eyes. He's working his arse off to make the shop his triumph. At the end of his first year he had squeezed through some tight spots. Traffic fell off when his regular clients went on vacation. He had to delay paying bills. Before cutting my hair one morning he gleefully announced that he had made his final payment to the electrician. It took him a year, much longer than he had anticipated. There were moments during those first twelve months when he was barely breaking even. He could have gone under.

But he didn't. Jack never gave up. He had the fortitude to turn his venture into a success because he never lost sight of his eventual reward. He had worked out a deal with the hotel chain that was his landlord: if he could make a go of it with this shop, they would let him open similar shops in their hotels across the country. Jack will realize his dream. He will be his own boss and he will feast on the abundant financial fruits of his labours. His risk was more than justified by his rewards.

Suppose this hadn't been the case? Imagine what Jack would have done if he had peered into his Risk-Reward Ratio's crystal ball and found that at the end of his struggle he would be no better off than he was when he started. Even if he came out ahead by a few dollars, would it have been worthwhile? Probably not. He might as well have kept working for someone else and spared himself the headaches of responsibility. The entrepreneur has to weigh the potential return on his sacrifice. You have to go into a venture expecting to become much better off than you are now.

You're convinced your venture is a winner. The research is done and the results back this conclusion. You have a reasonable idea of how much money you'll need to make the enterprise go. Now you can approach those financial sources we've already discussed. This calls for some selling. You want potential backers to catch your enthusiasm, persuading them to buy you and your project. Treat investors as a salesman would treat any valued account. Using your research notes and your projections, show them what your venture will mean to them: a good return on their money with a minimal risk and a successful client who will want to do business with them in the future.

In figuring out how much funding the project will require, you should remember that the biggest problem for most new companies is a shortage of capital. You can have the greatest idea and be the hardest worker, but if you run out of cash you can fail. Your best forecasts are going to miss their mark for sure. There is always something unforeseen that is bound to go awry. Projected sales can fall short of your worst fears. The refrigeration lines in your frozen food section may give out and have to be replaced. A strike by lorry-drivers prevents you from getting merchandise from your usual source and forces you to replenish your stock by paying higher prices to other vendors. A strike in your industry limits or shuts down your business for weeks on end.

You must be prepared with a reservoir of funds. Tell your investors or lenders, 'I want X dollars but I would also like a call on additional monies if needed.' With a bank, I would prefer to get a loan, backed up by a credit reserve that I can tap into whenever the situation requires it. Such a line is going to cost you money in interest, but it can be worth it. With a financial safety net stretched out under you, your company can survive if its product or service doesn't sell this season. The additional money will allow you the time you need to revamp the product line, draw up a new advertising campaign, streamline your service, or make whatever other changes are necessary to enhance your business's attractiveness. This security is priceless. Don't wait till the last minute to get it in place.

We've already seen how hard it was for me to find capital when Cessini pulled out of the jewellery business. This was not an unusual case. I know of a fellow who started a computer data base company two years ago. After failing to find private financing, he raised money for the venture by selling stock. The firm that floated the deal raised 4.5 million dollars. The founder had every reason to expect that this money would keep the company alive for two years. His projections backed this supposition. The projections were wrong. Having contracted to provide service to clients by the fourth quarter of the first fiscal year, he was compelled to hire almost twice as many employees as he had originally anticipated. The extra work force was needed to meet the deadline. Kinks in an untested system caused his software costs to double. The mountain of information that had to be loaded into the data base turned out to be much larger than anyone thought it would be. More employees were hired, and more computers were bought to handle the load.

Other unexpected costs, acting like a school of enraged piranha, greedily devoured the corporate nest-egg. This was an innovative venture in an industry steeped in tradition and resistant to new concepts. A wary universe of potential users was slow to sign on for the service. The number of clients the founder was able to reach agreement with did not live up to the projections listed in his worst scenario. Less than one year after the fanfare that had accompanied the public offering, the company ran out of funds.

Desperate to keep the venture afloat, the founder worked non-stop to come up with financing. He succeeded. However, the people who came to the rescue were well aware of what dire straits the company had been in. The blood that had been sucked from the company's monied veins had reappeared, transformed into crimson numerals haunting the data base's forlorn financial statement. The investors bided their time while the company's debts mounted. At the last minute, they stepped in and acquired 80% of the company not for a song, but certainly for something less than a short medley.

Whatever the figure was, it represents merely the monetary cost of propping up the data base. The entrepreneurial founder paid for its salvation with his dreams. The stock sale did not enrich him. Personal debts amassed, while trying to keep his enterprise breathing wiped out a larger portion of his take. After he was bought out, he held no equity in the company. He was just another high-salaried executive. The weekly pay cheque was insufficient recompense. His baby had been snatched from his arms and all he had left were visitation rights that were subject to the discretion of the new parents. This sad affair could have been avoided if only he had shown foresight and made arrangements for additional funding before the company was in crisis. Money is usually cheapest when you don't need it.

Since things don't always run smoothly with a start-up, you're going to need a healthy helping of entrepreneurial perseverance. Ellen and I had our tenacity put to stern test when we first started the Chinese jewellery business.

We had long been attracted to Chinese art, jewellery, and

artifacts. We would run across Chinese pieces in antique stores and we had got hold of some literature that featured examples of craftsmanship from China. The Chinese use of cinnabar, cloisonné, and the skill displayed in their intricate ivory carvings were particularly fascinating.

In 1968, I was the president of the Benrus Corporation. We had a jewellery division called Wells, Inc. that had become the largest seller of semi-precious earrings in the United States. In an attempt to maintain that position, we were always searching for exciting new styles of earrings or other forms of jewellery. I thought China might be a good source. Everything I had seen from there was eye-catching and I knew the country's labour costs were very low. It also occurred to me that, with its population of over one billion customers, China was an area any entrepreneur would want to explore.

I wrote a letter to the Chinese Ministry of Foreign Trade of the People's Republic of China in 1970. It expressed my interest in acquiring some of their crafts and jewellery as well as my intention to sell this merchandise in the States. Ten months after I sent the letter, I received a reply. Since the US had no relations with China, the correspondence came to me by way of the Chinese Embassy in Ottawa. Accompanied by a copy of *The Thoughts and Teachings of Chairman Mao*, the letter thanked me for my inquiry, but also informed me that there were no immediate plans to engage in trade with companies based in the United States.

This answer did not deter me. I wrote every year, making the same request and getting the same reply. Finally, in 1974, I did not receive the usual note turning down my proposal. Instead, I got back a letter inviting me to select merchandise from a black and white brochure, showing pictures of various samples of jewellery and listing their prices. I bought 3,000 dollars' worth of merchandise, though it was hard to tell from the pictures exactly what on earth I had ordered.

When my shipment arrived it was mostly made up of delicately carved fishes, decorated with a lacquered enamel. I was able to place them in five or six of our outlets just in time for Christmas. They were not a big hit, but I had opened the door to China a crack and I was determined not to let it close. I didn't care whether or not the initial venture had been a success. As an entrepreneur, I had to think long-term. I had faith in the products I knew the country could produce and I wanted to be on the ground floor of any business relationship the United States might have with the People's Republic. With this in mind, I did not care to continue ordering from a catalogue. I wanted to go to China and get an idea what kind of stock we could draw from. I also wanted to see if I could get the Chinese interested in any of our merchandise.

In January 1975, I petitioned the Chinese government for permission to visit its country with my wife and Mr and Mrs Wally Heinze. President Nixon had established bonds with the People's Republic during the previous year and the State Department had given me permission to forward my request. I was excited. Six weeks after I had sent the letter I received a telegram inviting our foursome to visit the People's Republic of China any time between 1 September and 30 November, 1975.

We flew into Peking on 3 September. As we touched down, the first thing we noticed was that there wasn't a light on in the city. It was 1 a.m., their time, and everything was pitch black. Only the airport runway was illuminated, a fact we all noted with deep gratitude. Apparently the lights in Peking were doused at 9 p.m. as an exercise in energy conservation.

Stepping off the plane, we were greeted by four armed members of the Chinese Army. They escorted us to a stark white room that served as the headquarters for the Office of Customs and Immigration. The officials were courteous, but their questioning had a pointedness that made us feel as if we were being subjected to an inquisition. They wanted us to tell them our life stories. It took us an hour and a half to answer their queries and even then we weren't finished. Each of us was given a form to list everything we had brought with us. We were asked to sign it and were then told the list would be checked just prior to our departure. They wanted to make sure we didn't sell any of our belongings while in China.

A representative from Peking Jewellery met us as we left customs. After accompanying us to the Peking Hotel, he and a translator made sure that our rooms were in order. They picked Wally and me up the next morning and took us to the jewellery company's main office. It was there that I got my first eyeful of the nuances of Chinese business.

It was immediately apparent that their marketing system was backward. This was supposed to be the government's sales office, yet no one had any idea what merchandise was arriving or when it was due. The manufacturing was done in various communes. The craftsman fashioned the jewellery out of whatever materials were available that month, so the sales office never knew what it was getting until the merchandise arrived. Once it was in stock it was up to the sales representatives to sell it. If buyers could not be found for everything, the government was required to purchase whatever could not be sold. One representative confided that the government had over twenty million dollars of unsellable jewellery sitting in a warehouse.

Colour was also a problem. If you wanted a specific style done in red and they didn't have the materials to make red dye that month, you would get your order in blue or green. There was also no way for them to produce mass quantities of any one item. When I asked if they could ship me 5,000 earrings, all of the same style and colour, they nearly fell out of their seats. They couldn't handle an order one-fifth that size. The more I investigated, the less practical became the idea of doing business with them.

Before we left the office, one salesman took us on a tour of their showcase area. Most of the items on display were one of a kind pieces fashioned from jade or ivory. The stuff was breathtaking. Wally Heinze thought it was the most beautiful jewellery he had ever seen. When we asked if any was for sale, the representative not only replied that it was, he quoted prices that were so low they were mind-boggling. I had Ellen, who had been out shopping with Wally's wife, come over to look at the pieces. She flipped over it and began buying everything in sight. The sales reps were so impressed with her spending spree, they invited us to come out to the government warehouse where they had tons of merchandise. We spent a week going through their stock. It was made up of priceless pieces that were being offered at rock bottom prices.

Ellen kept making purchases. One night I told her, 'Honey, we'll never be able to use all this jewellery you're buying. There's so much of it.' She said, 'Don't worry. Whatever we don't want, our friends can use.' A few days later, I said, 'Ellen, we've run out of friends. We've got to stop buying this jewellery. What will we do with it all?' Seeing my point, she replied, 'I know, but it's so lovely!' I countered with 'If it is so lovely, do you think Americans would be interested in buying it? If you do, we should buy some more and go into business with it.' That statement gave us both pause. After considering for all of two minutes, we asked ourselves why we hadn't come up with the idea earlier.

We bought twenty thousand dollars' worth of merchandise over the next six weeks. China's duty rates doubled the price we eventually paid, but it was more than worth it. When we got back to the States, we set ourselves up in business as the Friendship Collection. We borrowed the name from China's friendship stores. These shops had been given permission by the Chinese government to deal exclusively with a foreign clientele.

Just as we did when we started the Italian jewellery business, we ran the Friendship Collection from our home. We would set up the merchandise on our ping-pong table as a showcase for the various buyers. In February 1976, we landed our first big account: Jordan Marsh, a major department store in Miami, Florida. It backed the collection with an impressive promotion. The store took out full-page newspaper ads and bought radio air time. Ellen went down and appeared on local TV talk shows. She did a whale of a job selling the merchandise, though not everyone was impressed. Anonymous callers, claiming to be members of the John Birch Society, who of course are opposed to any contact with communist nations, phoned the station and threatened to blow up the store and Ellen if she mentioned that the pieces were from Red China. She made her entire pitch without once mentioning where the merchandise was manufactured. The store's ads also discreetly omitted this piece of information. It didn't hurt us. Jordan Marsh sold out half its stock within two weeks of its arrival. After that stores and boutiques across the country wanted to carry it. The Friendship Collection blossomed.

The test of our perseverance came when we went back to China in 1979. We had expanded our operation and wanted to make a deal to import more merchandise. Such an agreement would be vital to our continued growth.

Ellen and I had attended the Frankfurt Products Fair in Germany and had made arrangements to fly to Peking from Paris. When we reached the airport, we discovered that our flight had been cancelled. For some unexplained reason, there wouldn't be another one for two days. I was closing the negotiations to buy Remington in less than a week. Taking the delay into account, I told Ellen I didn't see any sense in going to China at all. We wouldn't have time to put together an agreement. That's when my wife gave me a lesson in entrepreneurial persistence. She said, 'In that case we'll have to find another way to get to China. Right now.'

I had no idea how we could pull it off. I certainly didn't want to go back to Germany and then dog-sled across Russia. Even an entrepreneur has to draw the line somewhere. Ellen went to an information desk and discovered we could get to China by way of Moscow. Fortunately, this involved taking another aeroplane. There was one flight a week from Paris to Moscow and it was leaving in one hour. We sent a cable to Peking Jewellery, telling them of our estimated time of arrival.

We sat through an eight-hour transit stop in Moscow Airport. I was somewhat flustered, but Ellen kept smiling through all of it. Our flight to Peking took off two hours late. When we landed, there was no one at Peking Airport to greet us. We learned later that the office had closed by the time our cable had arrived. It was six in the morning and the airport was cold and deserted. There was no way to get into the city. Turning to Ellen, I said, 'Honey, we just have to bundle up and wait till someone rescues us.' Five hours after our arrival someone did appear. She was an interpreter who had come to meet a flight that wasn't due for another hour and a half. She didn't speak English, but she did speak French. With a little bit of selling centred on an appeal to her good nature, I was able to convince her to drive us to our hotel.

Naturally, the hotel manager had no record of our reservations. Peking Jewellery had cancelled them when they found that our original flight had been called off. The manager kept insisting, 'We have no room for you. You go away. Maybe come back some other time.' I was too exhausted to allow us to be turned down. I looked at the manager and said, 'You say you have no room. Let me ask you something. If Mao Tse-tung were to appear magically right now, would you have a suite for him?' He immediately replied, 'Mao? Yes, yes we would have room for him!' I said, 'Good. I've got news for you. He's not coming. We'll take his suite.' Maybe humour is the universal language because we did get a room. When we got there, I don't think we even bothered to get undressed. We plopped on the bed and went right to sleep.

The next morning we called Peking Jewellery. Our translator, Mr Kuo, answered the phone.

'Mr Kiam, where are you?'

I told him I was in Peking.

'No, you not. Cannot be. Plane cancelled. You must still be in Paris.'

No, I assured him, we had taken a different flight.

'Where are you staying?'

I told him we were at the Peking Hotel and he replied, 'Cannot be! We cancelled reservations when we find out plane not coming. You're not here. Impossible. You play joke on us.'

When I told him I wasn't kidding and that we really were in Peking, he was astonished. Neither he nor anyone else at the office could believe that we had got there without any assistance, especially after our flight had been cancelled. They were so impressed with our perseverance – Ellen's really – that they told me, 'We come over right now and pick you up. You come to our office. You good people. We do business for sure.'

Knowing I was under time constraints and mindful of the trouble we had gone through to reach them, the Peking Jewellery reps did something very unusual in this part of the world. On the final day of our visit, they worked past closing time to hammer out a deal. They had dinner brought in and we ate it in their offices. We finalized our agreement at midnight. Because of my wife's stick-to-itness, we came away with the merchandise we needed and the Friendship Collection grew into the US's largest importer of Chinese jewellery and antiques.

CHAPTER SIX

Seeing it through: the art of negotiation

If business is a game, negotiations are its version of poker. As an entrepreneur, there will be moments in your career when you will be called upon to negotiate any number of things: a sale, a takeover or a contract.

One of my more gratifying negotiations occurred when I had to convince a valued employee not to leave Remington. He had come into my office one afternoon, announcing that he had just received an offer from another company, one that would give him a higher salary than he was presently receiving. The proposal also included a number of perks, including membership in a country club, use of a company car, and an annual trip to Puerto Rico for the company's winter sales meetings. Such perks are taboo at Remington. We try to run a mean and lean operation. He knew we couldn't give him any of those extras, nevertheless he insisted on discussing their offer with me, giving Remington the opportunity to match it before he accepted.

I went over the particulars of it with him. The other company's bid was generous in terms of salary. Remington couldn't match it. In his present position, the young man simply wasn't worth that much to our organization. I could, however, offer him a slight boost in pay.

Having agreed to raise his salary, I then proceeded to point out that the position he currently held at Remington had vast potential for growth and promotion. Though I couldn't match the other company's offer, I did remind him that everyone at Remington was rewarded on merit. If he was successful in his current job, the incentives built into the company salary structure would increase his annual pay substantially. He was already well aware of my plans for Remington's expansion and he knew that seniority was not a prerequisite for upward movement on our corporate ladder. At Remington, employees are rewarded on results, not on their length of service.

After reminding him of what he had going for himself with us, I then pointed out something he had already suspected: the job he was considering was virtually a dead end. Certainly, I admitted, it would pay him a few dollars more than I was willing to give him. And I wouldn't blame him if he found those perks attractive. But if he accepted this position, it was highly probable that he would be unable to move much further up in his new organization. This was not a comment on his ability. On the contrary, I thought he was quite gifted. It was just that the position in question didn't offer that sort of opportunity. He would be joining a family-owned operation and most of its members were related either by blood or by marriage. It would be tough for an outsider to break into the magic circle. Also, the line to the top in this conglomerate did not pass through his area of expertise. His strength was in sales; this company's base was in financial services.

After bringing this to his attention, I then made it clear that, unlike the company that was attempting to woo him away from us, Remington did not place any limits on the heights he could reach; he might even be sitting in my chair some day. I said, 'I really believe that you should have the same goal here that I had at Playtex. You should think about going all the way in this company because you've got all the tools.' We went over some of the things he had already accomplished with the company and I began to talk about the things yet to be done. *I was painting the vista.* He had no small confidence in himself and knew that I was not giving him pie in the sky. What I was saying was true; he could go to the top. He was a go-getter. As he left my office, he said our discussion had given him a lot to think about. He asked if he could mull things over for a day and then get back to me. I told him that this could very well be the most important decision he had ever made; it would have an impact on whatever direction the rest of his life would take. I wasn't being melodramatic. I simply wanted to make the gravity of the moment plain. I believed this young man had a tremendous future with Remington. I didn't want to see him toss it aside for a few extra bucks and some frivolous perks. A few days after our meeting, he came back to my office and told me he had decided to stay. If he had come to tell me that our sales were up 30%, I don't think I could have been happier.

When he first entered my office, it appeared as though I didn't have too much of a chance to retain him. How was I able to do it without matching the other company's offer? What was the key to this and any other successful negotiation? *Information!* I was well stocked with it in the situation just described. I knew the young man well enough to have little difficulty picking up the signals he was sending me.

The mere fact that he had come in to discuss the offer he had just received told me that he wanted to be persuaded to stay. Why else would he give me the details of the other company's bid and then ask me what I thought of it? He knew he had no chance of getting any perks out of Remington and I'm certain he didn't expect us to give him anything more than a slight rise in salary, provided we agreed to give him any increase at all. What he wanted was some sign that he had a future with us, that he was *valued*.

I also knew that this young man thought himself to be something of an entrepreneur. That was one of the reasons I had hired him. It was incomprehensible that he would want to be chained to a job that promised neither challenge nor a chance for advancement. He wanted to be part of an organization that would encourage his growth. Knowing this, I could easily point out the advantages of staying with Remington, especially those advantages I knew he would find most appealing. It was the vista that convinced him. The small increase in salary helped. It placed a tangible value on his already considerable contributions to the organization. But more important was the vista's ability to answer his real needs and to give him a glimpse of the wonderful future he could shape for himself within Remington.

Any time you're negotiating, you're selling. You have to convince the person on the other side of the table to buy your representation of reality. In this high-stakes confrontation you might not always have many cards to play. Don't fret. You don't need a full house to triumph. As long as your opponent doesn't have an inkling of the sort of poor hand you're holding, you can still walk away with the pot.

I was in a situation not too long ago where the other player held four aces and I couldn't even come up with a pair of twos.

Remington had signed an agreement with Charles of the Ritz, allowing us to manufacture the Aroma Disc Player. This was a gadget that allowed its users to fill their households with an interesting array of fragrances simply by placing a scented disc inside an electronic diffuser. Within minutes, the pleasant smells of roses, popcorn, ocean breezes, or other equally appealing aromas would be released through vents in the top of the machine and come wafting into the room. I was impressed with the disc player's potential, especially since it worked economically (one disc would give you more service than a large fragrance candle) and featured a variety of enticing scents. I was so enamoured of the machine that I asked that our contract also give us the right to sell it while paying Charles of the Ritz a royalty.

Though it was a terrific product, we had problems with it right away. The disc player was so foreign to anything Remington had done before that our sales force didn't quite know how to handle it. They were never really able to get behind the gadget and make it go. Despite this, we might have done all right the first year, but there was a delay in the delivery of the aroma discs to Remington. This tardiness on the part of Charles of the Ritz cost us a lot of momentum. Since then, I've tried everything I could think of, but I couldn't get the disc player to take off.

As the sales numbers, acting as harbingers of grim reality, came in, I decided I had to take a hard look at our involvement with the disc player. I realized it just wasn't a business for us. Charles of the Ritz had all the fragrance discs and that meant it was going to get all the repeat sales. That's where the business was long-term and there was no way I could compete in that market.

Since we had to get out of the disc player business, I wanted to make sure we did it as painlessly as possible. We had made a sizeable financial commitment to the product; to close it out would have put a dent in our pocketbooks.

Until I made the decision on what we would ultimately do, I wanted to give everyone the impression that we couldn't be happier with the business. I wanted Charles of the Ritz to think that we had faith in the disc player as a money maker. To create this illusion and to give the appearance that we were gearing up to give the disc player a big push, I sent bulletins out to all our accounts, announcing our lower-priced machine. This made it seem as if Remington was planning to become an aggressive force in the market.

When Charles of the Ritz got wind of what we were doing, they were not pleased. Their representative called me and said, 'Look, we didn't enter into an agreement with you so that we could have you as a competitor. Your lower price is going to hurt us. We're not looking to get into a dollar war with you, so let's find a peaceful solution to our problem. What would you say if we offered to buy back Remington's rights to sell the Aroma Disc Player?'

This fellow didn't know it, but I was General Custer at the Little Big Horn and he was John Wayne leading the cavalry to my rescue. Of course, I didn't appear overly grateful. It's true I still wanted out of the disc player business, but I also wanted to leave with the best deal possible. It behove Remington to appear bullish on the disc player industry and to loom as a threat to Charles of the Ritz. Having heard only a small part of his proposal, I replied, 'Are you kidding? This is such a tremendous business, why would we want to stop now? You've seen our bulletins. They're just the beginning. I believe this machine has a bright future. Think of the untapped market for it in Europe and the Middle East. I tell you, we're going to come on like gangbusters. I don't want to be bought out.' Of course this was only so much talk. In reality, when he first made his offer, I wanted to put on a pair of dark sunglasses so he wouldn't notice how my eyes had lit up. I had known long before he called that the only way out was to make Charles of the Ritz want us out.

The company made us a fair offer and I told its representative that I would consider it. I let a week pass. Then I called and said, 'I don't know. I hate to give this thing up. It's such a winner. But I don't want any hard feelings between our companies. I'm sure we're going to do other things down the line. I'll tell you what. If you insist, we'll give the disc player up. You can have the whole business and Remington will act as a manufacturer for you.' Then I pointed out the benefits of being the disc player's sole distributor. I created a vista and he reached for it. As with any vista, it wasn't painted with bogus oils. I actually believed that this was a wonderful product. It just wasn't for us.

No matter how much you think you have going for you, you will be unable to win every negotiation. Some people refuse to be swayed and are in a position to turn down anything that falls short of what they are demanding. In 1960, I was interested in acquiring the Jantzen Company, a manufacturer of swimwear and sweaters, located in Portland, Oregon. While working for Playtex, I had heard from a number of retailers that the company was up for sale. Gossip had it that the founding family, owners of 30% of the stock, wasn't happy with the direction the company had taken. They had recently been ousted from the board of directors and there was apparently a lot of corporate infighting taking place. To prevent a bloodbath that would produce no winners, it was decided to unload a huge portion of the company at what was supposed to be a bargain basement price.

I thought this would be a marvellous acquisition for Playtex. It was a related industry with a history of success. I couldn't, however, convince Al Peterson of the merits of the acquisition. At the time, they didn't think Playtex should be involved with this particular business. Though their resistance was firm, it didn't dissuade me from believing that the Jantzen Company was a hell of a pick-up. I decided to make a play for it on my own.

I put out the word through some friends in the financial community that I was looking for a backer to assist me in the attempted buy-out. One fellow, a private investor who was always looking to get involved with this sort of enterprise, expressed an interest. I gave him all the financial data I had acquired on the company. Having digested it, he went over my plans for the company and decided to throw in with me on the venture. He would finance the acquisition; I would receive equity in the enterprise and also run the company after it had been bought.

Once an agreement was reached between us, we had to decide how much we were willing to pay. Having looked over the financial prognosis I had drawn up for the enterprise, my backer instructed me not to allow our bid to exceed twenty-one dollars a share.

I flew out to Portland and met Jantzen's president and three members of the board. After a bit of fencing, they confirmed that they wanted to sell. Their price was twenty-three dollars a share. I knew what my ceiling was, but I also knew that twenty-three would still give us a good deal. I told the four that twenty-three was a bit higher than we wanted to pay. Before I could attempt to talk them down, the president smiled and said, 'Perhaps it is, but that's the price. We don't have to sell to you. There are other interested parties so we don't have to dicker. We won't sell for $22.50, $22.75, or even $22.99. It's $23.00 a share or nothing. If you can agree to our terms, you just bought yourself a company. If not, we'll just wait for another buyer.' I knew he wasn't bluffing. He was an owner in a seller's market. Internal politics more than anything else was forcing the sale. The company was making money. Having that information, I knew we had to up our offer. I excused myself, telling the four that I had to speak with my partner before raising our bid.

I called my backer from another office and told him what it would take to acquire the company. Before he could decide, I went into the numerous reasons why this was still a good buy even at the higher price. I painted the biggest vista imaginable. The colours blended together, forming a rich landscape. Had I created a second Mona Lisa, it wouldn't have made a difference. My partner wouldn't budge. I went back into the meeting and told the president and the board members that twenty-one dollars a share was our first and final offer. They bid me good-day and reiterated their lack of interest, but did agree to call me if they changed their minds. I'm still waiting for that call. Four months later, Jantzen sold the company to another buyer for twenty-eight dollars a share.

My failure in this case wasn't my inability to complete the purchase. The Jantzen people would not change their minds, no matter what I said, and they were right not to retreat from their position. The higher bid they accepted later justified their stand. My defeat came when I was unable to persuade my backer to raise the ante. I was hampered by a lack of information. I had done my homework on Jantzen; I had studied the company inside out. That's why I was certain that their refusal to consider our proposal wasn't a ploy designed to get us to go higher. What I didn't bother to find out was what would turn my own partner on. I had no idea what would make the venture more attractive than it already was. Maybe nothing could have turned the trick. But if anything could have enticed him, and I had known what it was, I might have been able to persuade him to loosen his purse strings for the additional $2 a share. The lesson is that in a negotiation you have to know *both* sides – your opponent's and your own.

Too many negotiations go down the drain because of greed

or self-centredness. As a negotiator, you can wound yourself whenever you are overly concerned with what you need to get out of the transaction. You should back off. Your needs are known; you're already close to them. If you've done your research, you already know what your bottom line is and will recognize immediately when a deal is unacceptable to you. What you have to ascertain is what the other person hungers for. From the start of any successful negotiation, the entrepreneur must try to view the proceedings through the other person's eyes as well as his own.

This point was driven home for me once again when I tried to induce a certain executive to join Remington. He had been involved with a large, stereotyped corporation for his entire business life and was reluctant to come on board our ship. I told him all the advantages of being with Remington and gave him an idea of the pot of gold at the end of our rainbow. After discussing what the company could do for him, I focused the discussion on what he could do for the company. I drew up a colourful vista. It seemed in vain. This prospective employee wasn't crazy about the way our company was structured. He had been with the same company for twenty-five years. He had become trapped in its corporate syndrome. His salary was stable. All the decisions made in his division were reached by a committee. He had little responsibility and even less risk. In our company, people are paid according to the goals they reach. If he hooked up with Remington, his starting salary would undergo a 20% slash. But, he would be given a position in which he could really shine. If he were successful – as I was certain he would be – he could make almost twice as much money as he was receiving now. Of course, if he didn't produce, he would make less.

I let him know how confident I was that he could do the job. I had a feeling that the challenge appealed to him. All he needed was a nudge. I almost had him ready to accept when his wife squelched the deal.

Two years before I had interviewed him, this fellow's company had transferred him. His wife had lived in a big city for her entire life and relished the hustle and bustle of a lively metropolis. The transfer had forced them to move into a more rural area. She hated it. The lifestyle didn't suit her and it took her forever to make new friends. She had only recently come to terms with her new existence. Unless switching to a new company meant a return to the city life she loved, she wanted no part of a move. When she was told they would have to move to Connecticut, she became more adamant in her refusal. She figured they would be living in yet another remote, rural area and that it would take her two more long years to get acclimatized to her new surroundings. Adding his wife's feelings to his own hesitations, the husband turned my offer down.

I had blown it. It never occurred to me to find out what his wife's objections were. I had lived in Connecticut and so did most of my executives. We loved it. I didn't think anyone would seriously object to having to live there. Had I known what the problem was, we could have addressed it. We could have brought the wife out and introduced her to the Connecticut lifestyle. We would have gone out of our way to make her feel at home and to show her that she would have no trouble making new acquaintances. I didn't think to do this and it cost me a good employee. I had failed to see through the other person's eyes.

Generally speaking, you don't discover the other person's desires in the first negotiating session. You have to take time to forge a relationship. Get acquainted with your opposite number. Go out for dinner or a drink. All the time you're with him or her, look for clues. *A negotiator should observe everything. You must be part Sherlock Holmes, part Sigmund Freud.*

You may have to put up with a lot to build that rapport. I was putting together a transaction with a fellow who had the attention span of a hummingbird. He couldn't light on any one subject for more than three minutes without going off on a tangent or launching into one of his four favourite anecdotes. I don't know how often I heard the same awful jokes. I wanted to pull my hair out. I never interrupted him. When he was with me, he was the most important person in my life and I wanted him to feel like a king.

At one point in our negotiation, we had finished for the day and had dropped into a nearby restaurant to discuss some more business and anything else that flittered across his imagination. I had to be home at nine for another engagement. As our discussion continued, I knew it was getting late, but he was being expansive and I thought we were making progress that would benefit our negotiation. I never referred to the time; my entire focus was on him. Finally, as we were about to leave, I did turn to him and asked him if he knew what time it was.

It was 8.45. We had come into the place at 6 p.m. for what was supposed to be a half-hour chat. I now had a problem, but I didn't make him aware of it. I wanted him to know that I had devoted myself fully to him and that nothing else mattered to me except his interest. If you're in a similar situation you shouldn't check your watch unless you can do it surreptitiously. If you're late for an appointment, excuse yourself and claim you have to check in with the office. A white lie. Call whoever you are scheduled to meet next, make your apologies, and get back to the table. Business is where you are and you mustn't ever pass up a chance to mine those nuggets of information.

I had to play Holmes and Freud when I negotiated the acquisition of Sarong, Inc. for Playtex. That deal was brought to me out of the blue.

My fun-loving friend Roberto called me one evening and invited Ellen and me to an Italian restaurant in midtown New York. When we arrived, we found Roberto in his cups. He grabbed me when I first walked in and said, 'You are going to thank me for what I'm about to do for you. Come with me.' He brought me up to the bar and introduced me to Dave Henley. Clapping Dave on the back, Roberto said, 'Dave, here's the guy I've been telling you about all evening. Meet Vic Kiam. I think the two of you will have a lot to talk about. You're both in the girdle business.' David was the majority owner of Sarong Incorporated. He had told Roberto that he was looking to unload the business and Roberto had suggested that Playtex might be interested. I was called in to see if I wanted to arrange the transaction.

I approached Wally Heinze at Playtex. He was well acquainted with the Sarong organization and readily agreed that it could be a wonderful acquisition for our company. They asked me to negotiate the terms. It was understood that if I were successful in securing the takeover, Sarong would become a part of International Latex; I would be installed as its general manager with duties equivalent to those of a president.

This gave me an enormous incentive to come away with a deal. I did everything I could think of to help David come to terms, but was unable to make any headway during the first week of the negotiation. I'd make an offer and David would hardly respond.

It was strange. He never rejected any of my proposals out of hand, he just didn't approve of any. I felt unable to turn him on. No matter how I structured the deal it got the same lukewarm reception. At first, I thought this was David's idea of a negotiating ploy, but, as the days passed, I realized it was something more than that. He wasn't playing hard to get. The fact that he never responded with a counterproposal told me he wasn't playing any kind of game. It became apparent that I simply hadn't figured out what Dave Henley wanted. Until I discovered that, I knew these negotiations were going to be futile.

I knew what I had to do. I decided to find out what made Dave Henley tick. I knew his background; he had inherited a fortune and had turned it into a success as a minor Hollywood producer. He had been involved with some of the last films starring Errol Flynn. He had met Roberto through the movie star. Though married, he had a reputation as a playboy. That's not to say he fooled around or tried to emulate some of Flynn's antics. It just meant that he was drawn to bright lights and loud parties.

In an attempt to get to know him, I started dining with him even when there was no business to discuss. I found that the public face of David Henley was all veneer. There was another David, desperate to be recognized. Sensing this, I began to probe, gently prodding him with questions about his background. The more concern I showed, the more he opened up. He revealed himself to be a thoughtful and serious man who wanted to drop the masquerade. His need to pour his heart out to me confirmed what I had suspected: David Henley was a lonely man. He had no one he could honestly relate to. He had tried to fill an empty life with nightclubs and strangers, safe in the knowledge that they could never give him the affection he both feared and craved.

David was fifteen years older than I, but I adopted him as though he were a son. I called every night to see how he was doing. Ellen and I invited him to our house for dinner. I took an interest in him that nobody had before. When you take an interest in a person during a negotiation, you win their trust. They know you're going to do your best to see they don't get hurt in the deal. Building this relationship with David wasn't hard to do. He was an immensely likeable chap and I was so touched by his need for friendship that I really did want to look out for his welfare. We became close friends. When it came time to crunch out an agreement, our personal relationship translated itself into a smooth negotiation. We came to terms and Sarong became part of International Latex. If I hadn't taken the time to read David Henley and respond to the signals he was sending me, the acquisition might not have happened.

Getting close to the person on the other side of the negotiating table is a strategy that can often involve enlisting the aid of that person's employees, co-workers, partners, and family. Again, *information is a negotiator's greatest weapon.* Getting it can be a tricky business.

In a recent negotiation, an acquisition I made, the owner of the enterprise was giving me a devil of a time in our confrontations. We'd seem to make some progress, then he would bring up some minor detail and we would slide back to square one. I couldn't get a handle on the guy and it was frustrating me.

I stepped back and analysed the situation. Had I lost sight of any red flag he might have been waving? During our talks, he often mentioned how little time he had taken off during the past thirty years. 'I can't remember my last vacation' was a frequently heard complaint. He had repeatedly mentioned how he had very little time for himself and how he had forgotten what it was like to have a good time. There was obviously something there. I was certain that no matter what the terms of the sale were, he didn't want any part of the business after it had been sold. This meant I couldn't use a vista portraying how we were both going to make the business better than ever. I had to find out what he wanted to do after he walked away from the company. I pursued this question with some of his executives and members of his family. Nothing sinister there. We just had a few informal chats. Somewhere during the conversation I would casually say, 'Gee, Charley looks all done in at times. I think he needs a rest. Maybe we should call an intermission to these negotiations and let him get away for a few days.' I hit a bull's-eye with that comment. Two of the people I conferred with said, 'Don't worry about Charley. He does need a vacation and a long one. He knows it. That's why he's selling the company.' With that as a start, it didn't take long for me to find out the particulars. Charley longed for retirement, not just from his company but from the business world. He was tired of working and didn't care who he sold the company to as long as he left the negotiations with one million dollars after taxes.

That would be the nest egg that would allow him to sit and count sea shells on some Caribbean beach or whatever else he wanted to do with the rest of his life. I structured my offer around that need. I didn't bother with any incentives I might normally have offered him if the company was successful because I knew he wasn't interested in them.

With his needs in hand, I went into our next negotiation armed to the hilt. I made it clear to him that the only way he could achieve his retirement goals was to sell his business, if not to me then to somebody else. I had gone over his cash flow, his profit and loss account and his balance sheet. He had a large portion of a 1.6 million dollar loan outstanding. His business brought him 200,000 dollars a year in pre-tax income. This meant he took home roughly $100,000 after taxes. I had some idea of the financial demands of his lifestyle. I had been sure to visit his house and observe him at close quarters. Even at a conservative estimate, I showed that it would take him the rest of his life to pay off that loan. Unless his business took a dramatic upswing, he would never be able to afford his cherished retirement.

When I pointed this out to him, he asked why I was willing to take over the company and its debt. I was honest with him. From my point of view the business was a worthwhile investment. It was a money-maker and it fitted in nicely with some of the things Remington was already doing. This made it especially attractive. I told him he had built up a hell of an organization and that I would be proud to maintain its position in the industry. I was giving him the Good News. There was no reason to tear down him or his company. He had done a good job with it. But, even if he hadn't, I still wouldn't take a shot at him. You never want to alienate the other party in any negotiation unless you want to call the proceedings to a permanent end.

As the session continued, I listed other reasons why I wanted to buy the company. Being in a related industry, we could duplicate many of the services his company was currently paying for at no additional costs to our operation. Our companies called on many of the same accounts, so my sales force could sell his products without having to be enlarged. He had a large accounts department managing the company's finances. I had this department already in place. These were just some of the areas where I could cut costs. With the money saved through a merger, the business would be more profitable than ever without adding so much as one new account. The Remington link-up would enable his business to pay off the debt very quickly. With his question answered and his need satisfied, the negotiation came to a rapid and successful close. He got his nest egg and I got the company.

In enlisting the aid of key executives of an enterprise you are negotiating to take over, you want to make it worth their while to push for the sale. Let them know they have an incentive for wanting the deal to go through. There is nothing shady about this; do everything out in the open. Tell the owner, 'Look, I've got to talk to your people. If I take over the company and your key executives leave, I'm in trouble. I want to get their feelings on the deal and I want to do anything I can to induce them to stay.' When you meet those individuals, start painting that vista. Let them know what great things you want to accomplish with the company and how you expect them to be an important part of your plans. Find out what they want from this new relationship. It's an especially good idea to ask the incumbent management what they would like to see happen with the company. Find out the vista they've painted for themselves and incorporate it into your overall canvas. Build the euphoria to such a pitch that the existing management and other employees will hardly be able to wait for you to take over. They will become your sales force with the present owner.

If there are agents or any other go-betweens involved in the transaction, enlist their aid in bringing the negotiation to a happy conclusion. They have a stake in the outcome; see that they earn their fee or commission.

A banker called me one afternoon to tell me about a young man who wanted to sell his apparel business. The owner had built the business up and had done well with it, but it had fallen on hard times as had a number of other ventures he was involved with. He was faced with a hard decision: sell the company or go into bankruptcy.

The officer of his bank knew me and thought I might be interested in buying the business. He arranged a meeting between the owner and me. Before the get-together took place, I went out and got all the information I could on his industry in general and his company in particular.

The owner – let's call him George – came to my New York

apartment for the meeting. The moment he walked in he said, 'I'm so nervous. Can I have a drink?' I knew immediately that this guy was trying to con me. If he had really been nervous he wouldn't have admitted it, he would have done his best to give the appearance of being calm. George had a boyish face – he had to be at least thirty years old, but he looked about twenty – and tried to come across like the bare-arsed babe on the rug. He dropped what I thought was a feigned nervousness two minutes into our meeting and starting singing arias about what a terrific company he had. I was supposed to believe that he was reluctant to part with this fabulous business. Of course, I knew if his company was doing as well as he claimed, we wouldn't have been having the meeting. Possibly realizing that that thought might have ambled across my mind, George assured me that the only reason he was even considering selling the company was because he had just got into the tax avoidance business, and it was so fascinating he wanted to devote all his time to it. It was all I could do to suppress my laughter. Then he went on about why he thought the apparel business was the perfect venture for me. I tell you, this guy wasn't painting a vista, he was giving me the whole Sistine Chapel. When he finished he told me he would let me have the company for two million dollars and claimed that if I didn't like the price, he knew of plenty of people who did. In a final summary, he reiterated, 'I don't really want to leave this business, but I think it's time for a change of lifestyle.'

I had listened to this drivel while keeping one eye trained on the balance sheet. Watching him concoct this fantasy world, I thought, 'Boy, is this kid in trouble. His business is sinking right before my eyes.' I hardly said a word through most of our meeting. I let him do all the talking, interrupting him only for an occasional query. At the end of his pitch, I said, 'You've made an impressive case. Let me think it over and I'll get back to you in a few days.' I could have started punching holes in his presentation immediately, but I had decided I wasn't going to be the bastard in this confrontation. I had an ally who was going to assume that role: the bank. George's company was into them for a lot of money and, if it went under, they would lose their shirts on the deal. With so much on the line, they should be the ones to squeeze him.

Calling the banker who brought us together, I said, 'You have some kind of nut here. You asked me to talk to him and I did. You and I know that this outfit is virtually bankrupt. It's dancing in the shadow of Chapter 11. In your honest opinion what is this company worth?' The banker admitted he didn't have any idea. I asked, 'Is it worth one million dollars?' He replied, 'Gee, did you offer him that? That would be an awful lot of money for this company.' I asked, 'Is it worth a million and a half?' 'No way.' Then I asked, 'Is it worth two million dollars?' The banker chuckled and said, 'Of course not.' I countered, 'Well, that's what he's looking to get for it, two million dollars.' The banker nearly gagged. He said, 'Are you kidding? That's ridiculous. How can he have the nerve to ask for that kind of money?' The banker was on my side now. I said to him, 'I think I can do something with this company, but we both know it needs a lot of work and new financing. I'm not going to do you down. In its present condition, this company is worth half a million dollars and not a penny more. That's my offer. Now I don't think I can sell him on that price. You're going to have to help me. Talk it over with him. If this company goes bankrupt, your bank is going to get hurt.' He agreed that mine was a fair offer and he said he would do whatever he could to see that it was accepted. He doubted any other buyer would be as generous. By stating my case plainly, I took the onus off me and forced the bank to drive home my negotiating points. The bank officials called George into their office and read him the riot act, making it clear what was at risk with his outlandish demand. The next time we got together, the discussion was a bit more realistic. Whenever George did try to play hard to get with me, I'd call up the bank and let them deal with him. I never really negotiated with him. We ended up reaching an agreement a lot quicker than I originally thought possible.

Let the agent or go-between know whenever the other party is asking for anything outrageous and let this intermediary know about any negatives you've uncovered with the company. It's in this person's interest to move the negotiations along. Agents don't get their rewards unless a deal is struck. Pump him for information. Let him prod your opposite number into the direction you've plotted. The intermediary will pull the seller back to reality by reminding him of his enterprise's worth based on the negatives you've cited. Don't let him be anything but your ally. He's getting that fee. Use him.

Unlike the owner of the apparel company, you have to know when you're in no position to make demands in a negotiation. After the buy-out of Remington, I made a trip to Michigan to call on K-Mart, our biggest account. I had gone over our records and realized that our position at K-Mart was tenuous. We were doing about one-eighth of their shaver business and Norelco was getting about six-eighths. Sunbeam had the other eighth. I knew we weren't very important to K-Mart, but I thought I could change that with aggressive marketing.

I met the K-Mart buyer to discuss future business. The meeting seemed to be going well. The buyer was friendly and appeared receptive to some of the ideas I had for marketing the shaver. Just as we were about to conclude our discussion, the K-Mart merchandise manager came in and said, 'I'm glad you're here because Remington and K-Mart have a problem. Actually it's your problem more than ours and I want to know what you're going to do about it?' I was unprepared for any bad news. I asked him what the trouble was and he replied, 'Your company sold us a large order of new shavers. At the time we made the purchase, Sperry (the former owners of Remington) promised that there would be a massive promotional campaign backing the product. We bought the shavers with the understanding that we would benefit from advertising on TV and radio. We also expected more than the usual exposure in the print media. If this hadn't been our understanding, we wouldn't have put in the order. Now I've just heard that you don't intend to do anything approaching the campaign Sperry had promised.'

I confirmed this. It wasn't that I didn't want to run the campaign. I did. But the Federal Trade Commission had forced me to change my plans. When Sperry first drew up the campaign, they submitted ad copy to the Food and Drug Administration. The FDA was in a position to challenge the ad's claim that the shaver helped prevent razor bumps. Sperry challenged this authority by claiming the shaver was a non-medical device and was therefore beyond the FDA's jurisdiction. The FDA bought that argument, but, just as a full campaign was about to be launched, the FTC entered the case. It ruled that the shaver *was* a medical device and that any claims made about its ability to prevent razor bumps would have to be supported by medical evidence reviewed by the FDA.

I took over Remington in the midst of this controversy. I

checked out the numbers and discovered that it would be too costly to run the device through any sort of extensive medical testing. It would also be too time-consuming. With these factors in mind, I decided to drop the advertising completely. K-Mart saw this as a breach of their understanding with Remington and they weren't happy about it. They were sitting on 30,000 shavers that had cost them thirty-six dollars apiece.

I didn't have a ready answer for this dilemma, but the merchandise manager had a clear idea of what had to be done. He said, 'I want you to take those shavers back immediately.' If he had told me I was about to be evicted from my home, I doubt I could have felt any worse. I had been with Remington for three weeks and was trying to nurse it through its rebirth. At this fragile stage of its existence, it could perish from the common cold. This request by K-Mart represented more than just a mild case of the sniffles; it was nothing less than a version of the bubonic plague.

Remington's cash flow was predicted on sales, not returns. I knew that if I agreed to take this order back, I would be jeopardizing our loan agreement. But I also knew that if I didn't allow the return, Remington's relationship with K-Mart was history. I was in a position where I was either going to have to risk losing a large portion of financing or lose our largest potential account.

I sat in the buyer's office with streams of perspiration winding their way down my back. Unaware of the position he had placed me in, the merchandise manager asked, 'Well, are you going to take them back or not?' What could I do? I figured there was always a chance that I could work out some arrangement with the bank; I knew there would be no negotiating with K-Mart. I did the only thing I could. I agreed to let K-Mart return the shavers.

As soon as I left that meeting, I ran to the nearest phone and called Remington's chief financial officer. I said, 'Don, you had better check out our loan agreement and then do a comparison with our cash forecasts. I've just taken back over one million dollars in shavers from K-Mart.' Silence. I thought Don had passed out. He recovered enough to blurt, 'Oh my God!' and then jumped off the phone to open his files.

As it turned out, we were able to arrange it so that we weren't hurt as badly as I thought we would be. I agreed to take the shavers back in March. By the time the paperwork went back and forth, it was late June before they were ready to return the merchandise. They didn't get all the shavers back for a long, long time; it must have taken more than two months. After they were returned, we had an additional thirty days or so to return their money. By then, we were in pretty good shape. Our cash flow was healthy and we were able to absorb the loss without suffering too much pain.

Three years later, our business was booming. We had 50% of the shaver market at K-Mart, not 12%. The merchandise manager, having since risen in the company, and I had become close friends. One day we were having lunch and I told him, 'You probably didn't know it at the time, but when you told me to take back all those shavers, you almost put my head in a noose. It could have ruined me.' I explained what our situation had been and added, 'But I knew we couldn't afford to lose you, so I thought it made good business sense to do what you asked.' He smiled and said, 'You made the right decision.' That was borne out shortly after my problems with the shavers had been resolved.

One of our competitors had run into a similar situation with another large account. This rival had introduced a beauty kit. The kit consisted of about twenty cosmetic items and a ladies' shaver. It retailed at $34.95 and it wasn't selling. The customer tried to return them, but our competitor hadn't been as co-operative with this account as I had been with K-Mart. Riding high at the time, they felt they could refuse. Their attitude was, 'You bought them, you own them.' This was a terrible misjudgement. This shaver company did a substantial business with this customer. They and Remington were the only lady shaver brands carried by the chain, with our competitor holding the majority of the business. They should have attempted to reach a compromise with their biggest account.

I was calling on this client in December 1981. Before I went to their corporate offices, I visited several of their stores in the outlying area. In each store I saw a most perplexing sight. My competitor's ladies' shaver retailed at $19.95. This beauty set, which included the shaver, was selling for $14.95. I called over a salesperson and said, 'Pardon me, but isn't this a mistake? You have this kit listed as $14.95, but you're selling the shaver for five dollars more. How can a kit, which includes the shaver, cost less than the shaver by itself?' The salesperson assured me that the price was as marked. I thought, 'What's going on here? Did the account make a special buy? Is my competitor cutting its pricing?' I went straight to the buyer's office to find the answers.

When I asked the buyer for an explanation, he said, 'No, we didn't make a special purchase and they didn't trim their prices. We're going out of that business with them and we're looking to unload our stock. Once we've sold out of the kits and shavers, you're going to be the only ladies' shaver in our store.' I couldn't believe it! I said, 'My goodness, how come the sudden switch?' The buyer replied, 'Don't ask. Just be thankful for small blessings.' Remington was being rewarded for always having the sense to take care of its accounts, no matter how badly it got burnt doing it. Our competitor was paying the price for putting its own interests ahead of the interests of its client. Unless you're an inept negotiator, you can never get hurt when you look out for the other guy.

Sometimes the other guy doesn't have to be looked out for. They know what they want and no matter what you do you'll never be able to dissuade them. In March 1976, while with Benrus, I had made a deal to sell digital watches to a sporting club in Kuwait. Kuwait was a soccer-crazy town. They had recently won the Pan-Arabic Soccer League championships and, in celebration of the feat, had built six soccer stadiums. To show you how much they loved the game, I should tell you that each stadium had a seating capacity of about 50,000. The population of Kuwait was only a little more than 100,000.

The wealthier fans of the national team showered team players with lavish gifts of appreciation. This one particular sporting club wanted to buy the digital watches for the players and all its club members.

Upon our arrival in Kuwait, Ellen and I were picked up by two Arabs in long flowing robes, driving a Cadillac convertible. They dropped Ellen off at the hotel and took me to the club.

When we got there, I walked in and was confronted by the sight of a small army of club members engaged in martial arts exercises. In another room, other members were fencing with padded scimitars and daggers. I passed through these work-out areas and entered a large room furnished only with a long mahogany table surrounded by plush leather chairs, and a huge stereo system that dominated the chamber.

The gentleman seated at the head of the table was an immaculately dressed Arab with fingers heavily laden with jewelled rings. He was the club president and he sat smoking from a water pipe and drinking thick Turkish coffee. Other members of the club sat around the table and listened to the stereo. I found out they were all waiting for the broadcast of the national soccer team's first game of the year in a European tournament. They were going to play a German team and the supporters at the sporting club were anxious for the game to start. I sat next to the club president and began to negotiate our deal. He said he wanted to purchase six thousand watches. I thought, 'Great. That's a big order, especially for a watch that Benrus is about to discontinue.' We had come up with a new style in digital watches and weren't going to sell this particular line any more. I expected to do very well with them. I knew the Arabs wanted the watches and they seemed to be such fanatics for anything that had to do with their soccer team that I doubted they would haggle very much if the price was fair. I was willing to let the watches go for little more than cost, so I figured there was no way I couldn't come away with a good deal. Weighing these factors, I decided to offer the watches for thirty dinars (twenty-two dollars) and then let them talk me down to twenty dinars.

Before I could even mention a price, the club president tells me the watches are very nice, but the most he will pay is the equivalent of 48,000 dollars for the whole kit and kaboodle. Eight dollars a watch! With that wide a gap between us, I knew we were in for a session of heated bargaining. We negotiated for the next four and a half hours. I had to sit through the entire soccer game and the only time we could talk was during the breaks. During our confrontation, I was faring so poorly that one of the members suggested I take a turn duelling with the scimitar. He said it might help me be a better negotiator. Much as I needed the help, I declined the invitation. Good thing, too. I didn't need to risk life and limb to learn how to negotiate and I proved it by coming away from this gruelling session with a win. I persuaded the club president to raise his offer. By twenty-five cents a watch. I was happy to get it. As soon as we signed an agreement, I got back into the Cadillac and headed to my hotel. When I got to our room, Ellen asked me how the negotiation had gone. I said, 'Not too badly, but I'll tell you one thing: I'm never going to negotiate in this country again without first working out with those scimitars and daggers. These guys work out with them all the time and it must really toughen them up. When they negotiate, it's all-out war and they don't seem to believe in taking any prisoners.'

I was at a complete disadvantage in that negotiation. As it turned out, the Arabs knew I was looking to unload the watches at whatever price I could get for them. They were aware that we were discontinuing the line – it was common knowledge – and figured they could get a bargain. They also knew I had spent time and money trying to arrange the transaction and correctly surmised that I wouldn't want to leave Kuwait empty-handed. Finally, the club president used the soccer game with its breaks to control the ebb and flow of the session. All things considered, I was fortunate I didn't have to agree to pay them to take the watches.

At least my friend in Kuwait was willing to deal, though not at terms favourable to me. Occasionally you're going to run up against someone who doesn't really want to sell. If you choose to deal with him, start digging the trenches. You're in for a war of attrition.

In this situation, you're usually talking about a person who started the business and built it up into a viable entity. Having nurtured this thing from infancy to maturity, he's reluctant to part with it. I've seen this happen. I was negotiating to pick up a small appliance company several years ago. The gentleman who owned it was in his late sixties and had founded the company in 1941. There was nothing unusual about the negotiations. We quickly hashed things out and agreed to terms. But when it was time for him to put pen to paper, I couldn't get him to sign. He kept waffling and finding excuses not to close the deal. Things we had gone over and agreed upon before, now had to be reviewed for a second time by a battery of lawyers and accountants. As soon as he started the nit-picking, I knew he was gone. His emotional involvement with the company was so strong he could not bring himself to make the break, despite the fact that it was he who originally proposed the transaction.

I sat down with him one afternoon and said, 'You really don't want to walk away from this company and it has nothing to do with money. We have a pretty good offer on the table and you know it. I'm not going to try to talk you into accepting something that you really don't want. Let's forget about the deal for now. If you decide to sell the company later, please give me a call. I'll be as interested then as I am now. You have my offer. It won't change and I doubt anyone will top it. I also want you to know that if you do change your mind and if you do call, there's no reason why we can't arrange for you to remain with the company in the same capacity. In fact I would want you to stay. Your knowledge of the business would be invaluable to us, especially during the period of transition.'

By having this chat, I was doing two things. I was drawing the negotiation to a close. Unless the seller changed his mind, any further discussion would be a waste of time for both parties. I also addressed the only obstacle to the sale. By offering to allow the owner to remain with the company, I thought I was answering his need. Looking back, I realize he was sending signals to me throughout the entire negotiations, but I was so sure we had a deal, I hardly took notice. But his nit-picking forced me to take a closer look at what he was trying to tell me. I had to figure out why he seemed bent on tripping up the deal with all those minutiae. Once I reviewed the situation, it seemed clear enough what the solution was. I made my offer to retain him with the company, folded my tent and left. It was the right thing to do. He still hasn't reopened the talks, but he's not trying to sell to anyone else either. I doubt he'll ever let go of the company under any circumstances.

A problem of this nature rarely exists when you're trying to negotiate with a corporate entity rather than an individual owner. With the corporation, a board of directors has probably told its representatives to unload a company or a division. A committee of individuals may be selected to make the deal. It's unlikely that any of its members will have any affiliation with the company or division to be sold. There are no emotional intangibles, it's just dollars and cents. If the board tells its chief negotiator to sell the thing for ten million, he'll spend a certain amount of time trying to do exactly that. Failing, he might come back to the board and say, 'I did my best, but the highest bid I can get is eight million.' The board will probably give him all the leeway he needs to complete the sale. They're not looking to be difficult. They just want to unload an unwanted appendage. The fellow negotiating for them hasn't lost face by his inability to sell it for ten million. He's not responsible for the loss in the company's value because he wasn't associated with it. The board will almost welcome this seemingly bad news. They'll congratulate themselves for dropping a company they thought was worth ten when it was actually only worth eight. They'll believe that they got rid of it just in time and be thankful that they hadn't held on to it for another month or two, when its value might have dropped even further. The division or company in question is probably buried in their corporate structure and won't be missed.

By contrast, if you're dealing with an individual who thinks his company is worth ten million, and you offer only eight, you're going to have a tough time selling him on your price. Often this company is the owner's last chance at a big score; he is going to hold out for every last penny he can get. Whenever you're dealing with an individual the obstacles can be far more complex than if you're putting together a transaction with a corporation.

As in selling, I like the good news approach in a negotiation, but it must be used with discretion. A negotiation has an ebb and flow to it. When you start out, you don't want to knock the other person's enterprise, hoping to drive down his price. You'll only alienate him. Let the person know what a wonderful company he's built up and how much you want to acquire it. If the owner is going to retain a position with the company after the sale, paint a vista depicting the wonderful things the two of you are going to accomplish as a team. Make him feel good about himself and his business. You can point out that if he hadn't done a good job with it, you wouldn't be interested in it. Only when you start to talk dollars and cents and he starts giving you a hard time, should you start to play it tough.

Start by trying to get the other person to commit to certain facts. For example, ask him what sort of profits he expects his company to make this year. He's trying to sell you and will usually come in high. He certainly won't underestimate his potential bottom line. I had a fellow answer that question by stating, 'We will do four million this year and that equals 400,000 dollars in profits.' He gave me a point of reference. I was able to go back to him and say, 'That's terrific, but what happens if you don't meet that goal? What is our protection? I'm sure you'll meet it if you say you will. After all, you're running a hell of a ship here. But the price of that ship is based on your estimate. You know better than I the number of things that can throw that off. If you don't meet that projection, do we get a reduction in price?' Once he had committed himself to a set of numbers, I could go in and pick the numbers apart. This was the first step towards winning a number of important financial concessions. For your part, try to commit to as little as possible. I believe the less you say and the more talking your opposite number does, the more success you'll have in negotiations.

Whenever you do have to point out the negatives of a company, do it as gently as possible. There is nothing personal meant by your observations. You bring in the bad news only to bring the true worth of an enterprise down to a more realistic level. If you like, you don't have to do this yourself. Take one of the people working with you on the deal – an accountant, for instance – and let him be the bearer of bad tidings.

At one point, while dealing with that fellow who claimed his company would do 400,000 dollars in profits during the coming year, I had to tear the glitter off a few of his numbers. I said, 'Harry, the accountant wants to show you something. He's brought up a point, though I'm sure it's something you're already aware of. We're probably going to have to set up a receivables reserve of about half a million dollars. I'm not sure if it's necessary, but the accountant insists on its being done. It is a sound accounting practice considering the way your company looks. This could bring down the company's net worth and will mean we have to take a much harder look at the price tag you've put on it.'

There may come a point when you will have to take an even stronger position. This generally occurs when you're dealing with a Mad Hatter, a fellow who doesn't have even a nodding acquaintance with reality when it comes to the worth of his company. In the negotiation mentioned in the preceding paragraph, my accountants eventually discovered that Harry's projections were the stuff of dreams and nothing more. I had to fire from the hip, saying, 'Harry, I was impressed with your company, but now the accountants tell me it might be a goddam disaster. You claim the company will make 400,000 dollars next year. My people show me it will be less than half of that. There's even a possibility that your net earnings could fall below the break-even line. I can't believe this, but if it's true, we have to restructure the deal completely. I'll still buy the company, but not at the price you've been quoting.' By putting Harry on the defensive with the facts,

I forced him to take a less idealistic look at his company. When he came back to deal, he brought along a far more realistic price tag.

Though negotiations are a tough game, you should never allow them to become a dirty game. Once you've agreed to a deal, don't back out of it unless the other party fails to deliver as promised. Your handshake is your bond. As far as I'm concerned, a handshake is worth more than a signed contract. As an entrepreneur, a reputation for integrity is your most valuable commodity. If you try to put something over on someone, it will come back to haunt you.

I had a signed agreement with a European distributor for Remington. We had promised to spend one and a half million dollars on advertising in his country on a campaign that would last a full year. The distributor agreed to put up 20% of the money. Four months after the campaign was launched, I went over to his country to see how it was faring. Remington's managing director for all of Europe joined me in a meeting with the distributor, his head of sales and his chief financial officer. We were looking over the results of the campaign – things appeared fine, though it was too early to take a sure reading – when we started to discuss payment of the monies owed. I said we would send them an invoice for 20% of what had been spent so far. A grave look passed over the distributor's face as he said, 'I can't spend any more. Our government has put restrictions on us and my business is hurting. I can't afford to spend the kind of money we're committed to contribute to this campaign.' I couldn't believe this guy! When I took out the agreement and tried to show it to him, he ignored me. I didn't know what to do. I could have stooped to name-calling but, outside of making me feel better, what would that have accomplished? I could have threatened legal action against him, but I was in a bit of a bind. If you sue your distributor, the chap who's selling your product, how much product is he going to sell for you? There was nothing I could do except swallow my pride, though I was certain the son of a bitch was pulling a fast one on me, and offer a compromise. I had to do something because I didn't want to lose the money he already owed me. I said, 'We have a deal, but I can understand your problem. Here's what I propose. You pay us what you owe us plus an additional 20% of what you would have paid as a cancellation fee and we'll forget the whole thing.' He agreed to this and we shook hands.

When we left, everybody, including myself, seemed happy. The first chance I got I cut the fellow loose. I never did business with him again. If he had come to me and said, 'I'm sorry. I know we have a contract, but the economy is tight and I'm hindered by government restriction. Let me pay you for what you've done, but allow me to delay any future investment,' I could have understood that and would have been glad to work something out. This was my distributor; I wanted him to be happy. I probably would have assumed the full cost of the campaign and allowed him to pay us back in the future. But the way he had violated our agreement without so much as an apology went against the grain. That's why I never dealt with him again. He brought it on himself. The entrepreneur should always be mindful that if he steps on too many toes by double dealing or failing to honour his commitments, someone is going to cut off his foot.

CHAPTER SEVEN

Turnarounds

In a turnaround, entrepreneurs assume the roles of firemen: they are running into a situation everyone else is trying to leave. However, just as the trained fire-fighter doesn't rush into a building and start spraying water helter-skelter, the entrepreneur must enter the turnaround with a well-drawn strategy. If I had come into Remington without a plan, you wouldn't be seeing any of those commercials about how my favourite entrepreneur liked the electric shaver so much, he bought the company.

I had first heard of Remington's availability in 1976. Dewey Roberts, the account executive for Wells-Benrus at Young and Rubicam, our advertising agents, had told me that Y&R handled the Remington account and that he had heard that Sperry-Rand was looking to sell it. Dewey wondered if I was interested in purchasing the company. I didn't know anything about the shaver business and I had a full-time involvement with Wells-Benrus, so I told him I couldn't even begin to consider it.

Two years after my conversation with Dewey Roberts, I was tending to a Saturday morning ritual: reading *Business Week*. This particular issue featured an interview with J. P. Lyet, chairman of Sperry Corporation. In it he said, 'We'd rather sell one computer installation than 100,000 Remington shavers.' That was strange. Lyet had an interest in both companies. I wondered why he would denigrate the shavers by making such a comparison. Then I remembered my long-since-forgotten conversation with Mr Roberts. It was obvious that Sperry was still unhappy with Remington and was probably more anxious than ever to sell the company. I had left Wells-Benrus for reasons I'll go into later and was actively looking to make an acquisition. I had almost purchased a company called Maui Divers, a maker of fine coral jewellery. Located in Hawaii, they had a government licence to operate a submarine. The sub carried two passengers and they would patrol the ocean floor searching for coral. When they came upon a reef, they would use two huge crab-like claws to cut the coral. Once severed, the prize would drop into a basket attached to the sub and be carried off to be turned into delicate pieces of jewellery.

Among its many pluses, there were two points that would make the company attractive to any entrepreneur. One, the jewellery was first-rate and would fit in nicely with Friendship. Two, Maui Divers owned the exclusive rights to the coral. No other company could mine the oceans for these exquisite skeletons. Among the three or four ventures I was exploring, this was the most exciting. I was prepared to make an offer, but the two other investors who had agreed to join me in the venture didn't hit it off and pulled out at the last minute. By the time I came up with alternative financing, I had read about Remington.

In Chapter One, I mentioned that an entrepreneur must be decisive and must also be prepared to grasp opportunity. *Procrastination is opportunity's natural assassin.* I wasted no time in finding out the particulars of Remington's situation. Having read that article on Saturday, I called J. P. Lyet first thing on Monday morning. He confirmed that Remington was on the selling block and then he switched me over to Ty Garcia, Sperry's chief financial officer. Ty was handling the Remington divestiture. He informed me that several individuals and groups had already made inquiries about the company. After ascertaining that my interest in Remington was genuine, he offered to make Remington's books and records available to me. That's all I had to hear. When he asked me when I would like to come in, I know I surprised him by saying I could pick up all the necessary material in an hour. 'Boy,' he said, 'you really are serious about this, aren't you? Will it be any trouble to get over here that quickly?' I assured him that it wouldn't inconvenience me at all. Opportunity had asked me to dance; I didn't want to allow opportunity a minute to change its mind and choose another partner.

Commandeering a cab, I raced over to Sperry headquarters and lugged the books and records back to my apartment. There were twenty-six volumes of material and countless pieces of paper packed with facts and figures. These numbers told the story of Remington's entire domestic and overseas operations. It took me an hour and a half to arrange and spread the material out on the dining-room table.

When I started to pore over the books, I saw that Remington was more than just shavers. They had operating companies that were producing a wide range of products for different countries: watches in Mexico, steam irons in Italy, clocks in Germany, hair-care products in France. I didn't see any cohesion in the operation. The only product that was common to each nation was the shaver. Knowing that it was ridiculous to try to manage so many different products in so many different locales, I decided to rule out the secondary branches of the operation and confine my study to the shaver business.

Rearranging the material so that I would have all the pertinent information in one place took another thirty minutes. I was just about to begin the research when my wife came home. She was not enthusiastic about my turning the dining-room into a mission control centre. She asked if I could clean the table off in preparation for dinner. I moaned, 'But it took me so long to set everything up! Can't we eat in the kitchen?' Ellen wasn't crazy about that idea, so I started clearing the table, slamming the books down on the floor as I went along. The racket got her attention. She asked, 'What are you looking at, anyway?' I told her I was reviewing the Remington company as a possible acquisition. Ellen said, 'Remington? They make electric shavers, don't they? How can you even think of considering that company? You've never shaved electrically in your life.' She had a point, but I reminded her that I had been in the brassiere business for thirteen years and had never worn one of those either.

The next evening, Ellen presented me with a present: a Remington shaver. I raced into the bathroom and shaved electrically for the first time in my life. How good was the shave? Well, as I've said more than a few times, I liked it so much I bought the company. It gave me the best shave I had ever had and when I threw on aftershave it didn't burn. Anyone who has ever shaved with a razor and has had to endure the sting of their favourite cologne immediately afterwards can understand my unbridled joy at this discovery.

The day after this experience, I decided to conduct my own market research. I went out and bought the top of the line shaver of each of the leading brands. Each morning I would conduct a test. For example, I would shave one-half of my face with a Norelco and the other half with the Remington. The next day I would have the Remington square off against a Schick or a Sunbeam. By week's end, I knew the Remington was the best electric shaver on the market.

My research didn't end there. While investigating a potential takeover, an entrepreneur should take advantage of any avenue of information open to him. Many of the same retailers who carried the Benrus watch had also carried shavers. I called several of them and asked them to tell me anything they could about the shaver business. I was careful not to mention Remington or my possible involvement with the company.

Everyone I spoke with told me the same thing. The market was dominated by Norelco. Sunbeam survived because of its low pricing. Ronson was dormant, and Schick was on the rocks. Despite Norelco's number one rating, however, the general consensus held that Remington had the best product. Unfortunately, the Remington management didn't seem to know how to sell the shaver. With such a clear field, Norelco was doing almost 70% of the electric shaver business in the country.

After further research, I decided I wanted to make a deal. It didn't bother me that the company had lost over thirty million dollars over the previous four years. I knew the product was a winner. With the right management and improved marketing, the company could be turned around. The retailers were hoping that a shaver besides Norelco would start to emerge as a power. Retailers don't want one company to dominate the market. It gives that company almost autocratic powers and makes it very hard for retailers to turn down their demands. It was in their interest to have another strong company that could be played against Norelco.

Even with my enthusiasm, I knew acquiring Remington wasn't going to be easy. There was the small matter of the twenty-five million price tag Sperry had attached to the company. I didn't have that kind of money. I had left Wells-Benrus because the company's board had decided it wanted to turn away from consumer products and become an industrial company. They felt this would give them a more stable market. I wouldn't stay on that basis, though I did agree to handle the company's divestiture of the watch and jewellery business. In exchange, I was to receive a consulting fee of ten thousand dollars a month for two and a half years. This gave me a good living, but the rest of my money was tied in Wells-Benrus stock. As a controlled shareholder, I could only sell an amount equal to 1% of the entire stock of the company every six months. I owned about 300,000 shares. The total capitalization of the company was two million shares. This meant I could sell only twenty thousand shares – worth in the neighbourhood of $60,000 at the time – every six months. I had close to one million dollars in stock, but I couldn't sell. I could have unloaded those shares in a secondary offering, but that was an alternative the board would not consider.

I did have some paintings to sell, but the earliest auction I could arrange wouldn't take place until the autumn of '78. Too late. Looking at the numbers, I wondered where I could come up with the capital I needed. I told myself there was little chance of convincing an equity investor to join me in the venture. Who would be willing to cough up the money I needed to purchase a company that had been on such a long downward spiral? How could I expect to find anyone who was as crazy as this Kiam lunatic? I couldn't. I knew if I was going to make this deal, it would have to be done as debt.

Leverage buyouts were not commonplace at the time. I didn't know very much about them, but I did know they were debt-oriented. After talking to some knowledgeable friends and associates, I decided that it was probably the best route for me.

In simplest terms, the leverage buyout is a purchase that is built around three components. The first allows the purchaser to borrow to the maximum against the assets of the company being sold. The second revolves around the amount of paper or notes the seller is willing to take back in exchange for the sale of the company. The third involves the amount of equity brought to the sale by the purchaser. In most cases, the company's liabilities will be retained by the seller. The potential success or failure of an LBO can be determined by projecting the company's cash flow. If it appears that it will be able to cover the debt that is being created, the prognosis is very good.

I thought Remington was a good candidate for an LBO. With this in mind, I knew I had to find a bank that would give me debt. I had several prospects. The one that stood at the top of my list was Chemical Bank. Only the month before, I had met Oliver

Mendahl, a senior vice-president with the bank. He was a friend of my lawyer, Arthur Emil. I had liked Oliver. In our brief meeting, he was effervescent, well-spoken, and seemed to know his business. At my request, Arthur arranged for the three of us to meet over lunch.

I explained the deal to Oliver. He suggested I come in and meet Michael O'Connell of the bank's corporate finance department. At that meeting, I brought Michael all the information I had on Remington and laid it out on his desk. I told him I needed to know two things. First, I needed to know how much I could borrow on receivables and inventory. Then, I needed to find out where on earth I could get the money.

About a week later, Michael called to say that if we could get Sperry to agree to certain conditions concerning debt and if we could get financing on the building and equipment, we would probably need between three and five million dollars of equity.

I knew I would realize about half a million dollars from the sale of my paintings. That meant I still had to raise a considerable amount of equity. It wasn't easy; no one was willing to take the risk until the rest of the financing was in place. I did find one fellow who was willing to put in two million dollars, but he wanted two-thirds of the company in return. I wasn't entirely against surrendering so much of the company, but that deal would still have left me far short of the required capital.

Michael O'Connell agreed with me. He felt that I should be able to raise the required amount and still retain control of a third of the company. I made a deal with him. I hired his bank to help facilitate my search for funding. Normally the bank received a hefty fee for performing such a service: a non-refundable fifty thousand dollars down and an additional fifty thousand if they pulled off the deal. I couldn't afford that. Instead, I countered with a more entrepreneurial offer. I would pay the bank $5,000. If they were successful they would receive an additional $200,000. With some hesitation, Michael accepted my proposal.

There were probably many days when he wished he hadn't. The first institution we approached was his own Chemical Bank. Michael took me to Chemical's assets-based lending division. Its representatives came to the Remington factory and seemed reasonably impressed. Afterwards, when I was going over the virtues of the deal, I brightly added, 'One of my strengths in this venture is that I've discovered that I know this business better than I imagined. It's just like the watch business.' When I said that, one of the Chem Bank people said, 'Just like the watch business! Forget us, my friend! We just lost our shirts with the Gruen watch company bankruptcy.' Talk about a 'Chemical reaction!' My well-meant comment had squashed any chance we had of getting any financing from the bank.

Undiscouraged, Michael and I tried other banks. We quickly discovered that all of the major banks were already involved with other principals who were interested in acquiring Remington. The list of potential buyers had grown. This forced us to approach second-tier banks, but none of them could handle a transaction of this size.

We decided to try state and federal government agencies. The Economic Development Administration, a now-defunct federally funded project that lent money on current assets, seemed willing to guarantee a loan for thirteen million dollars. We were certain we could get an additional three million dollars from the Connecticut Development Authority. It would lend money on Remington's fixed assets only. That would give us sixteen million dollars. We would ask Sperry to take three million dollars in paper, and then try to cut the asking price by another three million. That left us with three million in equity to raise.

Sperry had given me seven weeks to come up with the financing and time was running out. They had promised not to close a deal with anyone else during that period, unless they received an overwhelming offer. Even then, I would receive a call and be given a chance to match it.

With one week left before we reached our deadline, we still didn't have any of our financing in place. This despite the promise-filled murmurings we had heard at the government agencies and our tireless efforts. With complete faith that we would still come up with the money, I asked for a meeting with Al Mosher, Dick Brown, and Mike Stanton of Sperry. I was accompanied by Michael O'Connell and Arthur Emil.

Once the meeting was convened, I outlined what we had done and what we felt we would be able to offer. Adding in the government loans which we still expected to get, the notes, and the three million in equity which we still hadn't obtained, the package came out to $22 million. Al Mosher shook his head and said, 'This is all very well, but the price is $25 million and we're not going to lower it. We can make certain concessions on interest rates and time frames, but we're not going to sell this company for less than book value.' I thought we were in trouble, but as it turned out things weren't as bad as they seemed. Mosher wanted me to buy the company. He was a lovely man and Sperry truly cared about the fate of their employees after the sale. I was the only prospective buyer who was willing to promise not to move Remington out of Bridgeport for at least five years. I was also the only interested party who had submitted a marketing plan that predicted a decrease in first year sales rather than an increase. I wanted to make sure we would still be profitable even if our sales dropped off during our period of transition. Mr Mosher seemed impressed with my realistic forecast. He said, 'I want to be honest with you. Of all the people we've dealt with, we feel you are the best suited to run this company.' I nearly fell over! At that moment, I knew in my guts that we were going to come to terms somehow.

Mosher continued, 'We have some ideas of our own on how you can finance this transaction. If you'll accompany Mr Brown to his office, he'll explain our proposition.'

Brown told us that Sperry was willing to give us a four million dollar mortgage on the Remington factory and property. This was completely unexpected. We factored that in with our numbers, but we still came up short. Brown came back with another idea. He said, 'The European end of our operation is valued at six million dollars. It represents almost 25% of the deal. You don't have to pay us for it now. We'll give you a loan on that amount at no interest for the first six months and prime for the second six months. The loan must be paid at the end of those twelve months.' We put those numbers into the hopper and came up with a proposal. Brown looked it over and agreed to submit it to Mr Mosher.

The meeting took place on the Wednesday before Thanksgiving. Brown said he would call Mosher at home, lay out the proposal, and get back to me as soon as he had an answer.

I was elated when we left the meeting. I kept thinking, 'We got the deal! We got the deal!' Thursday, Friday, Saturday, and Sunday passed with no word from Dick Brown. Instant depression. I couldn't have got more than two hours' sleep on

Sunday night. I kept going over our proposal again and again, wondering how the deal had slipped through my fingers. At 6.30 Monday morning, what little sleep I could grab was interrupted by a phone call from Dick Brown. He explained that he had been unable to get in touch with Mosher over the weekend, but that he had used the time to re-work our proposal. He asked me to meet him at the Sperry offices at 7.45 a.m., in order to review the changes.

To make the plan more feasible, Brown had offered to give us three and a half million dollars in notes, payable over fifteen years. I wasn't sure Sperry would assume the risk. Brown, however, was. He explained, 'The gamble is less than it appears. We're giving you a four million dollar mortgage. No risk there. We know the factory and property are worth at least that much. Now we also have equipment in the factory and its liquidation value is something in the neighbourhood of $900,000. Taking that into consideration, we'll only be on the hook for an additional two and a half million. If these terms are acceptable to you, I'll recommend the deal to Mr Mosher.' I couldn't believe this! The three and a half million in notes would replace the three million in equity I needed. I wasn't going to end up with 25% or 30% of Remington. I would own the whole company! Having disclosed his plan, Dick asked me who was doing my financing. I told him I was still negotiating for the best rate, but that we were close to making a decision.

Naturally, we weren't as close as we would have liked. Mosher approved Brown's proposal, but Sperry attached a condition. We would sign a letter of intent. With that, I would give Sperry a cheque for $250,000. An additional $250,000 would be due thirty days after the signing. The auction of the paintings would bring in half a million dollars so I knew I would have that money. However, if I could not come up with the financing, the deal was dead and that first quarter of a million would not be refunded. That was a pretty hefty kill fee, but it was the only way the deal could be done. That money represented half of all my liquid assets. If I failed, the loss – both financially and emotionally – would have been crushing. Those funds could be used to help launch a less risky venture. Remember, at this point, I still wasn't sure where the financing would come from. I thought I could get it, but, until I did, I would be rollerskating on the edge of the volcano. Faced with this, I did the only thing an entrepreneur can do.

I accepted the deal.

We shook hands on the agreement on 30 November, 1978 and it took less than a week to draw up the letter of intent. We signed on 6 December. The following day – my birthday, as a matter of fact – a squib in the *Wall Street Journal* announced, 'Sperry Corporation sells Remington Consumer Products Division to company organized by Victor Kiam.'

I've always said that success was 70% hard work, 20% talent and ingenuity, and 10% luck. Michael O'Connell and his associates, Arthur Emil and I had contributed the hard work. Dick Brown joined us and brought along the ingenuity. The *Wall Street Journal* piece provided us with luck.

Three days after it appeared, a friend, having read the item, called to congratulate me. He also said he had a friend who had worked as a consultant for a group whose bid had been rejected. The fellow's name was Freddy Nichols. He already had his group's financing in place with Chase Manhattan. Since the deal had gone down the drain, my friend wondered if I might not want to look over Freddy's deal to see if it were better than whatever I had. *An entrepreneur must retain his equanimity.* Though the tell-tale heart was threatening to burst from my chest, I casually said, 'Well, I don't know. I guess it wouldn't hurt to meet the fellow.'

Freddy came to see me and we went over his plan. All the financing was in place; all he needed was the deal. After we reviewed the figures, he asked, 'How does this stack up against what you have?' Shrugging, I said, 'I don't know. In some ways it's better, in some ways it's worse.' This was the truth. His financing was better because it existed; it was worse because it wasn't mine!

We went through the numbers once more and finally I said that the plan was worth considering. Freddy said, 'Okay. I don't know what you have, but I think this is a pretty good deal. If you take it, I want fifty thousand dollars as a fee for putting it together.' With the financing in place, I was going to have to pay $500,000 to Sperry and $200,000 to Chemical. I wasn't going to quibble over another $50,000, especially since I thought it was a fair price.

One day after our discussion, I told Freddy I would go for his plan. He put me together with Chase and we consummated a deal. We closed during the first week of February. I had auctioned the paintings and had borrowed additional monies to take care of the fees. For a total cash package of $750,000, representing money given to Sperry, Chemical Bank, and Freddy Nichols, I had become the sole owner of a $25 million company.

The final negotiations between us, Chase and Sperry took about six weeks. During that period, I was doing further homework. I had asked Al Peterson, my former boss at Playtex, to join the team that would put Remington back on its feet. With the negotiations going smoothly, Sperry had given us permission to spend time with the people at the factory. This meant we could draw up a solid game plan that could be implemented the minute we took over the company. Those six weeks were vital to our strategy. In a turnaround, time is not a luxury. It's an oppressive taskmaster. If you take over a successful company, you can afford to take a few months to get the feel of the operation. Many of the changes you wish to implement can be introduced over a leisurely period of time. Your place of business rests on a firm foundation.

The turnaround candidate is another matter. It's the burning building I alluded to at the top of this chapter. Before you can rush into it, you have to have a strong inkling of what caused the fire, which areas of the structure can be saved and which have to be sacrificed. Once the fire is under control, you have to look for that hard-to-detect smouldering rag that could burst into another inferno.

You can have assistance, but you can't let anyone do this research for you. I got smacked in the teeth with this lesson when I bought the Benrus watch company. When I made the purchase, management claimed the company had nine million dollars in assets. I had auditors go into the company and they confirmed that amount. Four million of that figure was in watch cases warehoused in the Wells factory in Switzerland. Unfortunately for me, the auditors really didn't know the watch business. Having taken over the company, I flew over to Switzerland to visit the factory. The first thing I discover is that the watch cases are there, all right, but all of them are obsolete. The movements for them aren't being manufactured any more. Half the book value of the company was an illusion.

I telephoned my lawyer and described the situation. Entrepreneurial equanimity or not, I was enraged and was looking to sue the former owners.

My lawyer advised against it. He said, 'You can sue the principals, but they already have your money and a case like this could drag on for four or five years. You have a good case, but they can stall us with motions and they can stand behind that auditor's report. No matter how much you're in the right, this will be a mess. Considering your loss, you don't need the costs right now. Instead of wasting your time and money with it, you should concentrate on solving the problem internally and getting this company back on the right track.'

That wasn't exactly what I had wanted to hear, but I had to admit logic was on the side of learned counsel. Taking his advice, I asked around the industry and tried to find out if there was someone who could manufacture the movements I needed for all those cases. I did unearth one company. Its owner offered to make the movements for seventeen dollars a unit. Seventeen dollars! That was four times the price of an average movement. With that sort of cost, there would be no way I could sell the finished watches. I knew then that we would be lucky to salvage anything out of the stock. All we could do was melt down the cases for gold. The company ended up making ten cents on the dollar. I blamed no one but myself for the fiasco. Benrus recovered from the setback, but the experience taught me never to buy a company without first examining every bit of it.

When we took over Remington, a great many people asked how this fellow Kiam could possibly hope to turn the company around when a giant like Sperry had been unable to make it fly. The investigation Al and I conducted prior to the takeover gave us some clues.

Once we confirmed that the company was everything the figures claimed it was, we asked ourselves, 'Where have Sperry gone wrong?' The first thing we noticed was that Sperry, despite its size and well-deserved reputation, hadn't been comfortable with the shaver business for some time. They had bought the company in the late forties and had retained its founder as president. During his tenure, the company flourished. Sperry kept pretty much out of the day-to-day operation. When the original owner retired in 1967, Sperry named as president a fellow whose background was in engineering. They should have appointed a marketing person.

No one in charge knew what to do with the company's most important product. Marketing people were imported from Sperry, but they apparently had never been involved with anything like this business. They were good people, competent at their jobs. They just didn't know how to sell shavers.

One of the best examples of this could be found in management's overemphasis on creative design. Every six months, the engineers would introduce a new line of Remington shavers. They were having a field day. Sometimes the difference in styles was so subtle it was barely noticeable. In and of itself, this wasn't an offence punishable by death. But every time they added a new wrinkle, they would drop the previous line.

Retailers weren't happy about this. Shavers they had bought only six months earlier could become obsolete overnight. The engineers were having a marvellous time indulging their creativity, but they were alienating our retailers. Store owners and buyers were leery of stocking a heavy Remington inventory; they didn't want to get stuck. This hurt the company immeasurably. Our research told us that Norelco – which rarely changed its style – outsold Remington by almost five to one. It also showed us that stores stocked ten times as many Norelcos as Remingtons. They were going with the more stable product. If a consumer came in looking for an electric shaver, there was a good chance the Remington wouldn't be in stock. Was he going to wait six weeks till the next shipment arrived? No way. He'd buy the Norelco or some other brand.

Pricing was also a problem. Every time the competition raised their prices, Remington followed suit. There was no logic to it. One of the marketing directors told us that since Remington had such a small share of the market, the idea was to sell as many shavers as they could at the highest price possible. I knew we would change that philosophy as soon as we took over.

Al and I also looked to streamline the operation, particularly the non-productive areas of the company. As I found out when I first looked at the company records, Remington had been involved with a lot of products. But now we had only one product: shavers. The company payroll carried five product managers. With only one product, that was four too many. We trimmed the marketing department. With our combined experience, Al and I could carry the bulk of the marketing load. The ever-changing styles had been a problem. We solved it by getting rid of most of the engineers who had been doing the tinkering.

It wasn't easy to fire these people, but when the lifeboat is sinking, someone has to be thrown overboard. I chose to get rid of those people who couldn't row. I had to. The fate of the people who were toiling on the factory floor, the workers who were the backbone of Remington, depended on it. On my first day on the job I asked all the managers, including those who would be let go, to rate their employees. The best of this group would be retained to help put the company on its feet. Four days later, we sacked seventy executives. They didn't leave empty-handed. Each received severance pay equal to two weeks for every year they had been with the company. Some of them were absorbed by Sperry. With this one move I was able to trim over two million dollars of fat from the payroll without touching the labour force.

The day after the firings, a Bridgeport paper ran a headline about the bloodbath at Remington. I'm sure that must have disquieted the remaining employees. A large number of them must have wondered if they would be next. I was ready for that. The first Monday after the purge, I went down to the factory floor, called everybody together, and said, 'I had to implement a hard decision last Friday. As you have probably already heard, we had a lay-off that afternoon. I believe that is the only lay-off this company will impose. Unless we foul up everything, your jobs are secure.' I let them know that the people who remained, themselves included, were part of the team we knew could make Remington go. I could see this little talk was welcome news. With the air now cleared, we were all ready to get down to the business of Remington's survival.

Or so I thought.

Almost before I could press the start button on this new, lean machine I had fashioned, some of the parts started falling off. Many of the talented, key executives I had retained started to leave the company in droves. These were older corporate types who didn't believe I could turn the company around. Sperry was a five-billion-dollar corporation. I had just spent my last buck buying a failing company. In the past, when Remington ran out of money, it could dip into the almost bottomless pockets of Uncle Sperry. Uncle Victor's pants didn't have any pockets. At this point, Uncle Victor was lucky he had any pants. If we ran out of money now, Remington was history.

Many of the exit-ing executives were in their late forties or early fifties. They had mortgages to support and kids to put through college. When I told these chaps what a rousing success we could have with the company, they thought, 'This guy is either very good or he's not playing with a full deck. If he's right, terrific, but I can't afford the risk if he's wrong.' This attitude was hammered home to me when our chief engineer left. Oh, I hated to lose him. He knew more about our tools and equipment than anyone in the country. When he told me he had another job, I did everything I could to persuade him to stay. The vista I painted covered the office wall. It didn't help. He turned me down and summed up his bottom line by saying, 'I wish you all the luck in the world. I think you just might turn this thing round. But I've got to protect my family.'

Part of the problem was that Sperry had sent executives a letter announcing that they were all fully vested in the company pension plan. The plan reached full maturity in twenty years. A person with sixteen years in the company would be sacrificing a sizeable chunk of future income if he didn't choose to stay the additional four years. The letter changed all this. Once he was fully vested, he could leave early and lose nothing. This violated my agreement with Sperry, but there was nothing I could do about it. I wanted to sue. My lawyers advised against it. They knew the lawsuit would take at least four years and the costs would have been damaging. I also needed every minute I had to concentrate on the business; I couldn't be distracted by litigation. The negative publicity wouldn't have done anybody any good and I was still negotiating for parts of the overseas operation. If Sperry wanted to, they could really play tough with me.

I racked my brains trying to figure out a way to stem the exodus. I couldn't offer anyone an immediate financial inducement to stay. I didn't have the capital. So I had to sell everyone on the concept of Remington and what we were trying to accomplish. I needed a way to say, 'Sure, you can go out and get another job. That will be easy. You're all talented people or I wouldn't want you to stay. But wherever you go, it's just going to be another job. Stay with us, and you'll have a chance to be part of an adventure. You'll be part of a total team effort. A lot of people may say we can't turn the company around. Think of the satisfaction you'll have when we prove them wrong.'

To get that message across I had to turn the company into a cohesive unit. I called another meeting of the Remington employees. At it, I announced, 'Before I got here, there was a huge gap between the blue collar and white collar divisions of the company. As of today, that ends. There is no blue collar or white collar. There's only one collar: the Remington collar.' Then I ticked off the changes that would be implemented. Executive washrooms were among the first things to go. Medical plans and pay plans would be the same for everyone. Everyone was made part of a profit-sharing plan and they would be fully vested in six years. They were also put on an incentive programme. For instance, one executive was due to get a three-thousand-dollar rise as part of a 6% general wage increase. I called him in and said, 'Look, you can have the rise, but I'd like to offer you an alternative. If you pass up this rise and we make our annual budget figures for profit, I'll give you a bonus equal to fifty per cent of your salary. That's twenty-five thousand dollars.' I made similar offers to all the key executives. I was giving them something tangible to work towards. Then I implemented incentive programmes for all the other areas of Remington. If the assembly line people turned out more than a specified number of shavers, they were rewarded. If the advertising people could get us more return per dollar, they would see more money. Everybody would receive financial recognition for excellence.

By promising this, I was doing more than just painting a vista. I was giving these people a challenge, something I was certain would elicit a positive response.

I continued to eradicate the barriers between management and labour. As far as I was concerned, we were all labour and we were all working for Remington. I did away with all company perks. Company cars became an extinct species. Country club memberships expired and were not renewed. Remington also had twenty-seven memberships at a local luncheon club. I cancelled twenty-six of them. I told everyone that we would retain a card in one person's name. If they needed to make a reservation, they could do it through him. Either way, the club would be glad to accept their money.

A lot of howls were raised when I said no Remington employee could fly first class unless the flight was longer than six hours or they paid the difference. Everyone flew tourist or business class. To anyone who complained, I said, 'The back of the plane gets to the airport the same time as the front.' These weren't cost-cutting measures; the money they saved was minimal. They were just graphic illustrations that we were all part of the same team no matter what our position or salary.

Continuing with this theme, I told my executives that I wanted them to get close to the employees. I wanted them to be on a first-name basis with the workers and to know something about their lives away from the factory. This was going to be a family. Each of us had to care about the other. We started Friday morning coffee meetings. Ten employees would meet with different members of management for coffee and Danish pastries and discuss the company. Any suggestions, questions, or criticisms would be given a full hearing. Every quarter we would close the factory down for thirty minutes and I would give a state of the company address. Some executives at other companies thought I was crazy to be so forthright with the employees. I disagreed. This was *their* company. No matter how good I was, I couldn't make it without them. They had a right to know how we were doing. I was also confident that they would be hearing good news in short order. I felt they needed that. This company had been through the trenches and its workers' morale had been shot. For years, they had lived with the threats of rumoured closings and lay-offs. Anything that would ease the stress and pump up their morale had to be a plus.

None of this would have been successful if I didn't do my share and more. Many companies live by the principle of RHIP: Rank Has Its Privileges. There's no place for that sort of thinking in an entrepreneurial company. I told my executives to get close to the employees; I did the same thing. There isn't one person who works for me – and we now employ over eight hundred people – whom I don't know.

Management was told to forget about watching the clock. Their day was over when their tasks for the day were done. Business is where you are. I put more hours into the business than I did when I was a salesman working twelve-hour days, six days a week. The rest of the management followed suit. If I was on a business trip with one of my executives and he tried to carry my bags, I yanked them out of his hands. I made it clear that no one was expected to make any sacrifices that I wouldn't make myself.

Creating the proper atmosphere was only half a solution to our woes. The two-million-dollar payroll cut brought Remington into the black, but we didn't have any cash flow. Without receivables the company would be in a vulnerable position. We had loans to repay, contract conditions to meet, and our employees expected to see some tangible results with the new ownership. With everyone in the company pulling for one another, the salvation of the company rested with the shaver.

We had the best product on the market. But it was laden with chrome and fancy trimmings that inflated the price and contributed nothing to a smoother shave. For example, at one time Remington had a rechargeable shaver that featured a dial on the side. It was supposed to warn you that the shaver would need recharging soon by counting the number of shaves it had given. The engineers reckoned you would get ten shaves with each charge. That would have been terrific if we all shaved the same amount of time. But it stood to reason that a person who could shave in one minute would get twice as many shaves as the person who could shave in two. So what good was the counter?

The shavers came packed in a metal case that cost us two and a half dollars and weighed a ton. Did it improve the shaver? No. Was it an unwieldy item that was difficult for the consumer to carry? Yes. It was tossed aside. Shearing off that unnecessary chrome saved us another ninety cents a shaver. We wouldn't blind the consumer with glitter; we would dazzle him with quality. This was an easy choice. After all, we had the best product with the most powerful motor of any shaver on the market.

Despite that marketing director's comment about selling as many razors for as much money as possible, I felt Remington could do very well with a lower-priced shaver. We worked on it and came up with a dandy model that could retail at $19.95. This was unheard of at the time; the lowest priced shaver on the market was selling for $34.95.

Our new model was not a rechargeable. It was a plug-in that featured three shaving heads. We called it the Triple Head Shaver, and what it lacked in fashion sense it made up for by giving a sweet shave. When we test-marketed the shaver, it was a big hit. Some retailers were leery of it though. They thought we were changing styles again. But when we explained that this was merely a new addition to our line and that we weren't discontinuing anything, they were more responsive. With a recession going on, we couldn't have picked a better time to break ground with a new price point. *Entrepreneurs with new concepts or products can thrive during economic downturns.* The old merchandise and ideas aren't selling, so retailers are willing to try anything that might stimulate trade.

Our costs were further cut when I shut down all our overseas plants. Remington operations would all be centred in Bridgeport, Connecticut. We designed new marketing and advertising strategies. I'll discuss those in detail in the next chapter. Let me simply say now that I borrowed heavily from my experience with Lever Brothers and Playtex.

Much of what was needed to turn this company around and show some profits was now in place: a terrific product, a hard-working team (the new Remington *esprit de corps* had cut defections down to a bare minimum), reduced costs, a streamlined operation, and the improved marketing and advertising campaigns. The last step was to improve our distribution. This was vital. What good were all the other elements if we couldn't get this wonderful product into the hands of the consumer?

Many stores in the US would carry only Norelco shavers. They were dominating the market and had a powerful advertising budget. In some cities it was almost impossible to find a Remington. The stores that did carry them, as I mentioned before, were often out of stock. We changed this by banging on doors in every state. We painted vistas depicting what the new management was going to do with the business. The retailers were told that the lines were going to be stable and that if we received an order today, we would ship it out tomorrow.

We were also able to get them excited about the new low-priced shaver. We went national with it just weeks before Father's Day, 1979. It was a smash. We ended up selling over half a million of them in the first year. The first positive results that came trickling in convinced everyone at Remington that perhaps this Kiam character wasn't such a screwball after all. Morale went sky-high, our balance sheet took on a healthy glow. Remington was about to make its presence felt.

And then we were sued.

I guess Norelco didn't like the rumblings they were hearing from Bridgeport. Six weeks after we brought out our low-priced shaver, Norelco sued us for trademark infringement. We had called our model the Triple Head Shaver; Norelco had a shaver called the Triple Header.

Norelco hadn't registered the trademark and Remington had manufactured a Triple Head Shaver back in the late forties, so I wasn't going to cave in at the first sight of a subpoena. I knew we were right. Unfortunately, Sperry and the banks didn't take this as coolly as I did. You couldn't blame them. I had just gone through that almost disastrous episode with K-Mart and their large shaver return. Sperry could accept that; it was the result of decisions made and events that occurred under its administration. But Sperry management suffered a haemorrhage when I dismissed those seventy executives one week after taking over the company. They had barely recovered from that blow and what do I do next? I come out with a shaver that is priced so low the company will have to sell twice as many as any other model to make the same amount of profit and I get sued while doing it. By this time, Al Mosher must have been having some doubts about whether or not I really was well suited to run the company.

However, I was certain that, more than anything else, Norelco had brought the suit to scare the devil out of us. If we had lost, we would have been wiped out. Unlike the incident with the watch cases at Benrus, I knew the only answer was to square off in court. We countersued, charging Norelco with filing a false suit that interfered with my business. I claimed they were damaging Remington in the trade.

My action held Norelco at bay. We went right on selling Triple Head Shavers while the lawyers fought our case. It was settled to our satisfaction in 1982.

Though it took us almost three years to come to a settlement, the tremors the action sent through the company were shortlived. The Triple Head Shavers had become a monster, bringing almost four million dollars in extra gross profit. That would be enough to make sure we fell within the parameters of our loan agreement. It also enabled us to show a greater profit than projected at the end of the year. As much as anything, the Triple Head Shaver represented the sort of entrepreneurial risk that could make a turnaround possible.

Lawsuits, poor morale and the K-Mart affair weren't the only problems we faced in our first year. A lot of my time was taken up negotiating to buy the overseas operations. I had to visit each country and look over the operations.

Much of the negotiating was done with Dick Brown. We had some real knock-down drag-outs. Once we fought over two thousand dollars. The point of contention was the amount of reserves Sperry would establish to cover the future repair of hair-driers in New Zealand. No kidding. I thought the figure should be five thousand dollars; Dick would offer only three. We fought over this for two full days! It became a matter of principle for both of us. I lost that skirmish, but I wasn't too upset. Dick was a tough man at the negotiating table, but he was fair and conducted himself as a gentleman.

We had some difficulty in England. Before I took the helm of the company, Remington had ordered a shaver recall in Europe. A recall in this business is tantamount to a catastrophe. It means there is something awry with the shaver, either electrically or mechanically, and that it could be harmful to consumers. The recall hurts a company on two counts. It is terribly costly and it damages the reputation of your product.

The trouble started in July 1978. Sperry chose that month to announce that it would be closing its factory in France. Some of the French workers, perturbed by the suddenness of this decision, sabotaged an entire run of M-3s. This was the European version of our top of the line Microscreen Shaver. The workers had put metal filings in the motor. This didn't kill anyone, but complaints came pouring in from all over the Continent as consumers experienced an electric shock with their close shave.

Remington called all its European dealers and told them to ship all the unsold shavers back. Then they ran ads in every country. Anyone who had bought an M-3 in the last three months was invited to post it back to Remington for a refund.

Sperry had been honest with me about the incident. When we signed our letter of intent in November, they told me all the particulars and accepted responsibility for any repairs or refunds. I thought that was a fair proposal. It certainly seemed to resolve any problems we might have because of the recall.

When I got to England, I found out this wasn't so. Our deal with Sperry covered the financial repercussions of the recall, not the emotional. The action killed the M-3 in Europe. Retailers would not stock it and consumers acted as if it carried the plague. We had to change the name of the shaver to its American version, the Microscreen, before we could bring it back on the market. We also introduced a new advertising campaign designed to separate the two shavers as much as possible in the public mind. Even with all this, it took some time to rebuild the business.

My difficulty didn't end with the shavers' marketing. The motors for all the shavers that had been returned by the retailers had been stored in our factory in England. The returned M-3s had been cleaned out and rejuvenated with a new, safe motor. Going through the inventory to discover how many damaged motors were in stock, I made a discovery. It was Switzerland all over again! We were storing over 150,000 motors from discontinued shavers at our English plant. That was $600,000 of obsolete motors! The only use we had for them was in the repair of old shavers. I asked the president of the English company, 'Aren't you carrying too many old motors?' He didn't think so. He said, 'We'll use them. You'd be surprised how many repair requests we get for those older models. And at the worst, we can always put them in the Microscreens. I assure you in three years they will be gone.'

I thought this excess should bring down the price of the English operation, but the negotiators were adamant that, based on their knowledge of the market, the heavy stock was necessary. Reluctantly, I gave in on the point in exchange for some concessions on their part.

One year later, the inventory of the English operation showed they had indeed used those old motors. All of ten thousand of them. I called the company president on the phone and said, 'What's going on? You said you could unload those antique motors in three years. One year has passed and you still have 92% of them!' He replied, 'Well, I thought there would be a lot more repairs.' It took all the self-control I had to prevent me from taking a huge bite of the telephone receiver. I yelled, 'Do you know what we have on our hands? Over half a million dollars of useless goods!' At it turned out, we eventually used forty thousand of the motors. The rest had to be discarded.

Despite these and other minor problems, Remington thrived. The bank loans were paid off in less than twelve months – nine years ahead of schedule. We paid off all our notes with Sperry before they were due. As far as I'm concerned our biggest achievement was our ability to keep our promise to our employees. The Friday Afternoon Massacre was our last lay-off. In fact, during a period of recession we created over 400 new jobs.

As we grew, we did everything we could to ensure that Remington would have the best product on the market. We instituted 100% quality control at our factory in Bridgeport. No shaver leaves our plant without a meticulous inspection.

To review, you have to remember that this turnaround began with the product. I could have been blessed with the powers of Merlin, but, if the shaver wasn't any good, the company wouldn't have survived. Revitalizing Remington's cash flow was a top priority. The new pricing on all the shavers and the groundbreaking Triple Head Shaver combined with cost-cutting measures to kick us into the black. Improved channels of distribution and new advertising and marketing strategies put our product into the hands of the consumers. And, of course, there were the people, the Remington employees. The turnaround wasn't my triumph; it was our triumph. Those hard-working loyalists teamed up with this crazy man to prove all the experts wrong. With this combination, we went from a company with one of the smallest pieces of the shaver market to the company with the largest. It only goes to prove the soundness of something I once read. It was a quote from Al Burak, the president of Helena Rubinstein: 'You can make big money buying trouble.'

And, if you do it with a leveraged buy-out, you can buy it with very little equity.

CHAPTER EIGHT

Spreading the word: basic tenets of advertising and marketing

I don't recall who it was, but I remember once hearing some advertising executive boast, 'We could sell horse manure wrapped in cellophane with the proper advertising and marketing campaign.' I hate to burst his Madison Avenue bubble, but I disagree. Oh, sure, you might create a short-term success with a heavily hyped but shoddy product or some relatively useless novelty item. But for a service or product to enjoy a long and happy relationship with consumers, it must deliver quality. *The product or service is the selling point.*

A friend recently told me about an off-licence located near him on the upper West Side of Manhattan. The shop was doing a nice business until two huge off-licences, one part of a local franchise and the other a member of a national chain, opened within two blocks on either side of him. These two giants cut down the flow of traffic to the smaller shop to a trickle.

The two shops were impressive. Because of their size they were able to stock a large variety of wines and spirits. Able to buy in volume, they could offer these wares at low prices. The small shop owner couldn't carry that heavy an inventory; he had no place to keep it. He also couldn't compete with them on price. If he tried, the low margin would never support the costs of the shop.

Many people would have started to look for a new location. Not this fellow. He was an entrepreneur. He paid a visit to both of his competitors and looked to see if under all this sinew there wasn't some area of weakness he could exploit.

He found it. The first thing he noticed was that the people who worked at both stores weren't very good at their jobs. The employees at the check-out took too much time ringing up sales. Though the businesses could have supported it, neither store had an express line for cash-paying customers. These two circumstances resulted in long lines of grumbling consumers. Adding to a bad situation, the staff seemed sullen and did not appear to know very much about their merchandise. They were robots merely going through the motions with a weekly pay cheque as their only incentive.

The small shop owner found other foibles to add to his list. Though both super-stores had a large variety of spirits, neither carried any unusual stock. Both stores closed at 9 p.m., and neither offered home delivery on orders of less than twenty dollars.

Within a few days of his reconnaissance mission, that small owner took the offensive against his two larger rivals. He decorated his windows with colour action shots of professional wrestlers. These pictures were accompanied by the announcement, 'Don't wrestle with long lines or poor service. Come inside and get treated like a champion.'

It was a cute piece of advertising and it performed two important tasks: being unusual for an off-licence, the action shots caught the attention of passers-by and delivered the owner's message. However, eye-catching as this might have been it would have had little positive effect on his business if he had not backed up its claims in the following ways:

1 introduced free delivery on all orders in the borough;
2 kept the store open until midnight;
3 insisted that his employees offer service with a smile. He enhanced this courteous service by keeping wine and spirits reference books behind the counter; if one of his clerks didn't know the answer to a customer's query, he at least knew where to find it;
4 handed out lists of rare wines and spirits that could be placed on special order. The sheet included a tear-off form inviting customers to augment the list with suggestions of their own;

5 handed out sheets explaining which wines went with what foods; and
6 introduced the 'Recipe of the Week', a xeroxed copy of a recipe featuring wine or spirits as a prominent ingredient. Each Monday, a different recipe was made available.

The impact of his campaign wasn't felt overnight. It took some time, but as word of mouth built up, the store succeeded in winning back its old customers and adding new clientele.

Finding the USP

The owner of that small liquor store had built his ad campaign around a Unique Selling Proposition (USP). Simply stated, the USP is that characteristic of your product or service that is different from your competitors'. The tiny shop had at least five tangible USPs (free home delivery, late closing hours, recipe of the week, wine-food combining chart, and the rare wine list) not offered by its larger rivals. The sixth USP (friendly service) was an intangible that enhanced the value of the other five.

By something different, I don't mean the product or service itself has to be radically distinguishable from what's already on the market. You can take a new approach to advertising or you can package your merchandise in a manner that sets it apart from its competition.

For example, when we first came into Remington, I wasn't pleased with any of the recent commercials they had been running. They had one in which a helicopter, flying 1,500 feet over Death Valley, would drop a Remington on to a mountain top. I never quite understood the significance of this ad and I doubt many viewers did either.

Our first commercial was less elaborate. It featured a shot of the Remington Microscreen and announced 'The Remington Microscreen shaves as close as a blade or your money back.' *Shaves as close as a blade*. That was the USP.

After making the claim about the shaver's prowess it would continue to show how this marvellous performance was possible. We would zoom into the shaver and show the viewer the two flexible microscreens. The first screen shaves incredibly close, the second even closer. This was visual evidence corroborating our USP claim.

Our USP was further supported when we focused on the shaver's 120 cutting edges and its possessing the most powerful motor of any shaver on the market. This was a nuts and bolts ad; it explained what the shaver did and why. The answers were built around the USP, a claim that no other shaver company could make about its product.

I had learned the value of the USP at Playtex. When we first went into television, we featured what became known as slice of life ads. They were a wonderful education for me because we would write them ourselves. Nothing spectacular ever took place in them. You wouldn't see any rockets going off or marching bands strutting on screen, heralding the coming of a new age with the birth of some product. All we tried to do was recreate an everyday situation with which our targeted consumers – the women who made up a large part of the television audience – could identify.

In one, an actress in a supermarket would reach up to snare a box of cornflakes from the store shelf. A friend, shopping with her, would gasp in admiration and exclaim, 'Jan, how can you reach for that box of cornflakes? Doesn't your bra bind you?' An ecstatic Jan would reply, 'Oh, no Gladys, not since I've been wearing the Playtex Living Bra. It's all elastic and so it moves with you.'

The consumer was given the Unique Selling Proposition in that last line. *The Playtex living bra was the only all elastic bra on the market and it didn't bind the wearer.* Those were the things that set our product apart from the others; we wanted the consumer to remember them when she went shopping for a brassiere. Other bras bragged about the support they offered; we zeroed in on ease of movement. Whenever a woman went into a store looking for a bra that gave her a comfortable fit, we wanted her looking for a Playtex. Our USP also ensured that we didn't get lost in a crowd of bras promising super support. This approach should be especially appealing to the entrepreneur. He wants to stand out. It should make sense that he should want the same thing for any product or service he is selling.

You don't want to do what everyone else is doing. Remember some years ago when the Western world was suffering through the oil drought. All the car dealers in the US and Great Britain got it in their heads to sell the consumer on the prospect of getting better gas mileage for his money.

After you saw one of these commercials, they all looked similar. The difference between each model was almost nil. The information wasn't always clear either. An ad would promise that its car would deliver 26 miles to the gallon in the city and 30 miles to the gallon on the motorway. Another car might give you 28 miles to the gallon in the city, but only 39 mpg on the motorway. When I saw these commercials, I wondered, 'How do I figure out which car is the better buy? Do I have to take out my calculator and compute how many miles I drive in town and how many on the motorway?' It was so confusing.

When I looked at a car, I didn't care about mileage. The slight dissimilarities from model to model weren't going to help the salesman get the order from me or a good many other consumers. I was interested in comfort. During this mileage mania, how many advertisers said anything about the comfort of a car or the elegant beauty of its interior? In the US, we did finally get Ricardo Montalban singing the praises of Corinthian leather. It's no coincidence that this is the only commercial I remember from that period. It was so successful, variations of it are still running today.

Your USP doesn't have to be a major item. One Spanish restaurant in Manhattan is famous for its garlic soup. It started out as just another offering on the menu, but its reputation spread rapidly. It was unusual fare for those not used to Spanish cuisine and was exceptionally well prepared. With its growing popularity, it became the focus of the bistro's print ads. People began to know it as the restaurant with the best garlic soup in town. What did this mean? Well, if you had never had this unusual dish and wanted to give it a try, where would you go for it?

I found this story especially interesting because we're in the process of opening up a restaurant now. It will be located near our factory in Bridgeport. The menu isn't complete yet, so I've had to look elsewhere for the USP. I didn't have to look far.

The area we've decided to open in is surrounded by factories. There are a lot of fast-food places there, but they all deal in takeaway orders. There really isn't anywhere you can meet for a leisurely lunch or dinner and enjoy both the food and the conversation. Ours will be such a place and that mix will give us a USP.

Maximum impact

How can you be sure that your advertising campaign is having the greatest potential effect on the largest possible number of consumers? The management of Playtex felt that the ideal campaign should operate on the same theory that aided in the development of their presentation books. The pitch should appeal to as many of the senses as it could. It should occupy the full attention of the viewer. This was especially true of the television ads. When we showed Jan once again reaching for those cornflakes, a voice would come on and extol the freedom of movement offered by the Living Bra. At the same time, superimposed words would appear reinforcing the commentary of the announcer. Jan, meanwhile, would transform into ectoplasm. This allowed the viewer actually to see the bra move gracefully as Jan performed her chore. The viewer's sight and hearing were bombarded with images.

The positive message of the commercial could also be reinforced with an epilogue. After Jan had taken her cornflakes from the shelf, Gladys might say, 'If it does that for you, then I'm going to run right out and get a Playtex Living Bra.' Cut to the next scene. The same two actresses are in the supermarket. This time Gladys reaches for the cornflakes and says, 'Now that I have my Playtex Living Bra, I can reach for the cornflakes too.' This may seem like something out of the Stone Age now, but it helped sell a lot of Living Bras. And the basic concepts which led to its creation are still used in advertising today.

Look at our Remington commercials. When I say, 'The first microscreen shaves incredibly close,' those words appear on the screen. The same thing happens throughout the commercial. You hear me talk about the shaver, you see an illustration of the shaver's performance, and you read the commentary. Each element adds strength to the other.

When advertising on television, it's necessary to hammer home the USP at least three times. Listen to how many times I say 'The Remington Microscreen shaves you close as a blade.' There's a good reason for this. When a commercial comes on, the viewer often turns a part of his attention away from the television. He might use this time to play with his dog, or leaf through the TV magazine to see what's on next. By repeating the USP at quick intervals, you're increasing the chances of catching his entire attention (or boring him to death). Also, no matter how elaborate your presentation is, keep your message simple. You have only 30 seconds on that screen. You don't want to overwhelm the viewer with data or too many concepts. No one will be able to absorb it in such a brief amount of time.

Though we've been discussing television, the rules are pretty much the same when you advertise in print or on radio. Build your ad around the USP. If it's a newspaper ad, you lose the advantage of sound. You can compensate for this by having a vivid picture of your USP. That Spanish restaurant I mentioned earlier featured a picture of garlic soup that was so lifelike, you wanted to stick a spoon in it. With radio, you have only sound. Be sure your message is clear and that it's hammered home.

Consistency is the key to any successful ad campaign. Once you've found the theme that best serves your USP, stick with it. The purchase cycle of your product or service will decide how long it will take an ad campaign to create a demand for your wares.

For instance, suppose you were selling washing machine detergent. Let's say that on the average a person will run out of this detergent every two weeks. This means you can reach everybody who is going to run out of the product during a two-week period. Your first run of advertising should cover at least that period. Each succeeding cycle should run a minimum of two weeks.

At Playtex the purchase cycle for our bras lasted three months. If we had run our ads for only two weeks, we would have reached only one-sixth of those women who would be looking to buy a bra. However, a thirteen-week run would deliver our message to 100% of the market.

Marketing

Your marketing programme starts with the conception of your product or service. The moment you have an idea you want to run with, you have to begin thinking in terms of marketing. Your marketing plan should be built around a time-table outlining the period encompassing the birth of the idea to its introduction on the market and beyond.

At Remington, the marketing plans are specific. Each step of the programme is carefully laid out. The time parameter for each step is listed together with the person who is responsible for the implementation of that step. You should be able to follow the entire programme on one or two pieces of paper. Part of your outline may look something like this:

Marketing plan for solar typewriter

1 June	Final prototype due	Bill Bevens
15 June	Packaging due	Len Boehmer
22 June	Place orders for quantity production	John Griffiths
1 August	Production ready	John Griffiths
15 August	Released to sales force at National Sales Meeting in Dayton, Ohio. Needed at meeting: presentation books for salesmen, copies of storyboards for commercial, ad lay-outs, counter cards.	Lee Lowenfish
1 September	Shipments to the trade	Mark Bradley
20 September	National advertising begins	Anne Palizolla
1 October	Co-op advertising begins	John Collette

Your final plan will be more specific than this. It will include all the information necessary to give your marketing team a road map illustrating where the product is going. Besides those listed as being responsible for the plan's various steps, you will appoint one person to be responsible for the plan's overall execution. If production is two days late, this person can notify everyone connected with the product about the delay and let them know how it will affect their plans. He will also work closely with the other managers to see what can be done to make up for the lost time.

A key element of any marketing plan is the name of your product. Naturally, you want a name that will prove attractive to the consumer, but it's even better if that name tells you something about the merchandise.

When I first got to Remington, the lines were identified by

numbers. The top of the line shavers were the XLR-3000 and XLR-4000. Other models were identified by the letters PM and a number.

I asked one of the marketing people what these obscure codes meant. He said, 'There's a car called the XLR. It's very popular and so we thought it would be a good name for the shaver.' Did the advertising call attention to the connection between the car and shaver? Not that I would have wanted it to, but did it at least say something like you'll get as smooth a shave with our product as you would get a smooth ride with theirs? Of course not. When I asked what the PM stood for, the marketing fellow replied, 'That's an internal nomenclature. It means promotional model.' Oh. Gee whiz, I thought, that will certainly sell a lot of shavers. I asked, 'What on earth does that tell the consumer about the product? What does he know from an XLR or a PM?' They sounded as if they were the names of Sperry computers.

In looking to rechristen the shavers, I went back to lessons learned at Playtex. The names of the products told you something about their USP. What did the Mould 'n' Hold Girdle do? It moulded the shape and held it firm. The Living Bra moved with the wearer. What was the XLR's Unique Selling Proposition? It featured the microscreen that shaved you close as a blade. The XLR became the Remington Microscreen Shaver. The PM, which would be streamlined into our lower-priced model, had three shaving heads. It became the Triple Head Shaver and that name would later evolve into the more descriptive Triple Action Shaver. Why Triple Action? Because it shaves three ways.

My experience convinces me that if you can make the name descriptive enough, you can sell the most compelling feature of the product through the name. At times, it can help the consumer visualize the product. If you've seen a Cross Your Heart Bra, all you have to do is hear its name to remember what it looks like and what it does. The name of the product can also create a mood. We developed a watch at Benrus called the Citation. When the consumer got it we wanted him to feel as if he was receiving an award. Citation gave this impression and it also had a certain elegance that gave the watch added value.

Many of the marketing ideas I've used at Remington were variations of concepts I've picked up or developed at other companies. I have notebooks filled with marketing ideas going back to the early fifties. I review these notes a couple of times a year and always come away with something I can apply to the businesses I'm involved with now. The Fountains of Youth, a display holding tubes of girdles in various sizes, was Playtex's way of getting its merchandise out from behind the counter and on to the selling floor. As I've explained, sales staff couldn't stack those tubes; they would roll on to the floor. They had no choice but to arrange them in our displays. This was important. At Remington and Playtex, we learned that a sale can live or die in what we called 'the final three feet'.

Those three feet represented the imaginary distance between the clerk and customer at the point of sale. Somewhere in that final yard, you wanted your product at least to catch the consumer's eye.

When I took over Remington, I discovered we had a problem in this area. Shop owners were afraid to keep shavers out on the counter because they were an easy item to steal. They kept their models under lock and key. At many of the big customers, you could wait from now to sunset before an assistant was free to attend to your purchase. With the shaver imprisoned, you were unable to pick it up and take it to a check-out. This cost us sales and I had to figure out a way to get our shavers into those last three feet. How did we do it? We came up with a box that was just large enough to make it difficult to steal. Once the shavers were placed inside, these packages would be shrink-wrapped in cellophane. This made it difficult for the thief to open the box to get at the shaver. With this packaging, we were able to persuade retailers to put the shavers out before the public. As a result our sales increased dramatically.

I had seen the same thing happen when I was selling cosmetics for Lever Brothers in 1951. I found that if I could get my jars piled up on the store counter, so that there wasn't any way the customer could miss seeing them, we were going to sell more. There was a popular song during that era called *Out of Sight, Out of Mind*. It could have been the theme song for all salesmen because if the consumer didn't see your product, it was as if you didn't exist.

During those days with Playtex and Lever Brothers, I also discovered that educated sales staff could be your most important ally. The more they knew about your product, the bigger the advantage it had over the competition. Knowing this, Playtex salesmen did everything they could to acquaint the staff with the details of their products. We would get the customer's permission to give classes to their employees. These were informal affairs. Armed with coffee and cake for the students, I would come to the department forty minutes before the store opened and give a seminar on the wonders of the Living Bra or the Mould 'n' Hold Girdle. The goodies were part of a trade-off. They gave me their time and attention, I gave them breakfast. Having gone through this class, the staff were now prepared to answer almost any question the consumer could ask about our products. If a woman wanted a non-binding bra, the assistant could not only recommend the Living Bra, she could also tell the customer why it was the best bra for her. This helped sell the product. The seminars also gave us a chance to develop a relationship with the staff. It was tangible evidence of our interest in our product and them.

I can tell you of one idea, developed at Lever Brothers, that I've used throughout my career. When we introduced Pepsodent, we gave away small tubes of the toothpaste whenever a customer bought one of our toothbrushes. I used the same idea with a different product at Playtex. When we brought out a line of bras, we gave them away with our most expensive girdle. At Wells-Benrus, we sold a charm bracelet. If you bought three charms, you got the bracelet free. This accomplished two things. It introduced the charm bracelet to the consumers and it guaranteed the consumer would return to buy more charms. She couldn't wear a bracelet with only three charms hanging from it. It would look ridiculous. All three of these promotions were successful and they were nothing more than variations of the same theme.

An entrepreneur can also do take-offs of his competitors' marketing ideas. Keep in mind that this will be successful only if you can add something that will point out the difference between your promotion and theirs.

In Britain, rivals of Remington's instituted a trade-in policy: if you brought in your old shaver, they would give you five pounds off a new one. The brand you returned did not necessarily have to be the brand of the company giving you the rebate. I said, heck, let's go one better. We developed the no trade-in trade-in. If you liked our shaver, you kept it and continued to get the best shave you'd ever had. If you didn't like our shaver, you brought it in and traded it in for a refund. We did the same thing in America, touting the shaver as the one that 'shaved you close as a blade or your money back'. That campaign was a big hit. I might proudly add that we get refund requests from less than half of one per cent of all our customers.

Another competitor inspired me to change the name of the Remington Home Haircutter. It had brought out a beard trimmer that looked exactly like our haircutter. The only difference was it didn't have a thinner as our device did. You couldn't thin a beard with it; you could only trim it. I called in our designer and asked him if our haircutter could also trim and cut a beard. He thought it could. We ran a test, stacking our haircutter against the six leading beard trimmers. The names were stripped from the trimmers and they were coded so that we could tell them apart. Not one of the 100 test participants knew which company's device they were using on any given day. When the test was finished, eighty per cent of the participants said they liked our trimmer. No other trimmer could score as much as eight per cent. Shortly after, we were shipping Remington's newest item: a combination home haircutter and beard trimmer and thinner. The retailers loved it because it was two products married to form one stock-keeping unit. If they had carried a haircutter and a beard trimmer as separate items, it would have given them two stock units. Double inventory. By repackaging an idea we made an awful lot of people happy.

If you have national advertising and local tie-in advertising, make sure the message and presentation are consistent in both. A tie-in ad is run in conjunction with a local shop or shops. Today, unlike years ago when your company and the store would share the costs of the ad, the product manufacturer usually pays the advertising expenses. If you're not careful, a store can make your product the secondary feature of an ad you've bought. Make sure the final copy focuses on your USP and not what a wonderful shop Mr Jones has for carrying yours and other products.

If you have educated staff, consistent advertising on all the relevant levels, counter displays, and open channels of distribution that deliver your products on time, you will have a successful product. However, you must pay attention to every detail of your marketing campaign. Often, it's the little things that can foul up your best-laid plans.

To cite a painful example, Remington developed a photo-electric cell for bathroom deodorizers. We tested it in the bathrooms of our employees and it worked beautifully. When the bathroom light went on it activated the unit. If you turned the light off, the unit shut down. This meant the scent would waft through the room only when the light was on. It wouldn't be a constant, overpowering presence. It would also last longer than the average deodorizer.

There was only one problem with this marvellous product. None of those who tested it had fluorescent lighting in their bathrooms. However, when we turned the product over to a focus group, about a third of the participants did have fluorescent lighting in their bathrooms. They all had the same experience: the photo-electric cell refused to activate the deodorizer.

We had already manufactured 100,000 of these units. The only option we had was to send them to the market with a notice on the side of the box, warning that the product didn't work under fluorescent light. That killed me. The worst thing you can do with a product is connect it with a negative. Had I used my noggin, we would have done an analysis of bathrooms. We would have found out what sort of lighting was used in what percentage of homes and then tested the impact of the various types on the photo-electric cell. I didn't think to do that and it taught me a valuable lesson: in marketing, nothing is too small to be overlooked.

'I liked it so much, I bought the company!'

I've often been asked how I came to do my own commercials. Believe me, it was strictly an accident. When I flew over to Britain to discuss our 1979 advertising campaign, the thing furthest from my mind was becoming the Remington spokesperson.

We had put together our nuts and bolts ad with an off-screen voice explaining the virtues of the Remington Microscreen Shaver. It had tested well in the States and we wanted to run it worldwide. When I brought it to England, our ad agency here was not as enthusiastic about it as we were. The head of the agency said it was good, but that they had come up with something better.

I asked to see theirs. It featured a blade shaver with an electric cord. The narrator said, 'If you could have the comfort and convenience of an electric shaver, but the closeness of a blade shaver, you would have the perfect shave.' As the narrator spoke, the blade's cord was plugged in and the blade started to vibrate. The spokesman continued, 'Introducing the perfect shave, the Remington Microscreen Shaver.' At that point, the vibrating blade shaver was replaced by the Microscreen and the narrator proceeded to tell why the Remington gave such a close shave.

After viewing the commercial, I said, 'Well, it is attention getting, but I don't think it's believable. The part with the shaking blade is so far-fetched, and we don't associate the Microscreen with the USP quickly enough. I'd rather go with our ad.'

The agency people wouldn't hear of it. They argued that their commercial cut through the clutter and that it had won an award after running the prior autumn. I countered that argument with a reference to our sales report from that period. 'If it's such a great ad,' I asked, 'how come our market share at Christmas sank to its lowest level ever?' They responded that the ad hadn't had enough time to achieve maximum impact. We argued over that contention for a few minutes and then someone suggested we break for tea.

During the respite, a member of the agency asked, 'How is it a bloke like you could walk off the streets and buy a large company like Remington? With all the money leaving England right now, that sort of thing just doesn't happen here.' I explained how I had negotiated the purchase, including the part about how my wife bought me my first Remington. Midway through my story, I noticed an eerie silence had settled over the rest of the group. When I asked if anything was wrong, one of them said, 'No, no. We want to get the rest of your story. It's so interesting.' Hearing that, I wondered out loud if the average Briton would also be interested in the story. Everybody seemed to think he would, so I said, 'Why don't we build a commercial around that?' They agreed that it wasn't a bad idea. One person thought they could get Kevin Keegan to star in it.

That idea had no appeal for me. I asked, 'How can Kevin Keegan come on TV and tell how he bought the Remington shaver? Everyone in the UK knows who he is. They'll never believe it. At best, he can only describe how some fellow walked off the street and purchased the company. That just won't cut ice. I hate to say this, but if you really think this is a sound idea there is only one guy who can do this commercial. And you're looking at him.'

I'd love to be able to tell you how everyone agreed that this would be brilliant casting, but, if I did, I'd be fibbing. Instead, each member of the agency came up with at least one reason why I was wrong for the spot. One pointed out that I had never acted. This wasn't true. I had played an angel in a school play when I was ten years old. Another diplomat said, 'You know you're not such a young fellow.' I think he was trying to imply that Robert Redford wouldn't be losing any sleep over my new career. He wondered how much appeal I would have on the screen. A third expert said he couldn't be sure how the British public would react to an American as the star of the commercial. I replied that I wouldn't be the star; the shaver would take centre stage. I was only the straight man.

After hearing a few more of their objections, I said, 'You've all made some good points, but all this is theory. I have an idea. The only way to find out if it will take off is to try it.' Right then and there, we sat down and wrote the commercial. Ninety per cent of what you see in the ad now was created that day.

After writing the copy, we taped it. Reading from a hand-held script, I smiled at the camera and said, 'Hello, I'm Victor Kiam. I was a dedicated blade shaver until my wife bought me a Remington Microscreen Shaver. I was delighted and impressed by the shave it gave me. So impressed, I bought the company. The Remington Microscreen shaves you close as a blade or your money back. Here's why. The first microscreen shaves you incredibly close, the second, even closer. The Remington Microscreen will cost you about twenty pounds. The company cost me considerably more. The Remington Microscreen shaves you close as a blade or your money back.'

That was it. We test-marketed the commercial and the most negative comment came from those who asked, 'If you must use an actor in this bloody commercial, why not use a British actor?' That was the reaction of about 4% of the test participants. The general response to the test was highly favourable. We had a few more trial runs, got the same sort of feedback, and then decided to shoot a full commercial.

It wasn't easy. In order to get both out in time for the autumn campaign, we had to do the radio and the TV spots at the same time. This meant I had to stay in Britain longer than I had originally intended.

The agency people wanted to shoot the TV spot in an office setting. They had found the perfect office for their needs on the twenty-second floor of one of the few London skyscrapers. On the morning of the shoot, a limousine was sent to pick me up and deliver me to the set. Eat your heart out, Tom Selleck!

We started to shoot at ten in the morning and we ran into immediate problems. There was a bay window behind me that lent the commercial a breathtaking view of London. My make-up and the lights were adjusted to the amount of sunlight pouring through that window. It was an exceptionally bright day when we started the shoot, but then that London weather amused itself with some well-known pranks. The sun kept playing hide-and-seek. Every twenty minutes or so, often in mid-shot, it would duck behind a cloud mass and refuse to show itself. We'd have to stop shooting and readjust the lights and make-up to allow for the change in sunlight. Naturally, as soon as we made the alterations and got the cameras rolling again, the sun would appear, necessitating another delay.

This was my first time in front of a TV camera. I couldn't get used to the stop-go aspect of shooting. I would fluff a line, we'd start all over, and then the sun would disappear again. I've read how Marlon Brando, directing *One-Eyed Jacks*, drove his actors crazy when he delayed production two full days waiting for the ocean waves to be properly choppy. Apparently, the ocean had never heard of Stanilavsky. I can sympathize with my fellow thespians. Between my miscues and the uncooperative sun, it took us twelve hours to shoot a 30-second spot. Fortunately, the radio ad went a bit more smoothly though that session too had its share of problems. Studios were going on strike and we got our commercial taped just minutes before ours was forced to shut its doors.

The commercial premiered in the UK on 1 November, 1980. Shortly after its appearance, Remington sales skyrocketed in Britain. We released it in Australia, France, Norway, Canada and Hong Kong, and got the same reaction. One year later we put the commercial on in the States. The success there was not as immediate as it had been overseas. It takes a campaign much longer time to gain momentum in the US than in Europe. Gradually, however, there was a snowball effect. By the end of '81, I knew we had a winner.

I think the commercials have proved so popular because they represent something almost everyone would like to do. Many of us would love to have a financial stake in a favourite product. I'm still smarting over my missed opportunity with Velcro. An even greater number of people have watched actors in TV commercials and thought, 'Gee, I could do that better than he can.' If they were watching one of my commercials, they were probably right. I went out and actually fulfilled my fantasy and I think it touches the Walter Mitty in many of the commercial's viewers. The evidence of their eyes is also heartening. I'm an average-looking fellow. They correctly understand that if I can live my dreams, so can they.

With that observation, I do have a warning. If you want to buy or start your own business, go for it. Inspiring that sort of thought is the reason this book was written. But if you want to do your own commercials – something an increasing number of entrepreneurs are doing, whether their businesses are large or small – I must tell you the drawbacks.

You sacrifice a certain amount of privacy. Strangers recognize you in the street and have no compunction about stopping you for a chat. I don't mind that at all; I love meeting people, but if you're an introvert, it could be a problem. You also become more image-conscious. Before the commercials appeared, if some rude individual squeezed in front of me in a queue, I'd tell him to step to the rear. Except for me, I doubt anyone else would have noticed, unless the intruder was particularly obnoxious. In that case, I might even be applauded.

Now, however, if I were to ask that person to move his carcass, a lot of people might assume I was playing the part of the TV big shot and would side with the underdog, that obnoxious queue-jumper. The next time they viewed the commercial they would tell their friends, 'Oh, I saw him when I went to the cinema. Who does he think he is?' For this reason, I try to keep a low profile in public.

Doing a commercial has one more drawback. You become so closely identified with the product in the public's mind that your viewers have a hard time disassociating the two of you. You become the product. This reminds me of a story a *maître d'hôtel* once told me. A world famous fitness instructor, whose name graces an international health club franchise, came into his restaurant for dinner. He gave his order to the waiter: split pea soup, gulled fish fillet, fresh green salad, unbuttered baked potato and the mandatory glass of Perrier. When the waiter commented on what a healthy meal this was, the body-builder replied, 'Well, I usually eat like this at home, but I'm especially careful to watch what I order in public. When you're in my business and are as well-known as I am, you can't even afford to be seen walking a fat dog.'

There are those lazy Sunday mornings when I have to go out, but I don't feel like shaving. During those days, I know exactly how that body-builder feels.

CHAPTER NINE

The A-Z of fine-tuning

Going through the manuscript for this book touched off a few more thoughts on entrepreneurship. I'd like to share them with you.

Adaptability

An entrepreneur must be able to adapt within the corporate sphere. You're in a company. Before joining it you asked yourself what direction its management seemed to have in mind for its future. It appeared to be in the area of marketing, so you joined the company in a marketing position. Fine. That was an entrepreneurial move because it places you in a direct line to the top of the corporate ladder. But suddenly, after a series of setbacks, a change in the industry, or other reasons you can't fathom, your company switches its stance. It becomes financially oriented. Eschewing market share as its chief priority, it focuses its attention on bottom line profits. You must be prepared to change course or move on. If you intend to stay with the company and still have an eye on the top spot, you had better register for some financial courses. Better still, do this before a change takes place. The entrepreneur should not be a specialist. He should be well-rounded and able to adapt to change.

Be a leader

This principle also involves a bit of risk-taking. The entrepreneur should always try to be the innovator in his field. At Remington, we changed our outer packaging from a hard box to a soft box. Our competitors did the same thing. Our shaver had a heavy stainless steel carrying-case.

Carrying-case? Combined with the shaver, it weighed almost two pounds and was a wonderful item if you had just completed three years in intensive submarine training. Lugging it around was just the thing to keep those muscles toned. We developed a leatherette travel case which was light, attractive and easy to pack. Once again, our competitors followed suit.

Being a leader in your field might even mean being the first to change prices. During 1984, Remington spent a lot of money on advertising and promotion. Our sales were good, but our margins were down. This was worrying. Foreign competition has a significant advantage because of the strength of the dollar. I needed to get our top-of-the-line shaver into the hands of the consumer because I knew if he used it once, we had a lifetime customer. The only way to make the public aware of this terrific product was through heavier advertising. Common business sense told me that we would have to raise the price of the shaver two dollars in order to partially absorb the cost of the campaign.

When I told our sales manager of my plans, he nearly had a heart attack. He said our customers wouldn't pay the new price. When I asked why not, he said, 'Because the competition costs less.' That didn't disturb me. I reasoned that we had the best product on the market. *Consumer Reports* had only recently given it top rating. I told him, 'If we're successful with the new price and the shavers sell out of the stores during Christmas due to the extra advertising, what customer is going to throw out the US number one shaver? You think they're going to do that because we raised our price 4%? Even if they don't raise the price to the consumer, they'll still make more money than ever because of the increased volume. That increase will allow us to devote two million dollars more to advertising.'

Everyone at Remington, except me, was against the plan. They pointed out that if the sales dropped by only 10% we would lose everything we made on the extra two dollars. Our customers weren't too thrilled with the proposal either. Almost all of them said, 'No one else is raising their price. If you do this we will have to look very, very carefully at whether or not we should continue carrying the product.'

I wouldn't give in. We raised the price. Our market didn't fall off. In fact, our volume increased and, four weeks after we made the move, our major competitor raised the price of a comparable shaver.

By taking bold actions that succeed, your enterprise's image as a leader becomes fixed in the minds of your customers and consumers. Gradually, they become more receptive to whatever new programmes or products you introduce. They'll say, 'Let's get behind this campaign. Sure, it's never been done before, but it's obvious that this company is plotting the future direction of the entire industry. We don't want them to pass us by.'

Consensus opinion leads to mediocrity

You're in a meeting called to discuss a new idea. The idea could represent anything, a new product, a new marketing approach to an old product, an innovative service that your company is about to offer. Perhaps you called the meeting or were invited to sit in and give an opinion by a superior. At some point, someone is going to make a proposal to resolve a course of action concerning the idea. If there are eight people at the meeting and seven of them think the proposal is fabulous, but you disagree, you have to voice your opinion. *Don't have the courage of someone else's convictions.* As an entrepreneur you are always striving to stand out. How can you do that, how will anyone be able to measure the depth of your talent, intelligence and creativity, if you keep your mouth shut when you believe you are right? You should be prepared to risk the jibes of your peers, but if you have a better way of doing things you have to express it and be willing to fight for it.

When I was at Playtex, I wanted to adapt a promotion that had met with great success at Lever Brothers. In that campaign, a toothbrush was given away with every tube of toothpaste. In my version for Playtex, it was proposed that we help introduce the first all-elastic bra by giving it away with our top-of-the-line corset. Everyone thought I had lost my mind. They looked askance at any idea that would force the company to give anything for free.

Usually, I would agree with them. But I thought this was a marvellous way to get the bra into the hands of the consumers. I knew it was the most comfortable bra on the market and that once a customer used it, she wouldn't want to buy any other brand. Also, I made it a point to give the bra away only with our most expensive corset. With the right promotion, we would be able to trade up a lot of our customers from the $3.99 corset to the $11.99 model. Despite disagreement from all corners, I was able to convince the company to give my idea a chance. It was a smash and its triumph helped convince me that the majority shouldn't always rule.

Consultants

I don't like to hire consultants. They're like castrated bulls; all they can do is advise.

Don't be frightened by your first lawsuit

When I was younger and a comparative novice in the world of business, I imagined that being sued was the worst thing that could happen to anyone. I was certain that a subpoena represented the blackest mark that could be struck against someone.

It didn't take me too long to discover that this simply wasn't so. The way things work in the United States, especially today, you can sue anyone for anything. This isn't the case in many European countries. There, anyone who sues and loses is required to pay all costs and legal fees. That keeps the number of lawsuits to a minimum, but it also works against the little guy who can't risk losing a legal battle to a major corporation. The costs can be ruinous. The US system is fairer to the small man but it has helped to turn us into a society of litigants. So getting sued is not unusual and it won't leave you with an indelible brand.

The other thing I discovered is that – unless the case is settled out of court – it can often take years before it comes to trial. Add on appeals and there is no telling how long it will take to be resolved. This means that if someone slaps you with a subpoena, it probably won't have its full impact on you for a year or two. Considering the amount of time involved, it makes no sense to panic at the first sign of litigation. This is true of the UK too, so even though my lawsuits may not be particularly relevant, try to stop me telling you about them!

I was involved in my first one in 1959. My wife and I and another couple had planned to spend the weekend at a beach resort, which offered a nice weekend package including all meals. I rented a car for the weekend.

We left Manhattan shortly after 6 p.m. on Friday. Ten minutes after I turned on to the Long Island Expressway, the right rear tyre blew. This was not a major catastrophe. All I had to do was get everyone out of the car, jack it up, and put on the spare. There was only one problem. When I opened the car boot to take out the jack and the spare tyre, I discovered only the jack. The car rental service had neglected to give us a spare. Now we were in a pickle. Both wives were pregnant and we had to walk them almost half a mile before we got them safely off the motorway. Then I had to walk an additional mile before I found a petrol station that had a tow truck. One of the mechanics drove me back to the car, took off the damaged tyre, and took it back to the station to be patched. After it was repaired, he brought it back to the car and put it on. The entire episode took over two-and-a-half hours. By the time we got back on the road, we knew there was no way we would arrive at the resort in time for dinner. First chance we got, we pulled over and ate at a restaurant.

The dinner bill and the cost of the tyre repair added 140 dollars to the price of the weekend. When I got back to the city on Sunday evening, I returned the car. The rental was on a charge. I asked for a copy of the receipt. The next day, I photocopied the restaurant bill and the bill for the tyre repair. These expenses were greater than the cost of the car.

I wrote a letter to the car rental agency, explaining what had happened and telling them that I felt the added expenditure was the result of their negligence. I told them I didn't expect them to return the difference between their charge and my costs. I did feel, however, that my expenses cancelled any debt owed them.

The agency didn't quite see it my way. One month after the incident, I received a bill for the car rental from my credit card company. I refused to pay it. The letter I had sent to the rental agency, accompanied by copies of the bills, was sent to the credit card company as an explanation for my action.

Four bills arrived over the next four months. I answered all of them in the same manner as I had answered the first.

I received a surprise in the fifth month. No bill. I supposed the rental agency had decided to admit their error. One afternoon, I discovered that it was I who had erred. The doorbell rang and, when I went to see who was calling, I found myself face-to-face with a pleasant-looking gentleman whom I had never laid eyes on before that moment. I was about to ask who he was when he asked, 'Are you Mr Victor Kiam?' I nodded yes. He smiled and said, 'How very nice to find you home. I have something for you.' It was a subpoena! This grinning assassin was a summons server. The rental agency wanted their money and they were going to haul me into court to get it.

I could have paid the bill; it wasn't that large. But I felt there was a principle to defend here. Calmly, I reviewed my chances. I knew that, if needed, I could get the mechanic who changed our tyre to testify that there wasn't a spare in the boot. It was the agency's responsibility to provide one. I had full documentation of our additional expenses, including a brochure from the resort proving we would not have had to pay for dinner if we hadn't been delayed. As far as I could see, the agency had no case. I was so confident, I decided to act as my own attorney during the pre-trial deposition. If it went to full trial, I would consider enlisting the aid of counsel, though it would have been less costly to pay the original bill.

The question of legal fees and court costs helped me formulate an entrepreneurial strategy for dealing with the suit. In selling and negotiating, I always tried to put myself in the other fellow's shoes, to find out what his needs were. What, I wondered, was the purpose of the rental agency's suit? Were they trying to stand by a principle? Since they never attempted to come to terms with an obviously dissatisfied customer, I doubted they had any principles to uphold. Did they want to make an example of me? Hardly. No one knew who I was. If I lost the case, I couldn't quite envisage their posting my picture in all their agencies as a warning to any future quarrelsome customers who attempted to mess with them. No, the only interest they could possibly have in the suit was the retrieval of the money. Knowing this and sure I was in the right, I decided to make it very costly for them to try to get it.

At a pre-trial deposition, the side that initiates the action is responsible for all court costs including a stenographer. I knew a court stenographer was paid something like ten cents a word. When the agency's attorney asked, 'Did you use the car?' I replied that I had. When he asked if I had paid for the privilege, I told him that I had not.

Up to this point, there was nothing out of the ordinary about our exchange. But then, the attorney asked why I had refused to pay the bill. Keeping in mind the cost of the stenographer, I proceeded to tell my story in great detail. 'This whole episode started,' I began, 'when I left my office at 5 p.m. on the Friday in question. I took the bus that stops in front of the office building to the rental office. I got to my stop at 5.21 p.m. I knew the time because I kept checking my watch. Traffic was terrible and it was a much longer ride than usual. Reaching my stop, I got off and had to walk two blocks to the rental agency. I stepped inside and waited to speak with an agent. It was five minutes before one could see me. That's not a criticism of the agency; it was a busy time of evening . . .'

Twenty-five minutes into my testimony, I still hadn't got to the part concerning the flat tyre. The lawyer for the agency and its representative were pulling their hair out. They were well aware of how much my testimony was costing. The attorney interrupted my testimony and asked the court stenographer to be excused. Through clenched teeth, he said, 'Okay, Kiam. We're dropping the suit.' I had won! I had beaten those pirates at their own game. Had I panicked and allowed the subpoena to intimidate me, I would have turned over the money on demand and then spent the next few weeks kicking myself for giving in when I knew in my heart that I was right.

I did panic when I got wind of my first corporate lawsuit. It was a case of liability against Wells Jewellery. We had sponsored a series of pierced earring clinics throughout the country. One of these was held at G. Fox in Hartford, Connecticut. It was quite a success, attracting a large number of women who stood in a long queue while waiting to get their ears pierced.

One late arrival apparently didn't want to be bothered with the queue. She tried to bully her way to the head of it and almost succeeded. Only a solid wall of resistance kept her from her goal, but she still managed to push herself in front of most of the early arrivals. Many of these women had voiced their objections to her intrusion, but no one seemed willing to do anything about it. One woman, however, did take exception. Spinning the interloper around, she reared back and hit her across the mouth with her umbrella! The force of the blow knocked the intruder to the ground and dislodged several of her front teeth.

The injured woman sued her assailant, G. Fox, and Wells

Jewellery. When I first received notice of her action, I called a meeting of all the members of upper level management. I told them I wanted people sent out to G. Fox immediately and that they weren't to come back until they had taken depositions from every available witness. I kept badgering the lawyers for information on the strategy we should take. I was concerned that other stores would overreact to a suit and cancel the clinic. None of them did and despite my worry, the lawyers for the opposing sides weren't able to get together for almost six months. When they did finally meet, it took them only a few days to come to a settlement. The umbrella-wielding woman agreed to buy her victim a new set of dentures. G. Fox and Wells agreed to pay the complainant five hundred dollars each. We could have gone to trial and I believe we would have won, but the legal costs would have been much higher than the cost of the eventual settlement. Considering the time it took to resolve the issue and the final result, my fears were unjustified.

Though you shouldn't live in trepidation of lawsuits, you should do whatever you can to avoid them. It is a foolish entrepreneur who leaves himself open to litigation. At Remington, we do everything we can to make sure we are on firm legal ground. Any time a promotion is launched or a claim is made about one of our products – even if that claim is meant only for the eyes of our sales force and accounts – we talk it through with our lawyers. We satisfy any demands for proof of authenticity that the lawyers require and are prepared to defend any claim we make.

An example of our preparedness can be found in an accident involving the US magazine *Consumer Reports*, very similar to your *Which?* They had designated one of our rechargeable Micro-screens as the top-rated shaver in the country. Winning that accolade from a respected, dispassionate panel was a wonderful boost and we wanted to trumpet it in our advertising. Unfortunately, the magazine is very touchy about having their praise used in ads. In fact, they forbid companies from using their ratings or raves in commercials or the print media. I thought this was nonsense. The magazine is sold on newsstands. It was available to the general public. If that public was going to see we were the top-rated shaver in the magazine, why shouldn't they see the same thing in our ads? We did not solicit the magazine's kudos. They received no benefit from us for giving the shaver their top rating.

Therefore, their integrity could not be questioned if we put their rating in our advertising. Our lawyers, after long and careful consideration, agreed. They felt we would be well within our rights if we used the magazine's rating in our ads.

Consumer Reports was not pleased when we did this. They sued Remington and tried to force us to remove the information from our advertising. Already armed for such a confrontation, we fought them in court and were vindicated when the judge dismissed the suit. The legal preparation we did before doing the ads had convinced us that we were on solid ground. I was sure we wouldn't lose.

Another reason not to fear a lawsuit is that though many more people sue today than ever before, very few of them are anxious for their suits to be brought to court. As I mentioned before, the costs can be staggering. Even if you're staring at a certain lost cause, you can often settle long before your case comes to trial. There are, however, two instances when a settlement may be hard to reach: when your opposition is looking for revenge or when they want to set a precedent.

I was in that position not too long ago. I had secured a patent on an expanding suitcase. Without my knowledge or permission, two leading US department stores started importing these suitcases from Taiwan and selling them in direct violation of our patent. Their collective volume wasn't very large; each store would sell about one hundred dozen each. The loss to us was about $800 in each store.

Several friends advised me to forget about it. They felt the volume was too small to merit my attention. It would take $25,000 in court fees to retrieve $1,600 in profits. That didn't seem to be much of a Risk-Reward Ratio. I disagreed. You can't always measure your Risk-Reward Ratio in pure dollars and cents. Common sense also has to be a factor. The attorneys and I felt that if I allowed these two stores to get away with it, we would have a difficult time blocking similar actions on the part of other stores and merchants. Our patent would be worthless. We went to court and won the case, establishing a precedent that was inviolable.

Don't do business with friends

This can be worse than borrowing from friends. If you go into business, you might be tempted to have your friends as your first customers. Or you might wait to use friends as a source of supply for the materials or services your company needs. Don't give in to this impulse. If you do, and one of you fails to deliver, the friendship can be damaged. A schism can also happen if you find a better source of supply. You're in the position of having to take business away from a buddy. Who needs that headache? Try not to use friends as a source of investment. Unless he's a venture capitalist, a friend is usually not in the business of lending money. Banks and other lending institutions are well aware of the risks involved when they decide to get behind an enterprise. A friend might not understand the depth of his gamble.

Borrowing from a friend places you in an uncomfortable position. If your venture starts to sink, you'll feel enormous pressure if a buddy's savings are tied into it. If the venture does fold, your debt to him could engender bad feeling. I've seen friendships torn asunder by failed business deals. When that happens, the emotional interest on the money borrowed is much too high.

In a small company, with few employees, you're going to become close to everyone working under you. A familial relationship is bound to be spawned and that's a good thing. You want everyone to feel as if they're in this venture together, even if they don't have any equity in it. However, you must always remember that this is a business. The time may come when you might have to fire one of these people or chastise him for the good of the company. If such a decision has to be made, you don't want your personal relationship with your employees to cloud your vision.

Depending on the level of business you're involved with, don't use friends for their expertise unless you're both clear whether or not a fee will change hands. Always let people know when you're talking on a professional level.

If someone volunteers advice in an effort to help you with your venture, don't take it and then disappear into the night. This friend has sat down with you on the understanding that a fee wasn't involved. He gave you his help as an act of friendship.

You've probably asked him numerous questions. The investment of his time makes him an interested party. Whether you use his advice or not, keep him abreast of how the venture is faring. Don't pick his brains and then neglect to call him for six months. He'll feel used. The next time you call him, you'll get a cold reception. You'll lose him as a friend and an adviser.

Stay away from negativists. If the people around you spend most of their time telling you why things can't be done rather than helping you figure out how they can be done, keep your exposure to them at a minimum. The power of negative thinking is as strong a force as the power of positive thinking. You can't afford to have your enthusiasm undermined.

Get into debt

Start building a credit base as early as possible. In lectures given across the country, I've always given the same piece of advice to high school and college students: Get into debt.

I hope that got your attention as quickly as it gets theirs.

When I suggest that they get into debt, I'm not entreating them to go out and become wastrels. I believe that anyone, no matter what their age, who hasn't got a credit history, should go down to their local bank and take out a small loan; $500 would be a nice start. Deposit it in a savings bank. If you deposit it, the interest accrued on savings will help offset the interest accrued on debt. Using this method, a loan of $500, paid off over a year, will cost the borrower less than thirty dollars. Later, after the loan is repaid, go back and borrow $1,000. You'll have an easier time securing this loan because you've proven to be a good credit risk with the first transaction. Pay back this loan, and you've built up a credit history. This base will come in handy when you apply for a mortgage or need equity for your entrepreneurial venture.

Hire a maverick

At Playtex, we didn't want to hire the eccentric. The company had a psychological test which was given to all job applicants and only those who scored between 60 and 80 were hired. Under 60, they assumed your were practically comatose. Over 80, they assumed you were too brilliant. You might not fit in with the company. Playtex did not want to risk hiring you. They could spend a sizeable amount of time and money and then lose you. You might spend most of your time questioning and fighting management's decisions. Or you might become easily bored and quit for something more interesting. You might be Einstein's clone, but you were dangerous.

As an entrepreneur, I want those dangerous people working for me. I'll take those people in the 60 to 80 group, but I also want those people in the 80+ bracket. They need nurturing and I'm willing to spend time with them and give them a freer rein than I would give the others. These people are my prodigies. They're going to come up with crazy ideas, but they'll also draw up some brilliant plans. The others are going to do well without my help, but if I can harness the prodigy's potential without inhibiting it, he will bring more to the company than my other employees. The members of the 60 to 80 group will ably execute; this guy will create.

Investments

I have investments. I think it's good for the entrepreneur to have a diverse portfolio, but I'd rather put my money in something that requires my personal involvement. Buying shares is akin to buying a lottery ticket, but you should have some in your portfolio. They can come in handy. The money from my Playtex stock helped me buy into my first company. You should also look into real estate, though, as an entrepreneur, you may want to explore this option with an eye towards development. No matter what your investments are, you must be concerned with the liquidity of your assets. You don't want your money locked up when opportunity calls.

If you're one of those rare individuals who has nothing but money and all the time in the world, you can have a different investment strategy from someone who is running one or more ventures. You can take the time needed to keep track of small investments. But most entrepreneurs are *working* entrepreneurs. Small investments are anathema to us. We can't waste time on them because the return isn't large enough for the time and energy they cost.

If you invest in a venture run by someone else, a fellow entrepreneur who needs your financial backing, you must remember to give him the same leeway you would require if you were running the show. Don't contradict your own entrepreneurial principles by hampering him with demands that may give you a quicker return on your investment but would obstruct the growth of the company. Don't expect him to play it safe. You are investing in the entrepreneur *and* his vision.

Play fair

Business is a game and you should do everything you can to win, provided you play within the rules. When I was selling, I would get up in the morning and give myself a goal: 'Today, I'm going to get five orders and do at least $2,000 in volume. That's $400 for each order.' Then I would go out and fight like a hellcat to reach that goal. Making it would be my victory for the day. No matter how long it took, I would call on customers until I'd won. But I never tried to flim-flam anyone to achieve that success. I never overstocked a customer or painted a vista I didn't believe.

When I play tennis, unless it's in an organized tournament, like my opponent I'm on my honour when it comes to calling a shot in or out. I would never call a ball out when it was just inside the line. I would feel soiled if I achieved a victory by cheating. As an entrepreneur, money is not the final measure of your success, accomplishment is. If that accomplishment is tainted by cheating, how much gratification can it bring? In business as in tennis, you should never give a bad call. If you came to the Remington offices and opened our books, you'd find we sell to everybody at the same price. There are no inside deals. We do want to remain number one; we just won't do anything underhand to stay in that spot.

Postscript: selling

Many salespeople have the mistaken belief that making a sale is the last step in the selling process. Actually, it's the first. *Unless the entrepreneur can deliver a continuity of service, he will have a difficult time selling to the customer again.* You should think of your customers as partners, or better still, family. If your vista has turned the account on to such an extent that he wants to order more merchandise than he actually needs, give him the benefit of your knowledge. Bring him back to reality and go for the smaller order. If you persuade people to overstock your merchandise, you're going to come back in a month or so to a very unhappy customer. If it happens more than once, you won't be coming back at all. Your customer's happiness is the key to your long-term success. I stress this at Remington.

We give similar service to the consumer. Our shavers have a product life of five to eight years. If any consumer has any problems with one of our shavers, I want it taken care of immediately. When his or her shaver is ready for retirement after long and meritorious service, I want a satisfied customer coming back to the store to purchase another Remington. If I lose them to a competitor, it will be at least five years before I get another shot at them. Our company receives 1,000 letters a week. Many of them are just short notes praising the shaver. Some ask questions about our other products. I'm happy to say only a tiny number are from consumers who have experienced a problem with the product. We answer every letter and the problem ones are our first priority.

I don't think the head of a company should ever expect his sales force to be successful selling a product, a service, or a concept that he can't sell himself. I still go out into the field and sell Remington. Any chief executive with a sales background should be willing to do the same. If he doesn't have any selling experience, then the next highest executive who does should do it. I travel the globe six months of every year. Because of this I honestly believe that I know more about the world-wide electric shaver business than any of my competitors. I also know that when our sales force and our other employees see me actually going out and selling our products, the effect on morale is terrific. For them, it's just another illustration of the confidence I have in what we're doing.

When you paint a vista, remember never to make claims that you or your company can't live up to. You can't promise retailers that you'll run 45 TV commercials in their area in the next three months and then run only six. A company must be honest and it must insist that its representatives be honest. Some hyperbole is expected in any pitch, but never promise anything you can't deliver. If you do, you may get the order this time, but you'll never get another.

Don't sell on consignment. It's easy to get an order if you tell the client to keep the merchandise for thirty days and then allow them to return whatever they don't sell. That doesn't take any great selling skills. It is also my experience that selling on consignment doesn't pay off long-term. You want the customer to have a stake in moving the merchandise. When they buy on consignment, they are involved in a risk-free venture. It doesn't matter to them whether or not they sell your product. They're more concerned with selling the merchandise they've already paid for. If those products don't move, they're going to take a loss. By making them pay, you become partners with them and they will take an active interest in your merchandise.

When you're selling a product, you are its guardian. If your product isn't prominently displayed on your account's shelves, move it to a better spot. It is important to be able to catch the consumer's eye. Often the soap or toothpaste brand they decided to buy was the first one they saw. At Playtex, the salesmen were given dusters. They were expected to clean off any stock that was on display and were to make sure that it made a neat presentation. This was done just before the salesperson called on the store owner or buyer. We wanted whoever was responsible for the store or department and the consumer to know we cared about our merchandise. A product or service is like a baby. It needs tender, loving care before and after it is sent out into the insensitive environment of the marketplace.

In the chapter on selling, I dealt mainly with the selling of products. All the concepts presented in that chapter also apply to the selling of services. No matter what the merchandise, you have to find out the customer's needs and address them.

Public vs. private

The entrepreneur who wants to build a successful enterprise would be well-advised to operate his venture as a private company. By doing this, you avoid having to work for two masters: a concern for the good of the company vs. a devotion to what looks good to your shareholders. You'll be able to plan long-range strategy and shrug off cyclical swings which may not indicate how well the company is really doing. A person with a trained eye can read those swings, offer a higher price than your public shares are trading at, and walk off with the company.

On this same note, public companies are vulnerable to greenmail. This occurs when an individual or a group make a bid to take over a company. The buyers in these situations are not operating entrepreneurs. They already have equity in the company and they are hoping that management will thwart their takeover attempt. How? By buying them out at an inflated price. These people also take advantage of the vagaries of the market. They take positions in order to capitalize on short-term trends such as takeovers. These manipulators aren't really investors, looking to help build an enterprise. They are fast-buck artists, floating along whichever way the greenback blows and having the interest neither of the company nor its employees at heart. The future of the enterprise means little to them. Their biggest concern is any financial transaction that will result in an immediately higher share price or the sale of the company. Expansion and long-term investment are not part of their language. They are a bane to any entrepreneurial undertaking and their hoary spectres are always lurking in the shadows of any publicly-held company.

Another problem with a public company bares itself when poor management is able to entrench itself. Public shareholders are often lackadaisical and uninformed. Management will propose terms that protect their own interests. Most shareholders vote along with management on everything. It's part of the public company syndrome. These terms install management in such a way that it becomes almost impossible to unseat them. At one well-known US multinational, the shares were going nowhere – trading at ten to twelve dollars. An opposition group, owning more stock than the entire board of directors, tried to force management out. *It took them almost two years!* Now the company is growing and its profits are climbing. The shares are trading in the low thirties. The opposition knew what it was doing and they had the votes to take over. But it still took what must have seemed like forever to unseat those in control.

In a privately-owned company, you're not subject to any of these problems. At Remington, I make my own decisions and they're all made with only one thing in mind: what is good for the company? I also have an advantage over publicly-owned companies when it comes to making an acquisition. Suppose you're a public company and you're involved in a negotiation. Even if you sign only a non-binding letter of intent, you have to announce it. With that declaration, a rival company might say, 'My gosh, Company A is buying Company B for five dollars? Company B would be worth much more than that to us. We'll go in with a higher offer.' The next thing you know, you're involved in a bidding war or you've lost the acquisition. A privately-held company can operate without this handicap.

References

Try to gather an arsenal of business acquaintances to use as references. A word from the chief executive of a company is worth fifty letters from close friends. Those buddies of yours have never had any business dealings with you and their praise will carry small weight when you're applying for an important job.

When I was twenty-five years old, I bought one hundred shares of a twelve-dollar stock. I went down to the brokerage house and met the fellow who negotiated the transaction. While in his office, I was introduced to the person who researched the stock. Later, I made a transfer and made another investment, costing me close to $1,600. I went back to the same house to make the transfer and managed to meet the firm's manager. In time, he introduced me to a partner in the company. I was establishing relationships that would prove valuable if I needed to raise equity. They knew me as a fellow who bought and traded stocks with them and, as far as they were concerned, I was a good credit risk.

Having these sort of people on your side is important. When I get a reference that is typed on personal stationery, I give it less credence than one on the letterhead of a firm. In the latter instance, the writer is not merely speaking for himself, he's putting his company's good name behind his opinion. That speaks volumes to me. If Mr Howard Schaeffer's best friend, Mr William Altman, writes a personal note telling what a charming fellow Howie is and what wonderful personal habits he has, I'm not impressed. Good old Howie might have debts from here to Borneo and Mr Altman might not be aware of them. But if I get a note written by Mr Altman on the letterhead of Altman-Lang Associates, Inc. and it concerns a business relationship his firm has had with Mr Schaeffer, I'm going to give it serious attention.

Respect for the boss

I've worked for two companies, Lever Brothers and Playtex, in which I was not the chief executive. In both instances, I had to respect the person I worked for and I needed his respect. I loved my first boss, Keith Porter, at Lever Brothers, but when he left he was replaced by a fellow who was absolutely atrocious. He didn't work well with people and he had no respect for his employees. He gave way to a fellow who seemed interested only in playing corporate politics. He would screen every memo that went out to make sure there was nothing in it that would disparage his division. I couldn't live with so dishonest an approach. Everyone makes mistakes; you have to admit yours and learn from them. This fellow couldn't face his shortcomings. As soon as I could I transferred out of his division. What else could I do? I was beginning to lose my pride in the company. I felt that if they wanted someone as insecure as him to represent them as vice-president of sales, then this might not be a company I wanted to work for. Fortunately, the division I switched to was headed by an executive who had the same entrepreneurial bent as I.

The one time you may want to put up with a boss you don't respect is when you get something in exchange. I put up with Barry Ruff, the chap I mentioned in Chapter Four, because I was new to selling and wanted to learn the ropes. I also expected to move up rapidly, so I didn't expect to be under his thumb for long. I put up with his miserable personality, and managed to learn how to sell through the experience. I also learned how not to sell by observing Mr Ruff.

Tax shelters

These are only partly applicable in the UK, but you may as well have my views on them – for free. I'm not crazy about tax shelters. An entrepreneur should think about building his assets and the profitability of his company. He wants his money working actively for him. The tax shelter offers you a way to avoid paying taxes by lowering your tax rate. They can be tempting, but they don't build anything. Why get involved with a venture that does little more than just save you money? That goes against the entrepreneurial grain. It's true that a shelter offering a high write-off can make you think, 'Goodness, look at all the money I've saved!'

But what have you built? There are some tax shelters, however, that offer growth potential and they have some merit. For me, the financial benefit of the shelter is secondary to this potential. Unfortunately, whether we like them or not, shelters seem to be a necessary evil under the present tax system. If you must invest in them, get the advice of an accountant who understands your entrepreneurial philosophy before you make the transaction.

Vive la difference!

The status quo and the entrepreneur should never become bosom buddies. The entrepreneur should always be open to the unusual, even if his concept is only as good, or even not quite as good, as the way things had been done before. Just the fact that it is different and will change the basic habits of the consumer or client makes it worthy of serious consideration.

My 'Buy one, get one free' proposal, discussed in Chapter One, comes in this province. At the time, everyone was running 50% off sales. Harriet Hubbard Ayer, through your local store, would sell you a five-dollar jar of cold cream for $2.50. With my idea, you would pay five dollars for the cold cream and then get another jar of cold cream or some other comparatively priced Ayer item for free.

I thought the concept would work on several levels. First, it enabled us to run a sale without cutting prices and cheapening our product. There was some amateur psychology at work here. I felt that if you gave the consumer a one dollar item for fifty cents, she would think the sale price was all it was really worth. But if you sold it for a buck and gave them an item with a similar price tag free, they felt they were getting a top quality item plus a valuable gift. Second, with my promotion the consumer had to spend that dollar instead of the fifty cents. My campaign needed only half as many customers to do as much volume as the 50% off sale. Third, I wanted to build business. I thought a lot of customers would take advantage of the BOGOF (Buy one, get one free) promotion to try something else in our range. After the idea was 'borrowed' from me by my insecure superior, it accomplished all of these things. Today, it is a standard marketing tactic of many major companies.

Even a subtle difference can have value. If everyone holds their sales in January, how much enthusiasm can you generate by holding your sale at the same time? Why should anyone choose to support your sale as opposed to a competitor's? But if you were to hold it in February or March, it's going to stand out. It's still the same sale, but the unusual timing is going to excite your customers. Looking for the unusual angle will also keep the entrepreneur's creative juices flowing. Above all, you don't want to fall into a rut. Once an entrepreneur loses touch with his sense of adventure, he joins hands with business suicide.

Some wise words from a wise man

As I've said before, even the most successful ventures have their shares of ups and downs. Whenever you start to slide from the peak into the valley, I'd like you to remember the words of my grandfather. He was fond of saying, 'In these hard times, it's good to remember there were always these hard times.'

CHAPTER TEN

The Bigger Mo

In business and politics, there is a well-known American expression: the Big Mo. As you may know, it refers to momentum. Less celebrated, but in my opinion of greater importance, is the Bigger Mo: motivation. Without it, the Big Mo might just as well not exist because when it does come along, no one will care enough to notice or take advantage of it. An entrepreneur cannot function if he is unable to motivate himself or inspire motivation in others.

We've seen how the Remington turnaround was partly attributable to motivation. You don't have to wait to be a chief executive to motivate others. The principles applied to the Remington situation were originally picked up and used by me in my first managerial position at Lever Brothers.

I was lucky in both instances. The overwhelming majority of the employees at Remington and most of my nine-man sales force at Lever were first-rate. At Remington, they had experienced a lack of faith in a dying company and morale was at an understandable low. My salesmen at Lever Brothers had grown complacent. This too was not surprising. Lever Brothers backed its products with terrific advertising campaigns. It had smooth channels of distribution and product quality was first-rate. Many of the salesmen had discovered that their lines practically sold themselves. They were making good livings and didn't feel the need to put in any extra effort. It was also hard for them to get revved up about their products. As far as retailers were concerned, if the product was a major brand, there was little difference between any company's toothpaste or soap. Unless some salesman walked in with a monkey on his back, it wasn't going to be easy to get anyone excited about yet another tube or bar.

What I just described may seem like problems. They weren't.

They were needs that had to be answered. *Motivation is delivering the answers to your or someone else's needs.*

How did we restore faith, heighten morale and create an *esprit de corps* at Remington? By tearing down regulations, offering incentives and building relationships within the company. We became a team with a common goal: to prove that the rumours of Remington's death were greatly exaggerated.

The scenario at Lever Brothers was a bit different. We already had a success; I wanted to improve upon it. In order to do this I had to awaken these salesmen's slumbering pride and shake them from their complacency. *It's vital that the entrepreneur find something other than the promise of financial reward as a motivator. You want the people working with you to have an emotional investment in your enterprise.* An extra few dollars in commissions would not have been enough to stir those salesmen.

After giving it much thought, I drew up a motivational battle plan and implemented it at a meeting with the sales people. First, I had to give them a reason to put in greater effort. I had one. Our product, Pepsodent, was the number two toothpaste in the country. Colgate was number one. We wanted to overtake them. That wouldn't have meant much to those guys; Lever Brothers had been trying to do that for years. But now a new wrinkle had been added to the toothpaste wars. Proctor and Gamble had introduced Gleem with the heaviest promotional campaign ever built around any brand of toothpaste. As part of their strategy, P&G had recently sent a free tube of Gleem to almost every home in America. This was the first national sample distribution ever attempted in the US. With this sort of creative marketing and an aggressive sales force, Gleem had shot up to the third spot in the toothpaste ratings and was threatening to overtake us. I used that product and its threat as the common enemy that would help form my salesmen into a team. My speech at the meeting emphasized that it was going to be us against those upstarts from P&G and that we weren't going to let them pass us without one whale of a battle. And while we were beating them, we were also going to go after Colgate. I didn't want the salesmen to think we were merely defending our position. As Patton once said, we weren't defending anything. We were going after the enemy and we were going to grab him by the nose and kick him in the butt.

The idea of engaging in a war with the competition is often not enough to motivate anybody. It merely helps form a cohesive unit by giving the individuals involved a common purpose. With that done, you now have to focus on each individual's desires.

You go into this the same way you would go into a negotiation. Ask yourself, 'What does the person need?' I found my older salesmen needed to have their egos pricked. Speaking to them privately, I said, 'You guys have been around for a long time. You'll be retiring soon. Every one of you has earned his keep with the company. You've put in the hours, but Lever Brothers has made it easier for you by getting behind its products. National advertising and excellent marketing strategies have helped put a lot of money in your pocket. Now is the time for you to give something back. If you put in a maximum effort, those younger salesmen will be inspired. You guys helped build the company, they will look to you for an example. I'd love to see you fellows spend your last few years here going out with a bang. I would hate to have people say that when the company needed you, you weren't able to toe the line.'

My appeal to the younger salesmen was different. Since they had their careers in front of them, I was able to paint a vista. When I met them, I said, 'None of you would be here if you didn't want to move up the corporate ladder. You can do it quickly at Lever Brothers and I'm already area supervisor. I'm not going to be here long; I'm looking at that next step. There's only one way for any of us to move up to that higher rung: results. If we can show dramatic gains in the face of our new competition, we're going to get noticed. That attention has to benefit you in your drive for promotion. We're only a small area representing a tiny fraction of the company. We certainly can't turn the nation around in this battle with Colgate and Gleem. The other areas will have to work just as hard as we do. If they're up to it, we can win this thing. If they're not, then we will shine all the more for not having permitted our competition to get a stranglehold on this area.' The idea of this and any attempt at motivation is to give your team a higher purpose. I stressed to all the salesmen that we were working together and shouldn't be looking to cut each other's throats. I wanted everybody to be pulling for one another for the good of themselves and the company.

Had I only made a couple of speeches, nothing would have

happened. It's not enough to talk a good game; *an entrepreneur has to motivate by example.* I wanted my salesmen to put in twelve-hour days if necessary. If I had worked only from nine to five, they never would have put in any extra time. As I went from city to city, I made sure I was on the road with my salesmen at eight in the morning and I didn't leave until the last customer was visited. I let them know that I especially wanted to visit the accounts where we were doing badly and that I hadn't come to town merely to sop up the gravy where we were thriving. The entrepreneur has to be ready to carry his share of the heaviest load.

When I was with the salesmen, I rarely talked about myself. I wanted to build a relationship with my team. I did this in selling; we do it at Remington. You want the people working with you to know you care about them. You've already proved you care about your project or enterprise. They can see the hours you've put into it. But don't forget to take an interest in them. Without the team, you're nothing. I always made it a point to remember who liked baseball and whose kids had just started college. These are the things we chatted about while on the road. After a while, we were no longer a team; we were a family.

As positive results started to come in, I introduced financial incentives. Naturally, I couldn't do the things I did at Remington. I wasn't in a position to approach that grand scale. But I did reward salesmen by running small contests. One week, the salesman with the biggest volume in toothpaste would receive dinner for two at a fancy restaurant. The following week, the fellow who sold the most soap would get two tickets to a Chicago Cubs baseball game and twenty bucks to spend. I was turning work into a game and creating some more excitement with these little contests. By revolving the contest around a different man's strengths each week, I virtually guaranteed that no one player would monopolize the winnings and create envy among his team-mates.

Fully-motivated, this group out-performed my own expectations. The old pros did go out with a bang and most of the younger salesmen would eventually go on to managerial positions within the company. Our performance earned me another promotion. Every motivating tool I used in this situation has been adapted for use in my other enterprises with great success.

Of course, no matter what you do to inspire motivation, it will fail if you can't motivate yourself.

I wasn't always self-motivating. Oh it's true, I showed something of an entrepreneurial bent when I was a kid hawking cokes and model aeroplanes. But after I got out of the service, I was more concerned with having a good time than anything else. The tourist car company in France allowed me the freedom of a semi-Bohemian life. That venture was successful, but it was more of a lark than anything else. I wasn't particularly interested in business and I gave little thought to my future. I just wanted to explore Paris, read Sartre, listen to Sidney Bechet, and play tennis. In order to do those things I needed money; the touring car enterprise supplied it.

In the chapter on start-ups, I mentioned how I dropped the car business when I was accepted by the Harvard Business School. What I neglected to tell you was that going there was not my idea. My father had made my application without telling me about it. After he received the acceptance, the idea was presented to me as a *fait accompli*. My dad wisely ascertained that it was time I completed the transition from adolescent to adult. He knew I needed direction.

I found it at the Business School. It was there that I discovered I was handicapped. Many of my fellow students would graduate and immediately move into some high-paying position in the family business or use family connections to get a head start up the corporate ladder. Neither of those advantages was mine. It became clear that I would have to work my arse off just to keep pace with them in the business world and work even harder still if I wanted to come out ahead.

Why did the happy-go-lucky former American in Paris suddenly want to get ahead? Just a matter of logic, really. The Business School demanded a lot of my time. During the days I attended it, school was my life. This was a necessity; a lesser commitment would have led to my early dismissal. I felt that as long as I was going to invest time, I might as well also invest my best effort. We are only on earth for a limited amount of time. Why waste our precious moments simply going through the motions? I decided that whatever tasks I assigned myself, I would carry them out to the best of my ability. This opened up a world for me. I found out the meaning of boredom. You know what it is? It's that time in your life when you've stopped challenging yourself. How can anyone be bored if they strive for excellence every day? Since that realization, I can assure you, my moments of boredom have been few.

I think it should be mentioned that by challenging yourself I don't necessarily mean you have to do something that will change the course of mankind. If you're a sales assistant who thinks he's wasting away on a mundane job, find your self-esteem. You are a vital cog in the free enterprise system. You are the public representative of thousands of entrepreneurs whose products are sold in your store. When you go to work, set up a goal for yourself: 'I'm going to do $2,000 in sales today and I'm going to sell at least two pairs of those black satin sheets.' With the goal set, plan a way to reach it. Perhaps more courteous service will induce your customers to buy more merchandise. Better still, spend time getting well acquainted with your inventory so that you can be better prepared to make suggestions to customers who need direction. Many times a shopper wants to spend money but isn't sure what he wants to buy. Any informed suggestion you can make could become another sale.

You can do this sort of excercise on any job. Paying attention to the little details that help lead you to your goal leaves you no time to be bored. Business becomes fun. It's a game and you're playing to win.

Now that you've got your engine turning over, what is your long-range plan? Do you want to own a fleet of cabs? Open your own shop? Be president of your company? Whatever your dream, you can achieve it. If you don't believe that, please go back and read this book again. I went from being a management trainee – one of many in an international conglomerate – to the owner of Remington. I wasn't a child of destiny and I'm not exceptionally talented. I reached this position by working hard, grabbing opportunity, learning from my mistakes and allowing my imagination the freedom to dance. Don't tell me you can't do those same things. My life has taught me that we can do anything we choose. I'm asking you to choose to win.

If you're British, you're no stranger to making this choice. The history of your country is rich in tales celebrating triumph over adversity. At the start of World War II, you chose to fight a powerful and terrifying tyrant, one who set a new low for savagery.

At the onset, you were outnumbered and under-equipped. Many thought the British Lion's days were numbered. They should have known better. Joining with your Allies, you conquered the enemy. It wouldn't have been possible if you hadn't held the fort in those grim early days.

Your country is experiencing some grim economic times now. But knowing your history of Wellingtons, Churchills and Montgomerys, I'd never bet against your pulling through them. Of all the people on Earth, I can't think of any more entrepreneurial than the British. You've always dared to dream, dared to be great. I believe the examples in this book prove that those qualities are all you need to achieve victory. I know you will grasp every opportunity for success. When that triumph is won you will have proved what I've known all along: that the rumble emanating from Great Britain isn't the thunder of further gloom – it is the British Lion still full of fight, still able to roar.

Want some more motivation? Settle yourself in a quiet place and think about your ultimate goal. Make that image strong! Doing this, you may surprise yourself. The most powerful sensation you'll probably experience won't be one of wealth or power. It will be that feeling of subtle facial muscle strain as you struggle to keep a grin from enveloping your face. That grin comes with the glow of satisfaction you earn with success.

Isn't that glow worth its price? I haven't pulled punches in this book. I've told you that success is not easily won. It requires sacrifice and hard work. Even with these, you risk the pain of failure. Don't let that put you off. The Risk-Reward Ratio is on your side. I think the return on this investment is best described in Hooker's translation of Cyrano de Bergerac. In it, the Comte de Guiche, with reference to Don Quixote, reminds Cyrano that 'windmills, if you fight with them, may swing around their huge arms and cast you down into the mire'. A defiant Cyrano, speaking for all entrepreneurs, replies, 'Or up among the stars!'